Other Titles By This Author

Independence (and corruption) Comes to Zimbabwe.

This is a novel about one Godknows Kuzvida who, having grown up in racially segregated Rhodesia, finds himself travelling to the United Kingdom to further his education. Starting on the flight out, he experiences life in which, by and large, his race does not matter.

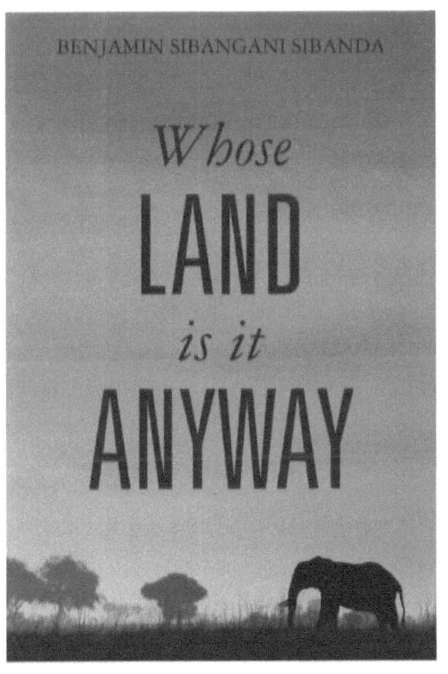

'Fast Track' Land Reform in Zimbabwe

Now, as Who's Land Is It Anyway begins, it's 2000, and some tribes have had enough. The Zimbabwe Patriot Alliance (ZIPA), a socialist organization, was supposed to right past wrongs, but ZIPA leaders became greedy and corrupt and did nothing to improve the plight of the displaced natives. Now a new political party is making promises...

ESCAPE

From

FREEDOM

benjamin sibangani sibanda

BENJAMIN PAGES PBC
36 Audely Street
Cranborne
Harare

benjamin@benjaminsibanda.net

www.benjaminsibanda.net

ISBN 978 -1-77929 -968 – 0…
Published by **BENJAMIN PAGES PBC,** 2020

This is a work of fiction. All of the characters, organisations and events depicted in this novel are products of the author's imagination or are used fictitiously.

This book is dedicated to the many Africans who have perished in all forms of political violence in their own countries or as a result of xenophobic attacks in foreign lands. It also remembers those that have perished as they attempt the hazardous journeys that they feel compelled to take as they escape from this vast continent that is blessed with so much; yet is cursed with poor leadership, an indifferent populace and abject poverty.

Acknowledgements

I am indebted to the following people who have stood by me through this project:

- My wife, Irelean Carol. My Pillar

- Professor Ruby Magosvongwe – University of Zimbabwe Faculty of Arts, English Department
- Tineyi and Gail Mawocha
- Stephen M Mpofu;
- Bruce le Fevre
- Thabani Maphosa
- Julian T Nyarota

All of whom have read the manuscript and contributed valuable comments as well as making corrections where necessary; as did my youngest daughter, Stabile (Star) Louise Sibanda.

Carlos George, my computer consultant and sounding board was of great help.

There are many, that I have not been able to mention by name, but whose unwitting contributions have been in telling the stories of their experiences with Gukurahundi, as well as other stories that have impacted this book .

'Breaking The Silence', a report on the disturbances in Matabeleland and Midlands by the Catholic Commission for Justice and Peace was a great source of information on the experiences of the time.

TO THE GLORY OF GOD

Cover Design By Creatvt Studio, Harare

CHAPTER ONE

"Good morning Sipho. Are you not going in today?"

Mr Mlambo was standing on his side of the four foot diamond mesh fence that was the boundary between our bungalows in Alexandra Township in Johannesburg. We had been neighbours for as long as I could remember – in fact, he had been there for many years before I made my appearance, yet it was only the previous week that I had had a more meaningful conversation with him beyond our usual *'good morning, looks like it's going to be very hot today'*. Only then had I found out that Mr Mlambo, like me, was from Zimbabwe!

He had called me from across the fence as he walked towards me.

"Psst! Sipho, can I have a word," he had said, looking and sounding somewhat conspiratorial. I was feeling rather tired, having just come home from my workplace, a restaurant in Sandton - one of Johannesburg's most up market locations. I was on my way to the outside toilet, after which I wanted to put my feet up and relax for a bit before starting on my evening chores – cooking and a bit of laundry. At twenty-six, I was still single and had not put any thought into finding a lifelong partner. The last thing I needed right then was a lengthy conversation with Mr Mlambo, who generally ignored me completely, but would from time to time hold lengthy monologues while I stood across the fence doing my best to show him that I was not really interested in anything he had to say. South Africans – I thought he was South African at this time – were very strange people.

"I'm going to the toilet, Mr Mlambo; and rather desperate I must say," I said as politely as I could master.

"Oh, I'll see you on your way back then," Mr Mlambo sounded unusually cheerful.

"You are from Rhodesia. Right?" Mr Mlambo asked as soon as I emerged from the toilet.

"It changed its name to Zimbabwe more than a decade ago and..."

"It will always be Rhodesia to me. Do you know that I come from Rhodesia myself?"

What? This man was incorrigible! Why would he lie about something like that? Did he need a favour from me and felt the need to invent a non-existent affinity?

"Mr Mlambo, I am very tired and I need to get some rest. What is it you want?"

"I am serious! I come from Rhodesia – rather, I came from Rhodesia in 1947 and I have lived in South Africa ever since."

1947! I could not even begin to imagine how long ago that was. But this man had never shown any interest in us '*makwerekwere's*[i]'!

"But, Mr Mlambo, you are a South African."

"Well, I am now. I mean, I have South African papers and have a South African wife and family, but I was born and raised in Rhodesia. I was sixteen when I insisted on coming with my uncle who had been here for a few years and had come home over Christmas. He had been telling us how beautiful it was in South Africa and how much money there was to be made. I was out of school and did not have many prospects, so I asked my uncle over and over again - until he agreed to take me with him."

I had stood there wondering whether this was some sort of joke. Mr Mlambo spoke the local languages – Zulu and Setswana– fluently, and as my own Zimbabwean language (IsiNdebele) was very close to Zulu, we had always communicated that way. In any case, a few years ago in South Africa, there had been some quite nasty attacks on foreigners and I, and many other people from *'Africa'*, as the locals referred to us as, had had to seek shelter literally anywhere - away from our homes until the problems subsided. Mr Mlambo had not had any such problems and while I had not seen him actually participate in the violence, he was never attacked. How could he now be telling me that he was from Zimbabwe?

"Ndiri kukuudza chokwadi!" he said.

Wow, Mr Mlambo was Shona! I recognised the language although I did not understand what he had just said. From his demeanour, though, I gathered that he was not only trying to convince me of the truthfulness of his statement, but also he wanted to prove his origins by speaking a language from Zimbabwe.

"I am from Melsetter in eastern Zimbabwe, near the border with Mozambique."

I had no idea what place he was talking about. The border with Mozambique was on the other side of the country and I only knew of a place called Mutare – the largest city in that part of the country. I knew nothing of this Melsetter. I came from Matabeleland in Western Zimbabwe, and while I did not exactly know too many Shona people, I knew that we did not like them and they similarly did not like us. I, of course had had no personal differences with the few Shona's that I had interacted with - but they were different. The ones that I had interacted with – by all accounts, were nicer than the average Shona person that I had heard of.

Back in the village for example, there had been this lady, MaMpofu, my uncle's wife. She was from Chivhu in Mashonaland but had met my uncle in Harare where they both worked in a shoe factory. I was about five or six when MaMpofu came into our home so I did not fully understand everything that went on, but I realised that my uncle's decision to marry a Shona had not been the most popular.

"They eat rats, you know," I heard one of my other aunties say one day when the women were gathered at the water well.

Rats! I was utterly disgusted. How could anyone eat that?

"And most of them are witches," one of the other women had piped in. "We are going to have to watch our children. Given the chance, they eat children!"

I had been squatting behind a bush relieving myself when the women came to fetch water. I had remained there hidden, because I did not want them to see what I had been doing – near the water well – when one of the neighbours, MaTshuma, had only a few seconds earlier, almost urinated on my face as she bent over to let fly a smelly full-flow jet of near yellow urine within a few inches of my hiding place. I had thus seen what I knew I should never have seen, and therefore did not dare show my presence then. They may have thought that I had hidden there on purpose. Besides, I was worried because I had always been told that seeing women's most privates would bring untold bad luck! Perhaps this would not happen if the women were not aware of my presence, I had reasoned, wondering what bad luck (*um'nyama)* was.

"And did you hear how bad her IsiNdebele is?" MaTshuma was shaking her ample posterior as she straightened up.

"At least she is trying," my aunt Sihle, my father's youngest sister, interjected. Everyone still called by her first name, Sihle, because she was still in her teens and seemed to have gotten quite fond of MaMpofu in the short time that she had been there. "She's used to speaking a different language and…"

"You call that a *language*?" MaTshuma interrupted to everyone's amusement, "sounds like she's cursing all the time!" MaMpofu had brought a niece with her and they would, when they were alone, communicate in their mother tongue.

"They probably think the same of our language," Sihle had persisted.

"Everyone knows IsiNdebele." Gogo MaDube was the oldest and most respected member of the group.

"Well, MaMpofu clearly does not know it," Sihle argued, while the rest of the younger women, I thought, looked at her disapprovingly.

"That's because she's a foreigner," Gogo MaDube was determined to have the last word, but the argument with Sihle seemed to carry on as the women lifted their water pots onto their heads and went back towards their homes.

The menfolk were no more accommodating of the new arrival than the women and my uncle had to cope with some awkward questions.

“So,” I had heard one of his friends ask him, “is her hole different from our women’s”

“I don't know,” ‘Ncane Peter sounded irritated by the question, “she was my first…”

“What do you mean she was your first? Don't tell me you never went with MaNcube?”

“Which MaNcube?”

“You know MaNcube! The mother of Sithembile…”

“That old woman? Why would I want to…?”

“Oh, come on now! Most of the boys in the village had their first sexual experience with her and she is quite a teacher!”

My uncle had looked quite disgusted by that comment. “She’s our mothers’ age, surely? You cannot be serious Phunyuka!”

“What has her age got to do with anything?” Phunyuka looked a bit embarrassed at least. “We all have to learn *somewhere*.”

“I'm learning with MaMpofu,” ‘Ncane Peter was looking at his friend pityingly.

“You are supposed to know these things before you get married. Otherwise you'll embarrass yourself on your marriage night!”

Of course, conversations such as this one were always spoken with some good humour, although Uncle Peter did not always seem to enjoy them. But some were quite scathing - like the comment from our grandfather's younger brother, who had become the family patriarch since our grandfather died, and who I only knew as *Khulu*.

"I see you've decided to *lift the dog's tail*," he had said during one of his frequent visits from his own homestead, several kilometres away. I did not immediately understand the sexual connotations of that statement at the time but it was clear from my uncle's reaction that he was completely displeased with that sentiment. When I did understand it years later, I could see why.

To everyone's surprise, MaMpofu had gone on to become one of the most popular and liked members of the family. She had a great sense of humour – in fact she seemed to be laughing all the time – she had learnt our language quite quickly and within a couple of years, could speak it quite fluently (albeit with an accent that was amusing, particularly to the younger members of the family), and she was also a hardworking and resourceful woman. I particularly liked her cooking and so spent a lot of time at her house. I never admitted it to the family but I got my only taste of 'rat' during one of these visits.

"Try it," she said. MaMpofu had caught a few field mice on the previous day and had dried them on her fire. She was eating one with such apparent relish that I found myself salivating, although I still told myself that I would never eat a *gundwane,* as we called rats and mice. She, of course was at pains to explain that they only ate *mbeva,* which are found out in the fields, not *makonzo,* which come into houses. To this day, I cannot tell the difference, but she clearly could because one day I killed a rat in our kitchen hut and took it to her proudly telling her that I had found a *mbeva* for her. She took one look at it and told me that it was a *gonzo - and* that she could not eat it.

Anyway, on the day that she was eating her *mbevas,* she eventually convinced me to try one of the tiny legs and, I have to admit that it did not taste *that* bad at all. But I never tried it again and I never told anyone in the family. It seemed that even those that had despised her to start with became her biggest fans although their admiration was always concluded with the explanation that she was the only *good* Shona. I had not known it then but for most of them, she was the only Shona they knew!

"Hey! Are you going to work or not?" Mr Mlambo's question brought me out of my daytime time reverie.

"Yes... No, I'm..."

"Are you sick? I've never known you to miss a day's work."

This was so true. I would even volunteer to go in on my days off. My boss, Mr Van der Merwe had been so kind to me over the years, so much that I felt like I owed him. In any case, he paid me double if I came in on my off days. But now he had fired me! He said he was suspending me for a month but I was convinced that when I went back to work, he would tell me that he had found someone else. I had not slept that well the night because I was worried about what would happen if I lost this job, the only one I had ever had and never having had to look for it.

"I've been..." I started hesitantly. Could I tell Mr Mlambo what I was thinking regarding my immediate future prospects? "I have taken a few days off. I need to visit my family in Zimbabwe." I blabbered. I had just made that up. The thought of visiting Zimbabwe had never come to me given the circumstances of my leaving the country.

"Good for you, young man. Do you know that I have never been back since I left? During the first few years of my stay in this country, I wanted to go back to Rhodesia every year, then it was 'soon'; but once I got married and had my own family, it did not seem important to go back."

I was surprised. Could I get to the point where I felt completely at home in this country? I missed many of the people I had grown up around and often wondered what had happened to them after I, and a few other boys and young men had left the village partly in search of our fortunes but mainly to escape from the soldiers who were not being particularly nice to the Ndebele people and had been responsible for a lot of misery in our area.

Anyway, having made that statement, I found myself wanting to go home. Would my mother and father still be there? Would

MaMpofu? In the early years of my exile, there had been some news from home. There were still people running away from the so called *Gukurahundi* who came with many horror stories of people being killed usually in front of their own people, being taken away by soldiers, never to be seen again, but my family had remained intact during those early years. But then the news stopped coming and I had had no idea for a few years now, how my family had fared. Of course the news that the soldiers had left the area after a unity accord was signed between the ruling ZANU-PF Party and ZAPU had been good, but I had not heard from anyone in my family or neighbours for some time.

"So, when do you intend to go?" Mr Mlambo was looking quite excited although I could not understand why until he said, "I regret never having gone back and I now believe that my people probably think I am dead."

"Why don't you go? There surely will be someone who will remember you," I said, trying to be helpful.

"No," he said quietly and thoughtfully. "It's been too long. Don't leave it as late as I did. I wish I had gone earlier but now..." He trailed off and looked almost as if he was going to cry. "Just go while you have the chance," he said with a sigh of resignation, and walked back into his house.

I was surprised. Mr Mlambo had always seemed so self-assured and confident. He came across as one who needed no one and had no emotions whatsoever.

Certainly the last couple of days had been something of a roller coaster for me. Only two days before, I had been looking forward, with guarded excitement, to the next day. Unbeknown to Mr Van der Merwe, I had been taking baking lessons. I was going to surprise him on his birthday and the cake that I had baked was looking really good after all the decorations I had put on it. It was a chocolate cake that I had become particularly adept at making. But it was the decorations that I had been particularly proud of. I had covered it with icing that I had made myself and finished it off with flowers and other decorations that I had bought from a baking supplies store in downtown Johannesburg. The finished product, I was sure, would not only make a fitting tribute to my mentor and benefactor since my arrival in South Africa, but it would convince my boss of an idea that I had had for a while – to open a bakery division in the restaurant, where people could walk in and buy various confectionary products for consumption on the premises or to take away for their office teas or on their way home. I had hoped that Mr Van would make me head of the division.

Anyway, I was taking it down the corridor to hide it in our kitchen at the restaurant for it to be revealed on the next day, when Rumbidzai came running round the corner and knocked it off my hands resulting in the cake landing upside down on the floor, completely destroyed. I had swung my fist instinctively, landing it against Rumbidzai's jaw and dislocating it. But I had not known about the dislocation immediately and had gone after her, picking her up by the scruff of the neck. Her shriek of pain stopped me punching her again and only then did I realise that there was something wrong with her jaw. By this time, everyone in the restaurant, including Mr Van der Merwe, was crammed into the corridor with all their attention on the injured Rumbidzai. My cake, needless to say, was getting trampled by all!

It was all Mr Van der Merwe's fault. Against the wishes of all his staff, he had employed a Shona! From the time the restaurant was opened, it had been an unspoken rule that no Shona was to be employed there. I had nothing against Shona's, personally; after all, I had known MaMpofu back home. It was just that I had met many Ndebele friends since arriving in Johannesburg and it seemed natural to want to work with one's own kind. In any case, when we did interact with Shona people, they were not particularly interested in us and they were not even sympathetic to our suffering at the hands of the soldiers back home in Zimbabwe. They kept reminding us that our ancestors had raided them and taken their women. What did that have to do with anything? It was such a long time ago!

I had been given the responsibility of letting our employer know of our displeasure at his employment of one that was not of *our kind*. He had clearly not been interested, giving us the lame explanation that Rumbidzai was qualified for what he needed – overqualified in fact as she was an accountant and all he needed was a book keeper! I later found out of course that she was doing an Accountant's job but earning a book keeper's salary. There was not much we could do about that, but we had agreed with my other colleagues that we were going to make her life as difficult as possible. As it turned out, we had not been able to achieve this either.

I fell in love with Rumbidzai as soon as I saw her. She was plumb without being fat, and had a smile that had all of us – the males in the restaurant – wanting to work in close proximity to her. She was extremely confidant and seemed unfazed by the fact that she was the only female – and the only Shona – in the whole establishment. I did not know it then, but all of us lusted after Rumbie, as we had started to call her; but none of us dared declare our interest because she was, well, Shona. I, of course, believed that my relationship with Rumbie was special, but the relationship was only at work. We did not socialise at all outside of our work at Mr Van der Merwe's restaurant – the Van der Burger. Except last Christmas, of course.

Every year at Christmas, Mr Van – as we all called him – threw a party for all the staff. It was the one time in the year when everyone let their hair down and we could even speak to our boss almost as an equal. As always happened, the bosses generally left early, at which point the party got louder and wilder. Most of my colleagues had been consuming alcoholic drinks that they were not used to and were thus more drunk than normal - and two or three had even passed out. George was having a heated argument about Gukurahundi with the other waiter, Khumbulani. It was the kind of argument they seemed to have every time they were drunk.

"The Shona wanted us all dead," George was saying, "I think that even the AIDS was all part of the Shona plan to kill us all…"

"But it's killing them too, this AIDS'" Khumbu retorted, "they were after the dissidents!"

"Did you see any dissidents yourself?"

"No, but I heard that they…"

"Aha!" George said triumphantly, "you only heard! In Lupane my friend, we saw women having their stomachs cut with those knives in front of their guns. They did not want them to give birth to future dissidents. Do you know that they made us sing Shona songs while dead people that we knew from the village were just lying there? They wanted us to see what would happen to people who supported dissidents."

"What about those tourists that were taken?" Khumbu still sounded unconvinced.

"My friend," George looked pitifully at his equally drunk friend, "those tourists were taken by the soldiers! They just wanted us to look bad so that they could kill us."

"*Egwelutshena!"* Kindness, the tea boy broke into a rendition of the old Ndebele classic, except that he could not sing it beyond the title word and, all evening, he had been breaking into the sporadic renditions then promptly drop his head onto his chest and fall asleep.

"SHUT UP!" George and Khumbulani spoke simultaneously.

Kindness looked up apparently confused, tried to stand, which proved too much of an effort so he slumped back into his chair.

"I miss home," he said to no one in particular.

The messenger, Fortune and the cleaner, Delicious, were lying side by side apparently cleaning the floor with their faces! As I watched, a pool began to form around Delicious as his bladder let go. It was not pretty. I was grateful that I had stuck to my usual drink –lager – and had thus remained relatively sober. Rumbie had had a few glasses of wine then declared herself drunk and started drinking water, so the two of us were the soberest – apart from the DJ, who seemed lost in his own world and was playing his own choice of music – I thought, slow and mellow.

"Come dance with me, Sipho," it sounded like a challenge and Rumbie, looking more beautiful than I had ever seen her stood over me, obviously emboldened by the wine, holding her hand out in an open invitation.

"I ...I don't dance," I said awkwardly.

"Come on, Sipho. Everyone can dance to this! Come, I'll show you." She had taken my hand and pulled me off the chair onto the dance flow. She held my left hand with her right hand and put her left hand over my right shoulder and neck, holding firmly and pulling me towards her. I was not sure what to do with my right arm so I let it dangle loosely on my side.

"All you have to do is sort of walk to the rhythm of the music like this - one, two three, she counted out the beats as she pulled me round the floor. My head was spinning. I had not been this close to a woman before– certainly none as beautiful as Rumbie. There had been, of course, the township wenches that had tried to entice me with their lurid dances on the few occasions that I had visited MaKhumalos, the local shebeen. They did not appeal to me at all and had rather put me off instead. Their interpretation, not entirely wrong, was that I was inexperienced in that department and was afraid of girls. The threat by one of them that she would tell all the girls in the neighbourhood that I was not a real man did nothing to change my opinion of them. Of course it also meant that I was reluctant to approach any girls in the area because I thought that they all knew of my lack in that area of life.

Rumbie was different. She smelt good and felt delicately soft. I could feel her breasts pressing against my chest and her breath on my neck. When she took my loose hand and gently pulled it round her waist so that we were as close as possible, it was all too much for me and I felt myself rising. I tried to pull back, afraid that she would feel my 'embarrassment', but she only pulled me back, almost as if she was enjoying it. Surely not! By the end of the song, I was so stiff that I could not let her go because of the fear that the bulge would be visible to anyone who happened to look. So we just shuffled round and round the floor, lost in a world of our own, holding each other tighter and tighter until my embarrassment became uncontrollable!

I felt my whole body stiffen as a sensation that I had only once before experienced – when a friend had said that he wanted to see if I could produce the *stuff* that would make a woman pregnant. That warm wave swept over me, and with what seemed like an uncontrollably violent eruption, I felt myself shudder and shiver and I clung to Rumbie even tighter. All too soon, the sensation was over and I excused myself hurriedly to go to the toilet to clean myself up. Had Rumbie realised what had just happened? I wondered. If she had, what did she think of me then? I thought of the many jokes that I had heard of men who could not hold themselves and released their sperm even before getting into the woman. Was she going to tell all her friends about my obvious inadequacy?

When I came out of the toilet, Rumbie had her coat on and was ready to leave. If she was aware of my embarrassment, she did not show it.

"Walk me home, please, Sipho."

She lived in an apartment not far from our work place and as the evening was nice and cool after a thunderstorm earlier in the day, we strolled rather leisurely to her home. She chatted endlessly with little response from me. My mind was racing. Surely she was not inviting me to spend the night, or was she? If she was, could I perform to her expectations, having had no prior experience? Perhaps she just wanted someone to accompany her home in the notoriously dangerous streets of Johannesburg. And how could I have let myself go like that? I was truly upset and disappointed with myself.

"I really enjoyed myself tonight, Sipho. It was a very good party," I heard her say and realised we were outside a block of flats which must have been the one she lived in.

"Yes," I said awkwardly. "Good party."

"Thanks for walking me home. You're a real gentleman." She held my hand for what seemed like an age and then said "well, its work tomorrow. Good night Sipho. Sweet dreams."

For a few minutes, I stood looking at the door through which she had gone, hoping without really knowing why, that she would come back and ask me to come in. She did not, so I trudged to the taxi rank to take a Kombi to my home in Alexandra Township

– or just Alex as the locals call it. I was still wondering how I had managed to… you know, without playing with myself.

My colleagues had somehow found out, probably from the DJ, that I had left with Rumbie. Nothing I said would convince them that nothing had happened between Rumbie and me.

"So, I hear you did the Shona last night. Was it good?" George was notorious for his womanising although most of the notoriety came from his own accounts.
"I just walked Rumbie home…"

"Yes, yes we heard that. Tell us all. Did she let you into her most private?"

"No! She needed someone to accompany her home. It was getting dark…"

"And we all know what happens in the dark hey?"

"Yes we do, don't we Sipho?" No one had heard Rumbie arrive and she joined the conversation with a statement that made sure that everyone was convinced about what happened the night before.

I had asked her about this when we were alone some time later.
"Why did you say what you said then?"

"When?" She looked genuinely puzzled.

"When you came in this morning. You know, when the guys were insisting that you and I…"

"Oh, that," she was almost flippant. "Well, they wanted to believe what they wanted to believe, so why not confirm it for them."

"But Rumbie, what will they think of you?"

"What do they think of me now?" She had answered with laughter in her voice. "To be honest, I don't care what they think."

"They'll think that you're easy prey for any man."

"Ah, so going with you means that I'll go with any man? Sipho, how can you underestimate yourself like that?"

"I didn't mean it like that! I meant that, mmm well, I have not exactly asked to date you, have I?"

"And how would your friends know that you have not asked me? Do you share with them every time you meet a girl you like and talk to her?"

"Rumbie! You can be so frustrating..."

"More frustrating than your friends?"

"What do you mean?"

"Well," Rumbie was enjoying herself, "when I came in, they were asking you if sex with a Shona was as good as sex with a Ndebele. I did not hear your reply."

"Well," I did not know what to say, "I don't have a basis for comparison because..."

"You've only slept with Ndebele girls?"

"NO! I haven't."

"Ah! You're a virgin then?"

I realised then that I had been smiling to myself as I thought of this episode. She had been right, of course. I was a virgin then but I was not going to advertise that fact to the whole world. If my colleagues at work preferred to think that I'd slept with Rumbie that Christmas party night, I had decided to let them. Of course it meant that I often offered to walk Rumbidzai home just to keep up the charade!

But now, I had broken her jaw. How was I ever going to keep up the pretence? How was she feeling? I was galvanised. I had to go and see Rumbie if only to offer my apology and see how she was doing. Of course I also needed to talk to Mr Van about my suspension. I needed to know if indeed my job would be there after a month, in which case I could travel home to Zimbabwe knowing that I would be able to come back to work for the Vans. I had no passport but I knew many people who travelled up and down to Zimbabwe without passports. I'd make inquiries after my trip to my work place.

CHAPTER TWO

I did not go to see Rumbie that morning. I decided to clean my two rooms instead; not because they were untidy – because I always cleaned them every morning before leaving for work – but I needed time to think about what I was going to say to Rumbie, and to Mr Van. So I took everything outside. The two sofas that I had bought at an auction, the table and four chairs that served as my dining room, kitchen, reading room and baking table, the two plate stove with oven on which I did all my cooking and had lately been practicing my new found baking skills – everything went outside. The only thing I did not take outside was my double bed which I had bought with the idea that I was, surely going to entertain a young lady or two but that had remained uninitiated in that regard thus far!

"Are you moving, Sipho?"

Sithembiso, my landlady's sixteen year old daughter was standing outside the kitchen door of her mother's house – the main house, as we called it. She wore a bright floral dress that I thought was a little too short and looked at me in the manner that she seemed to look at me a lot lately – directly into my eyes almost as if she was challenging me to invite her into my room. But she was like a little sister to me. I had been living on her mother's premises since she was eleven and I had watched her grow from a chubby little girl into a lovely young lady, who, unfortunately in my view, seemed to know the effect she had on many a young man and was not averse to take advantage of her charm.

"No, Thembie," I answered without looking back at her, "Just cleaning my house."

"Cleaning your house?" She sounded genuinely surprised. "Sipho, you have the cleanest house in the whole neighbourhood! In fact, you are always getting us into trouble with my mother! 'Look how clean and tidy Sipho keeps his rooms, and he is a man!' my mother often says." She walked across and peeped into my room. "What are you cleaning in there? If my mother comes home and finds all your stuff outside, tomorrow, we will be told to take all our furniture out and 'clean the house like Sipho!'" She put her hands on her hips and mimicked her mother's voice and manner.

"I'll be done by the time she comes home," I tried to reassure her.

"You better be. How come you are not at work today?"
"I took the day off..."

"To clean your house?" she said with raised eyebrows. "You are very strange indeed. I don't know anybody who would take time from work to spend the day cleaning a clean house, but why am I surprised? You are from Zimbabwe!"

She said that as if my coming from Zimbabwe somehow explained my 'strange' behaviour which included wanting to live in a clean space.

"I did not take the day off to cle... But how come you are not in school?" It had just occurred to me that she should have been in school on this day.

"I left school," she said simply, "I won't be going back there."

"Why?" I was surprised and shocked. Why would anyone want to leave school?

"They say I'm pregnant."

"Why?... I mean, how, who says you are pregnant?" I was confused. Thembie was so young and innocent. I didn't think she even knew what caused people to get pregnant. Some boy had probably taken advantage of her!

"Who's the boy?" I asked angrily.

"Who told you it's a boy?" She did not seem worried at all, but she clearly did not understand these things.

"You don't get pregnant from a girl, no matter how good a friend she is," I explained patiently, now convinced that she probably got raped and did not know what had happened.

"What about a man?"

"What about a man?" She was even dumber than I had realised, I thought to myself.
"A man can make you pregnant, can't he?"

"A man!" I shouted angrily. What grown man would take advantage of such a child? She laughed in my face.

"You don't know much about anything, do you, Sipho? So it's true what the girls have been saying; that you've never been with a girl?"

I was shocked again. Who talks about such things to a child? Then again, she was not a child anymore, was she? I looked at her again, not sure whether to feel pity or anger. I did not know her mother's history but I had seen how she had been struggling to bring up this child and her two younger brothers; how she always made sure that their school fees were paid and how she had such lofty dreams for her children.

"This one is going to be a nurse, or a doctor even", I remembered her saying just the other day.

"How does your mother feel about this?" I asked Thembie.

"She's not speaking to me. I think she is too angry even to beat me. This morning, she looked at me, shook her head and walked out without so much as a good morning. But I'm not worried. When Mr Mbambo comes for me…"

"The businessman? Why would he... You mean he is responsible. You poor child. He is a married man..."

"But he loves me! He told me that I'm the best thing that has ever happened to him and I am better than even his two wives put together!"

I was seething with anger. Why do grown man take advantage of young people like this? Why do young people let them? For some reason, I found myself thinking of Rumbie. Would I... Well, if she were my girlfriend, would I take advantage of her like this? Not a chance! But I needed to go and see her.

"Thembie," I tried again, "man like Mr Mbambo do not love anyone except themselves. I would be very surprised if he does not dump you after this..."

"Do you know Caleb? How can you say a nasty thing like that?"

"Is that his name? Caleb? I don't know him, but I know men like him. They prey on young girls' naivety and desire for 'nice' things that they can provide, but they don't..."

"Caleb's different," she interrupted vehemently, "you'll soon find out how wrong you are about him!"

I looked at Sithembiso with a mixture of pity and anger. How could she not see what seemed so obvious to me? She seemed so determined to throw her life away!

"In a few years' time, you'll regret this," I said without too much conviction.

"In a few years' time," she responded with childish confidence, "I'll be Mrs Mbambo, driving my own car – a Mercedes Benz - and you, Sipho, will still be my mother's lodger!"

In spite of my misgivings, I found myself admiring her confidence and determination. She was very pretty and would not be the first person in the world to get ahead just on her looks. Was she right though? How much longer was I going to remain her mother's lodger? Could I hope to have any chance with Rumbie while I was a lodger in Alex?

By the time I finished putting everything back in the house – with Sithembiso hovering around and making not too complimentary remarks about the state of my furniture – I decided that it was too late to try to go and see Mr Van. I thought it best to leave it until the morning.

My work colleagues seemed unsure quite how to treat me when I arrived at the Van der Burger, just after opening time. They were friendly enough but I sensed some distance, as if I was not quite one of them anymore. This only heightened my anxiety, which had been building up during a sleepless night and a tense journey into work that morning. Only George was being his cantankerous self.

"So, the Shona finally got you fired!" He said as soon as he saw me, "I told you she was trouble that one."

"When?" I retorted.

"When what?"

"When did you tell me that she was trouble?"

"Well, we've always known ..."

"Anyway, I was not fired. I was suspended!"

"Believe what you want, Sipho..."

"Good morning Sipho. Are you in control now?" Mr Van had just come out of his office without any of us noticing. "I expected you yesterday and *Rumbey*... well, come into my office."

Although Mr Van seemed friendly, I still felt quite nervous going into his office, and the looks from my colleagues did not help much. Many of them were quite jealous of my relationship with the boss and the thought that this was in jeopardy seemed to please them. Of course if I was going to leave, opportunities would open up at least for one of them.

"You got very angry the other day," Mr van said as soon as I sat down, "I've never known you to lose your temper like that; are you in love with Rumbey?"

"No sir!" This was unexpected, "I had spent so much time on that cake and I was just disappointed that you were not going to see it, or taste it!"

"I tasted some of it. It was good, I was most impressed."

"But how...?"

"Oh, there were little bits that had not been trampled on. It was not much but there was enough there to give me an idea of what you had done. It was a very nice cake."

I sat there, not quite sure how to respond. I had come expecting that Mr Van would be angry and disappointed with me and yet here he was praising my cake. Why was he prolonging my agony?

"Sir," I started tentatively, "I'm very sorry that I got so angry..."

"Are you sure that you are not in love with Rumbey...?" I hated the way he pronounce her name "There was so much passion in your anger! I mean it was an accident - she was rushing somewhere and had no way of knowing that you would be carrying a cake at that point..."

"I'm very sorry sir," I repeated, not quite sure what else to say. I was also wondering at this point why the boss was not saying anything about my suspension.

"Go and apologise to her, not to me. She is at home and I must say that she seemed disappointed that you did not come to see her yesterday!"

"I was embarrassed sir and I... did she tell you that she was disappointed?"

"No, Sipho, she did not say 'I'm disappointed that Sipho has not come', but I could tell. Anyway, go and see her."

"What about my job, sir?" My anxiety made my voice sound strange even to myself.

"You are still suspended for a month as I said. Come back after that and we can talk about your baking skills."

I was relieved but also disappointed that he was insisting on suspending me. He had seemed so agreeable that morning and I had begun to believe that he would have cancelled the suspension. Still, I thought to myself, I had a job to come back to after a month.

"Sir," I started tentatively again, "I was thinking that I may go to Zimbabwe during the suspension."

"Are you going to go and see Rumbey before you go to bloody Zimbabwe?"

"Yes, sir," why was he so insistent on me seeing Rumbie, "but I will need some money if I am to travel to Zimbabwe..."

"Of course, of course. You've never taken any leave since you started here so I'm sure you are due some leave pay. Did you ever get a passport by the way?"

"No sir but I am told there are people who can help you to get across..."

"They'll cost you a lot of money. You should try and get yourself a passport while you are there."

"Yes sir," I was not too sure that I would be able to do that. I had no birth certificate and was not even sure what the situation in Zimbabwe was and whether there would be anyone in the family to assist me.

"When were you thinking of going? I need a couple of days to work out your monies and then you can go. Now please go, I have so much work to do and, thanks to you, I'm two people short!"

"I'm sorry sir..."

"Stop bloody apologising so much. Go and see *Rumbitsayi*..." he was mispronouncing her name again... "and apologise to her!"

I had not expected Mr Van to have been so agreeable; to be honest I'm not sure what I had expected and although I had hoped that he would not have been against my travelling to Zimbabwe, I had half expected him to discourage me, at least. In fact, I was almost certain that had he even hinted at discouragement, I would have cancelled the whole thing. After all, Mr Van knew my whole history in South Africa, his son having found me on the banks of the Limpopo alone, afraid and wishing I had died with the others – I was convinced that my fellow travellers, all of them older than I was, had drowned in the flash flood that came upon us as we were crossing the Limpopo River from Zimbabwe, or been eaten by the crocodiles that had been basking in the sun not far from where we were attempting to cross the river.

"We have to cross fast before they become aware that we are here." Philani was the oldest in our group who also claimed to have crossed over to South Africa before although none of us could remember him being away from our village for any significant length of time.

"Are you sure about this, Philani? Those things are very fast when they get in the water, you know." Samson sounded worried, pointing at the crocodiles.

"Well," retorted Philani, "we've been walking along the river for a long time and this seems the best place to cross. If we delay any longer, it will soon be too light for us to attempt the crossing because the patrols on the other side will become very active."

"I've heard that crocodiles are very deceptive," Zenzo who was normally very quiet and hardly expressed any opinion. He jumped as the branch of a bush near him rubbed against his leg, "I thought that was a crocodile!" He looked very scared but everybody else laughed at him and said what a coward he was. Of course we were probably all as scared as he was.

I was shaking, partly from the cold at that time of the morning – even though I knew that it would get much hotter later – and partly because, although I had never witnessed a crocodile attack myself, there were enough stories told about how quickly they grabbed their victims and how strong they were. I looked across the river at our intended destination – South Africa! We were almost there and the excitement I felt was probably a little stronger that the fear of the threat posed by the crocodiles. Although the river was quite wide at this point, it was dry most of the way and there was only a narrow strip of water in the middle. It looked from where we stood, like one could just leap across it. We had come too far, I thought, to allow a small thing like the threat of crocodiles that looked half asleep and were perhaps a hundred metres from where we were, to stop us.

"Shhh," Zenzo said suddenly, with some urgency. We all went quiet and could hear the roar of what I could not imagine. For a few seconds, we stood paralyzed, not quite sure what to make of the sound that was not unfamiliar, but that none of us had ever heard with such ferocity. It was the sound of rushing water during flood season.

"Run!" Philani had started towards the river, "Let's cross before the water gets here!"

I ran as hard as I could, looking neither left nor right; just focusing on the narrow strip of water that I was aiming to leap across. But the water was a lot closer than any of us had realised. One minute I was struggling to make progress on the sand; the next minute I was travelling at breakneck speed down river, carried along by the raging waters. The trees on the banks of the river looking as if they were speeding in the opposite direction! I was out of breath because of the ferocity with which the water had hit me; I could not see any of my travelling companions although I assumed they were in the same predicament. I knew enough about drowning to realise that shouting would have meant I swallowed water which would only speed up the drowning process. In any case, no one would have heard me. Perhaps because of my young age, death never occurred to me as a possibility even though I could not see any way out of that particular situation. The last thoughts I remembered having were of whether crocodiles could still attack me in waters like these!

"Are you alright dear?" I turned round to see who the elderly white lady before me was addressing. There was no one behind me, so she must have been talking to me.

"Are you alright?" she repeated the question.

Only then did I realise that I had been crying! The thought of going back to Zimbabwe; the reality that I was actually going to travel back to my homeland had brought back memories of events that I had tried not to think about for a long time.

"I'm alright, Ma'am," I said feeling quite embarrassed, "It's the wind in my eyes," the explanation sounded stupid even to myself!

"Alright then," she said as she walked on, "I thought you might have a real problem."

I had to find a quiet spot in which to tidy up my face without being noticed. So lost had I been in thought that I did not realise how close I was to Rumbie's apartment block. I had one problem though. I'd never actually been to Rumbie's apartment; always only having seen her to her building and never having been invited in. I did not even know what number flat she lived in! I had to find someone to ask. A group of children were running around trying to play rugby with a round ball.

'Excuse me.' I said to the one who had stopped to catch his breath, "I'm looking for a woman from Zimbabwe who lives in this building."

"I don't know her." The little boy seemed in a hurry to get away from me. He gathered the rest of them around him and I could see there was some consultation going on. Finally, one of them came towards me, hands stuck deep in his pockets.

"Who are you looking for?" he seemed quite cocky.

"A woman from Zimbabwe..."

"There are so many *Makwerekweres* in this flat. What is her name?"

"Rumbidzai," I said feeling irritated with this youngster for the use of a derogatory term that many South Africans liked to use for anyone who came from Africa. Many other foreigners from all over the world had come to South Africa, but this term was reserved only for those who came from other African countries. What ignorance!

"Oh, you mean Rumbie from Zimbagwe? She's not so bad, for a *Mukwerekwere*. She lives in number five on the ground floor." He ran off to re-join his friends.

Rumbie was lying on a sofa dressed in a morning gown that was quite revealing and for a few seconds, she seemed unaware of my presence. I had heard her clearly say "Come in", so how come she lay there with her eyes closed allowing me a peak into her most private – well, as close as it could get. I stood there staring at the exposed flesh of her upper thigh and wishing...

"Oh, it's you Sipho!" She hurriedly covered herself as she sat up. "I thought it was one of my neighbours who just left. I thought she'd forgotten something. Sorry, I look such a mess, I was not expecting you..."

What I had just seen was anything but a mess. I kept looking at her hoping that the flimsy piece of clothing she had on would fall off her or something. What did she mean she was not expecting me? Mr Van had given the impression that she was rather looking forward to seeing me. Then again, I had dislocated her jaw only a couple of days earlier.

“How are you feeling?” I was suddenly aware that I had been thinking of things other than her welfare, which was the main reason for my visit.

“Please sit.” Rumbie indicated the sofa on which she had just been laying, “Let me tidy myself up.”

She left the room hurriedly with her gown clinging tightly to her body and as I watched her walk out, I had the distinct impression that she was not wearing any underwear, before the door closed behind her.

Left in the room on my own, I noticed how clean and tidy the room was. The furniture was simple but nicely arranged. Apart from the sofa I sat on, there were two other easy chairs. They were not the same as my one but were an approximate match. Against one wall was a cupboard in which I assumed she kept her plates and spoons and such like. To my right, separated from the sitting room by a low wall was what looked like a small kitchen. There was some untidiness there as the sink was full of unwashed dishes. Clearly because of her pain, she had been unable to keep her place as clean as the sitting room suggested she did. The cleaner in me had just won the debate on whether I should help her with the dishes, and I had just started walking towards the kitchen when Rumbie came back. She had changed into a simple white tee shirt and a pair of jeans. Somehow, I still saw her in her dressing gown.

“That must have been some cake,” she said, and for the first time, I noticed how much difficulty she was having with smiling. I was filled with an overwhelming sense of guilt.

“I'm so sorry, Rumbie, I don't really know what got into me.”

“Well,” Rumbie seemed amused. “According to Mr Van, it was an amazing cake - well worth an uppercut to the jaw...”

“Please Rumbie,” I pleaded, “don’t joke about that. I could have caused some really bad damage to your face.”

“Look, Sipho,” Rumbie sat beside me on the sofa, “I was very angry – and very sore – when I left work that day, but I’ve had some time to think about things and I know that you did not mean any harm. You just reacted and, yes, a fist in the face is not very nice but,” she shrugged her shoulders and tried to laugh, which caused her to wince, “I’ll live.”

“Thank you.” I could not think of anything else to say that would have been appropriate.

“You’re welcome,” her attempt at smiling caused her to wince again.

“Are you in a lot of pain?”

“Of course I’m in a lot of pain. I had a dislocated jaw!”

“I’m sorry...”

“I wish you’d stop apologising,” fleetingly, she patted my knee with her hand. It was only fleeting and she probably was not aware that she had done it - but I had definitely felt it! It felt as warm as a hug and I felt a reassurance in that touch, confirming that she was not angry with me.

“I hear you are going to Zim?”

“I’m thinking about it... where did you hear that?”

“Mr Van phoned and told me that you were on your way. But it took so long that I thought you’d changed your mind.”

She had a phone? I had not noticed it before but there, on a stool near the door, was a telephone. How come I did not know this? The number of times I had wished I could just talk to her – particularly during my days off – I could have gone to a call box...

“You never gave me your number,” I accused gently.

"You never asked," she winced again.

"Are you sure you are alright."

"Sipho, the jaw was dislocated," it sounded like an accusation. "It's been reset, of course, but there'll be some pain for a while. I am taking pain killers and now it's a matter of waiting for the flesh to heal, in its own time. There are no broken bones, okay."

For a few minutes, we sat side by side without speaking. It felt comfortable sitting next to Rumbie, but I still felt like there was something I needed to say about her jaw but could not think what to say. Rumbidzai broke the silence.

"So, when are you planning to go to Zim?"

"As soon as possible; Mr Van is going to work out some money that is apparently due to me because I have not taken any leave for so long. As soon as that comes through, I'll be ready to go."

"He's very fond of you isn't he?"

"Mr Van? No, he treats me like everyone else – in fact he is harder on me..."

"I noticed that," she interrupted, "but it's the kind of hardness normally reserved for those who are loved, like being taught at school by your father – as I was. I was positive that that man hated me – but now I know that he only wanted what was best for me." She stopped and looked at me as if she had just realised something. "Come to think of it, I'm almost certain that you and Mr Van der Merwe have some sort of special relationship, he's not gay is he?"

"NO!" I was shocked. How could she even think about me like that! "Mr Van found me, well, his son did."

"What do you mean, 'found you'?" She stood up then and went towards her kitchen. "How rude of me," she said over her shoulder. "I didn't even offer you a glass of water. What will you have? I have some orange crush from home."

"I nearly drowned when I crossed into South Africa, you know."

"What has that got to do with... you nearly drowned! You mean you came to South Africa illegally? You border jumped?" She looked so incredulous that I thought she was going to throw me out of her flat. People from our part of Zimbabwe had been crossing into South Africa for as long as I could remember and it had always seemed the most natural thing to do. I had heard of people who had crossed since the time my grandfather was a young man. Why was Rumbie so shocked?

"Young people from our part of Zimbabwe are much more likely to want to come to South Africa than they are to want to go and look for work in Salisbury..."
"Harare," she interrupted.

"Yes, Harare, or even Bulawayo. I had not really thought of coming to South Africa myself, but when stories of what soldiers were doing to young people in other parts of Matabeleland started reaching our village – and the incidences seemed to be getting closer and closer to us, it was felt that I had no other option."

"Where is your part of the country? I always thought that you came from Bulawayo."

"I'd never even been to Bulawayo," I admitted feeling somewhat embarrassed. Rumbie looked surprised and seemed to want to say something but changed her mind. "I come from an area called Maramani, which sits in South Western Zimbabwe quite close to where the borders of Zimbabwe, South Africa and Botswana converge. I looked it up on the map the other day and hey, yaaa, it's in the middle of nowhere. We fall under Beit Bridge but I've never been there either – I really know South Africa more than I know Zimbabwe, you know." I concluded lamely realising just how much I did not know of my own country. It was just as well I had decided to travel back there.

"That's so sad, but you were young when you came – sixteen, did you say? I don't know how much of Zimbabwe I knew at that age. But I had been to Harare at least." She smiled mischievously, "and I came to South Africa legally!"

CHAPTER THREE

I was transported back to the home that I had grown up in – a collection of simple mud under thatch huts built in a kind of semi-circle around a large Mopani tree. For as long as I could remember, the tree had always loomed large in my conscience and I had always thought that it had been there for a long time; probably since creation. Strangely, although the many Mopani trees in our area were responsible for one of the greatest culinary pleasures of my childhood – the annual harvest of *amacimbi* or the Mopani worm, as I had learnt that it was called in English – the big tree around which our homestead was built did not produce any and no one seemed to find this strange! It was a useful landmark for the many travellers passing the village on their way to and from the nearest road, several kilometres to the west of our village.

I had only ever been on this road once, when we went to visit the Thuli Game area as part of a school trip. I knew nothing beyond Thuli except for the stories told by adults of places further north with fascinating names like Gwanda, Filabhusi, Fort Rixon and of course Bulawayo which was said to be a very large city with many industries and where many young men who did not cross illegally to South Africa and to a lesser extent, Botswana, went to find work.

The big Mopani tree was also where my grandfather – and latterly my father and his brothers held court to discuss matters relating to the home and where occasionally – actually quite frequently – corporal punishment was meted out to the children for any misdemeanours! Thus whenever you were told to go and wait *ephaneni (*by the Mopani tree) or *es'hlahleni (*by the tree), you knew what was coming. It was, of course part of the adults' warped sense of humour that they would make you find the instrument of you torture from the nearby bushes and hold it while waiting for your fate under the big tree.

"Penny for your thoughts?" Rumbie's voice brought me back to the present.

"I.. err, I was just thinking about my childhood."

"It was a happy childhood then." It was a statement, not a question.

"Well," I hesitated, "parts of it were happy, but ..." I was not sure how to go on. "My early childhood was during the war of liberation and although I was too young to remember its full details, it's something that has always been in my conscience – the soldiers arriving in the village asking questions; the whispered conversations of the adults after the soldiers had gone. I even remember having to hide – or be hidden in the grain store while the adults went off somewhere we, the children did not know." I was surprised at these memories. I had not thought about those times for many years, but here they were –flooding in, fresh in my mind.

"But that was not the worst of it. There was palpable relief when the war ended and I remember the excitement of the elections and the disappointment that Joshua Nkomo, who all the adults supported and had been sure would win, had lost the election very badly. But it all meant very little to me. I was happy to go along with whatever the adults said."

Rumbie, sensing my mood, said nothing but somehow it felt like she had moved a little closer to me. It may all have been in my mind of course. How was she going to react to what I was about to say? Would it change our friendship? – I was sure we were friends. Would she speak to me again? Would it matter to me if she didn't?

"Our village had really not been that affected by the war, so its end did not make much difference to us. Many a young man from neighbouring villages had joined the war effort and there were families that were either celebrating the return if their young man (and some women) as heroes, or mourning the ones that did not return. In our village, only MaNcube was affected. Her husband and son had left for Botswana a few years earlier and had not been heard from since. It had generally been assumed that they must have gone to Zambia to join ZIPRA and when they did not return with the others, it was assumed that they had perished in the war. It did not help that none of the returning comrades had heard of MaNcube's husband or her son."

"Is that why she was like that?" Rumbie's question was confusing.

"Like what? Who was like what?"

"MaNcube. Is she not the one you said slept with all the young boys?"

I did not remember telling her that!

"Some boys claimed that she was sleeping with them; I don't know how truthful that was", In spite of all the stories, I still respected MaNcube and could not bear to think of her in those terms.

"I can only imagine how difficult it must have been for her; to lose a son and a husband and not be sure what happened to them." Rumbie was looking very thoughtful, "it must have been very difficult for her." She repeated herself.

"Well," I said tentatively, "everyone rallied around her and the men of the village made sure that her fields were ploughed and she had enough for her and her daughter."

"Did the women like her?"

"Of course they..." I hesitated. There had always been stories around MaNcube, particularly with regards to her relationship with the men of the village. I had unwittingly been privy to a heated discussion under the Mopani tree where she was being accused of sleeping with one of the village elders. I had come home from herding cattle feeling unwell and had gone into our bedroom hut to sleep without anyone noticing. The adults must have assumed that all the children were away – all the girls having been sent to the shops; it had not occurred to me at the time but it was very unusual that all the girls would be sent away like that. Anyway, I had been woken up by the loud voices as all the people seemed to be talking at the same time.

"She is a whore! And I am tired of her continuing to sleep with my husband. I have forgiven her in the past but she keeps luring my husband into her , her…" the speaker seemed at a loss as to how to complete that sentence.

I had got up and taken a peek outside without being seen. The men were sitting on one side on stools and other improvised seats like crates, plastic drums and so on, while the women sat on the ground opposite the men. MaNcube sat on her own - somewhat removed from the other women. She was crying. MaNdlovu, the accuser stood with her hands on her hips looking down at MaNcube very aggressively while her husband timidly examined the ground rather closely.

"Sa Themba, say something!" MaNdlovu turned her attention to her husband, "has she not followed you into the bush when you went looking for fire wood? Men cannot resist when women throw themselves at them like that!"

MaNdlovu had turned to the other women who all nodded their heads in agreement. I had noticed MaNcube looking up for the first time. She looked surprised at the vehemence of the accusations and even looked at Nkomo, MaNdlovu's husband rather pleadingly, but he was not looking in her direction.

"Whore! Bitch!" The other women seemed to be enjoying themselves at MaNcube's obvious discomfort. They were only silenced by the headman, Mr Moyo, raising his arm.

"Have you been sleeping with Nkomo?" The headman had asked MaNcube.

She had sheepishly nodded her agreement while looking at the ground.

"Sipho!" I had been so engrossed in the proceedings that I forgot that I was supposed to be hiding and MaMpofu had happened to look in my direction. "How long have you been there?"

"That was the last I heard of that story except for the beating under the Mopani tree during which I was made to promise that I would not tell anyone of what I had heard. You, Rumbie, are the first person that I have ever told that story," Rumbie was now sitting uncomfortably close to me and I had to adjust my position to not feel her breast that was pressing into my shoulder.

"Poor woman," she said almost as if she was speaking to herself. "Did you think that she was a whore?"

The question was so unexpected that I did not have an immediate answer.

"I didn't know what to think. She was an adult and I had always been taught to respect those who are older than me."

"But you do understand that as an adult, she had needs."

"I told you Rumbie, all her needs were taken care of by the villagers..."

"Not ALL her needs! And don't look so surprised, Sipho. Surely you understand that all adults need," she hesitated, "you know, intimacy."

She was looking directly at me. I stood up abruptly stammering something about needing the toilet. What was she saying? Did she have a need for intimacy too? I found myself thinking about the Christmas party and how she had seemed unbothered about my embarrassment. Was she looking to me to fulfil her need for intimacy? Then again, she was a very confident young lady and perhaps only spoke to me that way because she trusted me; or, like the girls in my neighbourhood, knew that I had no experience with girls and therefore harmless.

I came back from the toilet feeling calmer and less out of breath.

"As I was saying, there was a period of calm after the war of liberation although this was followed by a drought. Food was in short supply although again because I was so young, it really did not matter that much to me. There always seemed to be enough food particularly for the children. I later learnt that it was MaMpofu's industry and good housekeeping that were responsible for the availability of food. She worked hard and always kept something back after each good harvest."

For a good few minutes, we sat in silence. I had not sat next to Rumbie since my return from the toilet so that I now could watch her from a slight distance. She was so pretty, even though she was Shona, I was thinking.

"Then the Shona soldiers came."

"The Shona soldiers?" She sounded more curious than surprised. She certainly did not sound offended.

"As I said, there was a period of relative calm after the war, although there was some disappointment that ZAPU had not won the elections. Then we started to hear stories about some former freedom fighters who were fighting the new government. We did not experience any of this although people with radios told us about these things. The adults seemed reluctant to talk about it although there was some concern that the war – that many were relieved to have survived – might come back.

'What are these people fighting for?' I remember Khulu asking one day. 'We may not have won the election but we got independence, didn't we? We can contest the next elections in 1985, by which time these people will have messed up the country so much that no one will vote for them.'

Most of the adults had seemed more concerned about the lack of rain than by the prospect of another war. My father...."

"You've never said anything about your father," Rumbie interrupted my monologue.

"Well, my father was never really involved in my life. He worked in a faraway place called Antelope Mine and he hardly ever came home. When I was much younger, he used to come home regularly and I always looked forward to his visits, particularly at Christmas. But then he stopped coming – or rather came infrequently and we were lucky if he stayed overnight – always rushing back for his next shift!"

I was quiet for a few minutes as I remembered how difficult those times had been for my mother whose loyalty to my father was admirable even in the face of the many stories that he had another family at Antelope.

"'Your father is working so hard because he wants a better life for all of us', my mother would tell me although by this time I was beginning to doubt whether he was ever coming back to stay. Life was really tough and I saw my mother's struggles as she tried to eke out a living for us from the piece of ground she called a field. It had been worked for so many years that hardly anything could grow there. My father who had been sending fertilizers had stopped doing so."

The memories that I had not had for a long time came rushing back. They were so vivid and real that it seemed like these things had only just happened.

"My mother did what she could, of course but, it was tough, very tough indeed. The most painful memory of that time for me was when one of my friends, after an argument, insinuated that my mother was sleeping around to get food. I was so angry with him that, for the first time, I actually beat someone at a fist fight. I hit him so badly that for a few days he did not come to school!"

I chuckled as I remembered what school was like in those days.

"Not that there was much schooling happening. Most children were so hungry that they could not come to school and those that did were generally weak and hungry that they could not pay attention."

I was crying by this time. The memories were that painful.

"The teachers were also busy trying to find food for themselves and their families and teaching hungry, mostly absent children cannot have been easy for them to do. Thanks to MaMpofu's industry and housekeeping, we never went without although meals had been reduced to one meal a day!"

"Not bad for a Shona," I think Rumbie had meant that as a joke, but I was not in the mood.

"The insinuations about my mother never stopped. Even the teachers started to make comments suggesting that my mother was sleeping with the soldiers that seemed to be around a lot in those days. I remember one of the teachers asking when soldiers were passing our school, 'So, Sipho, which one is your father'? The other children thought this was very funny. I did not!"

I was surprised that I was sharing these thoughts with a relative stranger. This was not information that I had ever shared freely with anyone. It just seemed easier to talk to Rumbie about most things, possibly because I figured there was little chance that she would ever meet any of my family. But she also did not seem to want to tell me what to do. She listened, she sympathised where appropriate, and she offered some advice but never sounded like she was telling me what to do!

"It was my father who first told us about experiencing the nastiness of the Shona soldiers…"

"Why do you keep calling them Shona soldiers? Surely the army was made up of people from everywhere around Zimbabwe?"

"The ones that came in 1984 were definitely Shona soldiers. There was not a single Ndebele among them – at least among those who came to our village. But that was much later. Initially, my father, on one of his visits told us that there seemed to be a campaign to kill Ndebeles. In places far to the North of us – even further than Bulawayo, people were being killed by soldiers who apparently wore red berets."

"I don't believe that!" Rumbie looked genuinely incredulous. "People will sometimes use tribalism for political gain…"

I was surprised by that comment. Surely everybody had heard about what happened in Matabeleland and I would have expected someone of Rumbie's obvious intelligence to know about it and to sympathise with me. Was I wrong about her?

"I'm sorry, Sipho, that came out wrong. We did hear that there was some trouble in your part of the country but the government was fighting dissidents who had been killing your people, surely? I just find it hard to believe that they would have targeted people for the language they speak."

"Eventually it came to our part of the country," I went on, feeling that I had to make Rumbie understand how bad things were. "By this time," I continued, "I was old enough to understand a few things. There had been a drought for a few years and food was in very short supply. Yet these soldiers seemed determined to destroy any food that they found in homes. Shops were forced to be shut so that there was nowhere to buy food and even the donors were not allowed to come into our area."

"How on earth did people survive?" Rumbie's face showed real concern.

"Many died," I said simply. "MaMpofu came to our rescue again. She had found some caves in the area and got us to move some of the grain into them – at night of course. 'My grandmother always taught me to scout around for caves whenever I got to an area', she would say, 'caves saved their lives when the *Madzviti* (your people) came to raid!' The rations had to be reduced again but we stayed alive; one day at a time."

I found myself close to tears as I recalled.

"It was at this time that thoughts of coming to South Africa really gelled in my mind," I went on. "As I said, many young people in our area had ambitions of going to South Africa or Botswana. I had not really thought about it seriously because I thought I was still too young, but I was then overtaken by events.

The dreaded red bereted soldiers came to our village one afternoon. The men and the older boys had taken to spending days out in the bush hiding in caves for fear of the soldiers. When they came into the village, I was the oldest male there and I got most of the attention from their leader. Of course I did not understand a word he said because he spoke in Shona. This seemed to infuriate him even more and he shouted louder – as if shouting louder would make me understand a language I did not know.

Then he hit me. I had been hit before, by older members from the family for the many misdemeanours that young people will commit from time to time; by my friends at fist fights; by teachers at school and even my mother had slapped me now and again. All that now seemed to have been child's play. This soldier knew how to hit! It was so painful that I could not cry. I just stood there staring at him in awe, dazed.

After they had gone, MaMpofu explained that I had been hit because I was a dissident-in-training and I would grow up to be a problem for the army. Almost in tears, she explained to the elders that the village was no longer safe for me and the other young men.

'They will come back,' she explained, 'and when they do, who knows what they are capable of. We have heard of what they did in Matabeleland North and how many people they killed!'"

"She sounds like an amazing human being, that MaMpofu."

"She was – is. She is one of the people I am really looking forward to seeing when I go back home – if she is still there." It struck me for the first time that I had been so out of touch for so long that I did not know who was still alive. Not even my mother! I had to go.

"What about your parents?" Rumbie asked quietly.

"Of course I'm looking forward to seeing them, well my mother, at least. I'm not sure if my father will be there. He had long disappeared when I left home."

"Disappeared?"

"Yes. The Shona soldiers were rounding up men from all over the province and detaining them. The last we heard, my father had been detained in a place called Bhalaga and, according to some people detained with him (who had been released), he and a few other men had been taken away one night, and they had never been seen or heard from again – up to the time I left anyway. My mother continued to hope that he had been moved to another detention centre and that one day he would come home.

"I was not really sure what I felt about my father - a man I hardly knew. However the stories that the men from Bhalaga told, had given me a new respect for him. He had been picked up and accused of being a ZAPU supporter and with many other men, they were herded into the disused army base where living conditions, according to those released, were nothing short of horrendous. Food was scarce and the soldiers seemed to enjoy beating and torturing the inmates. So traumatised were some of the men who came from there that they refused to talk about some of their experiences.

"'Sometimes', I remember one of them saying, 'they would make male and female detainees have sex in front of them for their amusement'. He had shaken his head ruefully. 'Your husband's other woman', he addressed my mother, 'was tortured by having a sharp stick pushed up her private parts while her husband was made to watch! I will remember her screams for the rest of my life'. I saw my mother wince as though she felt the other woman's pain. 'That poor woman', she had said quietly."

Rumbie seemed to sense that I had gone into a dark place in the recesses of my memory and she said nothing. I sensed her empathy though and it seemed to me that she was genuinely shocked by what I was telling her.

"'But my husband was never political', my mother had said, 'he always said that he did not trust politicians as they were really looking after their own interests and only used people to…'

'That, Mrs Dube, did not matter to the soldiers. As long as you were Ndebele, you were ZAPU. It was as simple as that'."

Rumbie stood up, went to the kitchen and brought back a glass of water which she handed to me. She, clearly, did not know what to say, yet in that simple act, I felt that Rumbie and I were on the same side. Quite what that side was, I could not immediately define.

"'I'm sure they will soon realise their mistake and my husband will be released'. Even at that young age, I remember feeling angry with my mother. How could she possibly still believe, after all she had heard, that these monsters were going to release my father? I never said anything to her but I think that, at that point, I accepted the real possibility that my father was dead; although of late, I have found myself harbouring my mother's hope that he may still be alive!"

"She must have really loved your father." Rumbie said. "And now she doesn't know if her son is alive or not!"

I had not thought about that –not for a long time. In the early years of my stay in South Africa, I thought about my mother all the time, but as the years went by, she had become a pleasant but distant memory. I knew that I loved her dearly but I had lost all contact with my people after my near drowning crossing the Limpopo River. In the early years, I had written letters using the address of the primary school that I had attended but as these had remained unanswered, I assumed that the erratic postal service had not delivered the letters. I did not know it then, but in the ten years since I had left, the postal service had got even worse!

"After the encounter with the soldiers – I can still feel that clap when I think about it – it took a few days for me and three older boys to prepare for the journey south. The elders had debated the issue for a couple of evenings, particularly in my case as it was felt that I was too young. I could tell that my mother was very sad about my leaving but she had little say in the decision and was only told by the men what the right thing to do was. The only one who seemed to understand my mother at this time was MaNcube whose own experience of losing a husband and a son meant that she could empathise. My mother spent many of her afternoons at MaNcube's and when she came back, it was clear that she had been crying."

"And you? Did you feel for your mother in any way?"

"Well, I did not realise how far we were going and the excitement of going to *eGoli* outweighed any misgivings I may have had. All I was thinking about was how I was going to send money to my mother and make her life better. The stories I had heard of South Africa and the untold riches to be had convinced me that I was making the right move. MaMpofu encouraged me as well, although I could tell that she too was unhappy about my going. 'You'll soon be back', she would say although it felt like she was trying to convince herself of that fact. 'As soon as the soldiers leave the area, we will send for you'."

For a few minutes, I was overwhelmed by these thoughts of my leaving home. Was I selfish? Did I not care about my family at all? It had been ten years!

I found myself sobbing, uncontrollably. Why had it taken me this long? I knew that in the early years of my stay in South Africa, my thoughts were always about making enough money to be able to go home with money in my pocket, nice clothes on my back and some goodies for all the people in my young life – clothes for my mother, and MaMpofu of course, a suit for my father, a hat for Khulu, and my uncles and other cousins would get smaller parcels of ties of handkerchiefs or socks.

"Why, why, why did I forget?" I murmured.

"Don't be so hard on yourself." Rumbie had moved and was now sitting next to me. "It cannot have been easy to leave home like that but I think the thoughts of going back to a home where you felt unsafe must have been harder. In any case, you are going soon, you have a bit of money and I'm sure it will be a very happy home coming."

I felt a warmth towards Rumbidzai that I had not felt before. I cannot have been a pleasant sight at that very moment as my face was full of the dried fluids that had come out of my facial orifices when I was crying. I had even been wiping my face with my arm and I noticed what looked like mucus on my shirt sleeve.

"Go and wash your face," she reminded me of MaMpofu. She made me feel like I had no say in the matter, yet it still felt like I had made the decision.

"That feels better," I said as I emerged from the bathroom, having cleaned myself as best I could. "I have not cried like that in a long time. I am so sorry."

"A good cry never did anyone any harm." She was being polite, I decided, but she obviously had seen a side of me that she probably did not like. I was sitting next to her, having gone back to that position when I came out of the bathroom. It was the only place in the room that felt safe.

"So, how did Mr Van *'find'* you, as you say?"

"I lost count of the days but we seemed to walk for ever! The days were very hot so we generally walked in the early mornings, starting before light and walking until it was too hot, then we would find a nice shady tree under which we would sit or sleep until it was cool enough in the late afternoon. Our provisions, made up of some homemade bread, boiled mealies and an assortment of boiled nuts ran out after two or three days even with us supplementing our diet with wild fruits – when we found some – we even tried to catch some rats, figuring that if the Shona's ate them, they must be safe, but we were unsuccessful - and boiled eggs that we found in some bird's nest."

"What bird's nest?" Rumbie was looking part shocked part fascinated.

"I don't know," I said honestly.

"But Sipho, you could have poisoned yourselves!"

"Clearly we did not. But what would have been worse, dying slowly of hunger or dying of poisoning? Anyway," I said after a long pause, "we finally made it to the Limpopo and, well, I nearly drowned."

"Now you are making that up Mr Dube!" She said getting up to go to the toilet. "I'm already impressed with your trek through the jungle. You don't have to embellish it anymore!" There was laughter in her voice.

"But it's true..."

"Yes, yes Sipho," she said closing the door behind her.

I sat there listening to the sounds coming from the bathroom, my imagination running wild. She was now taking off her pantie, and... was that running water or was she...? It went quiet for a while and then the faint but unmistakable smell coming from the bathroom told me what else she was doing. I found myself laughing quietly. 'Even the pretty ones do that,' I said to myself.

She came out looking radiant, having clearly freshened herself up after the bodily function. She was pretty. For a Shona, she was very pretty!

"Like what you see?" I must have been staring.

"Yes... I mean, you are a very nice person."

“Ah! You’ve only just realised that?” I could not quite tell if she was joking or being serious. “Is that how you Ndebele guys look at nice women?”

“I said person. You are a nice person.”

“So, you always look at nice people like that?” Why was she being so difficult?

“Anyway, tell me about this ‘*drowning*’” – she made quotation marks in the air – “of yours.”

So I told her. In every detail. She listened, sceptically at first but I could tell that as the story unfolded, she began to think that there may have been some truth in it.

“The last thing I remember is thinking about whether crocodiles could attack in these waters,” I concluded.

“Are you telling me that this really happened?”

“Of course it did. Why would I make something like that up?”

“I don’t know,” there was mischief in her voice, “to impress me.”

“Why would I want to…”

“Impress me? Because, as you just said, I’m a nice person.”

I decided that I really liked this girl. She was capable of lightening even the darkest of moods with a well-chosen word or phrase, even just a gesture.

“That’s not what I was going to say,” I lied. “I was going to say, why would I want to tell you a lie?”

“People lie all the time for all sorts of reasons,” Rumbie looked serious and somewhat pensive for a minute or two, then seemed to quickly come out of that mode.

"Anyway," she said somewhat too cheerfully, "the crocodiles clearly did not eat you?"

"Presumably they were busy fighting off the flood themselves." I was fighting back the tears that had overcome me earlier, so I stood up and went to the window so that she would not see my eyes. The three children that were excitedly playing with one tricycle and taking turns to ride provided something of a distraction. I watched them quietly for a few minutes rather envying their enjoyment of such a simple pleasure. I, of course, had not had any such fancy toys to play with and I wondered how they would have fared in the world of my childhood.

In a few minutes, I had worked out who the owner of the tricycle was. He took every second turn, meaning that he rode twice as much as the other two. I remembered how, when my uncle, 'Ncane Peter had made me a catapult, I made sure that I took my turn after each one of my four friends so that for every one turn that each of them took, I had four! It did not improve my rather poor aim and everyone else took home their kills while I went back with my catapult, which I blamed for missing every bird that I tried to kill.

'Never mind,' MaMpofu had tried to console me, 'I'll let you have some of my *mbeva'.*

My mother had looked somewhat miserable as she went into her kitchen to prepare the evening meal of *isitshwala* (maize porridge/pap) and some wild leaves that she had picked for relish. There was no way that she would allow me to eat a *gundwane*!

"I'm not sure what happened," I said turning away from the window, "but when I came to, I was lying on the ground, naked except for the pair of torn shorts that I had been wearing as underwear. The sun was very hot, I remember, and for a few moments, I thought that I had fallen asleep while looking after the family's cattle. I got up – or rather tried to get up – hurriedly and found that I could not stand. It felt like one of those dreams I used to have as a child when I slept with my knees tucked up in the foetal position. I'd always be chased by something (or someone) and found it difficult to run. I would always wake up just before I was caught, usually sweating although I don't remember whether it was from the effort of running or from the fright."

"I used to have those kind of dreams too," Rumbie sounded as though she was surprised that someone else had also had those dreams. "Sometimes I would end up falling over a cliff and waking up just before I hit the ground."

"They used to tell me that if I ever hit the ground in those dreams, I would die!" I said, although I had often wondered how they knew this for a fact. After all if one died, they could not tell anyone that they died because they hit the ground in their dream!

"Anyway, I was not waking up from this dream because I was not asleep. The voices that came from my right startled me. I turned my head to see two white boys sitting on a rock and watching me from what I presumed was a safe distance in their minds. I could not understand what they were saying but was sure that the language they were speaking was not English. I had gone as far as Form two in school and English had been my favourite subject.

After some time, they seemed to realise that I could not understand them at all. One of them stood and came towards me with his hands in his pockets in that confident manner that all white boys seem to have. He pointed across me towards my left.

'Zimbabwe?' It sounded like a question.

I turned my head to look in the direction he was pointing and saw the river. I remembered then what had happened. So many questioned came to my mind; how had I got out? Where were my friends? Did they get out? Were they, like me, lying on the side of the river where I could not see them because my vision was limited to the left and right?"

The tears came flooding back as I remembered how alone I had felt at that time; how alone I had been since coming to South

Africa because I never did find out what happened to my friends. They were older and my mother had relied on them to look after me! I had tried to speak but my mouth was so dry that it felt as though my tongue was swollen and filled my whole mouth.

"'Zimbabwe?' He said again.

I had nodded without understanding. The two boys spent what seemed like an age, apparently arguing although I could not understand what it was they were arguing about. Eventually, the one who had spoken to me seemed to win the argument and again approached me.

'Running from Mugabe?' He spoke English! I nodded again and tried to speak, to ask for some water, but no sound came out.

'You want water?'

He had asked and without waiting for my answer, had spoken to his friend in the language I did not understand. The friend brought some water in a strange looking bottle and he helped me sit up and slowly put water in my mouth, a few drops at a time to start with and increasing the amount of water until I could swallow slightly larger volumes. All this time, he seemed to be making a running commentary to his friend although I could of course not understand what he was saying.

'Can't give you too much', my friend was at pains to explain to me what he was doing. I felt a sudden elation. The white boy had indicated that Zimbabwe was across the river. I had made it into South Africa! But I was still not sure what would happen. These were children whose parents might yet decide to hand me over to the authorities! That thought sent shivers up my spine. I could not go back! Having made it this far, I could not go back!

'Don't worry, my father will be here just now'."

"Who were the boys?" I had been so lost in my memories that Rumbie's question did not make sense – at first.

"What boys? Oh, my friends from the river. It was Piet, you know, Mr Van's son…"

"The Doctor?"

"Yes. I don't remember his friend's name and, to be honest, I don't think I ever saw him again. He did not seem too friendly anyway. Piet was only a little boy in shorts then, visiting his grandparents from Johannesburg where his father and mother lived and worked but I understand he was the one who talked his father out of handing me over to the authorities.

'He is about my age', he apparently told his father, 'how would you feel if I was in his position?'

Apparently nothing his father said about me being an illegal, who would probably turn out to be a criminal, could persuade young Piet! Even when his father tried to argue that Piet would never find himself in the position that I was in, he apparently got quite angry.

'How do you know that, dad? You think that the privileged life you lead under this Apartheid system is normal? You think that it will last for ever?'"

"He's always been quite liberal then? Piet I mean?"

"I think so. He qualified as a doctor and chose to go and work in Soweto, much to the disgust of his grandparents! His grandmother was particularly horrified. In fact, recently, when I visited them on the farm she was telling me how their son had spent so much money on Piet's education and all he could do was to go treat black children in Soweto Hospitals for a fraction of what he could get elsewhere."

"So, how did you come to work for Mr Van's restaurant in Johannesburg?"

"Long story. I quickly became one of his parents' most trusted workers on the farm and I went back to school – through distance learning. In fact when Mr Van suggested that I come to Johannesburg to work for him, his mother would not have it.

'He is the most honest worker we have', I heard her tell her son in Afrikaans, which I had begun to understand a little bit, 'and he is very intelligent'.

'And for those reasons, you don't want him to progress?' his son had asked casually.

'But he is illegal and in Jo'burg, he will get caught'.

'Don't be so dramatic, mother. He is more likely to be caught here than in the hustle and bustle of Johannesburg! In any case, independence is coming to Africa and sooner or later it will come to South Africa. Don't you think…'

'Never!' his mother had interrupted, almost shouting, 'we will never give up this country. Look what these people have done to the rest of Africa; the Rhodesia…'

'It's Zimbabwe now, mother.' He sounded like he was trying to appease her without giving in.

'Yeah, well,' Mrs Van Senior was smiling, 'we used to go to Rhodesia to visit the Zimbabwe Ruins, now they tell me that going to Zimbabwe is to visit the Rhodesia Ruins!'

They had both laughed at a joke that I was hearing for the first time but have since found out that it was a common joke among the whites.

'I was going to say,' Mr Van had gone on, 'don't you think it is better to have honest, educated Africans to take over when independence does come?'

'But he is not a South African!'

'Oh, mother, how many foreign workers have come to South Africa over the years and eventually been assimilated into South African society?'

'As far as I'm concerned, they are all foreigners!'

'Funny that,' Mr Van had responded, 'They think that you are the foreigner from Europe!'

'Oh, take him! Your father and I will have to do without an honest houseboy because you want to educate your future President!'

'Don't worry, mother. Piet will find you another one from the river.' I was not sure if that was meant as a joke."

"He was right of course," Rumbie was looking straight at me.

"Who was right about what?"

"Mr Van. He said that you would be assimilated into South African society and here you are…"

"I am not assimilated!" I hesitated. How much did I know about my native land? I had spent all my adult life in South Africa and I knew more about my adopted land than I did about Zimbabwe. I had to go back.

"Goodness! Look at the time!" Rumbie exclaimed suddenly. It was after nine in the evening. So lost in conversation that I had not realised how late it was. I panicked. Would I be able to get a lift home so late in the evening? I had never been out that late and therefore did not know how one could travel at that time of night.

"I'll have to phone for a taxi," I said, remembering that Rumbie had a telephone in her flat.

"Don't be silly! You can sleep here." My heart stopped for a moment, "I can easily make a bed for you here in the lounge." Oh, she was not inviting me into her bed then.

"Thank you, but what will your neighbours think? I mean when they see a man coming out of your flat in the morning."

"We'll have to make sure that you are not seen then. You may have to live at four, before anyone gets up."

"I can do that..."

"Sipho!" she had laughter in her voice, "I'm teasing you. Who cares what the neighbours think? If that's how they think they probably have reached those conclusions already anyway."

"And you don't mind?"

"Why should that bother me? You and I know the truth. That is all that matters."

She quickly made what looked like a comfortable bed on the floor of her lounge. She had offered the sofa, but with my height, I didn't think that I'd have been comfortable. It turned out that sleeping on the floor, which I had done at home for many years, was no longer as easy as I had thought it would be, so I did not sleep very well and I tossed and turned and thought about the events of the day- well, about Rumbie, really.

My first thoughts were about how she could trust me so much – I had not heard her key turn in the door after she closed it, so she clearly did not expect that I would attack her during the night. The elation that I felt at being so trusted soon gave way to other thoughts. What if she hoped that I would follow her into her room? I had been told many times that women could not tell men that they wanted to sleep with them. Men, the wisdom of most of my male friends dictated, had to understand the clues from a woman's behaviour and do what was expected of them without asking questions. But then, what were the clues in Rumbie's behaviour in this case? She seemed genuinely fond of me and she had allowed me to sleep in her home! Would she be disappointed if I did not, at least try to get into her bed? On the other hand, she seemed comfortable around me and had shown a tremendous amount of trust in me. Would I be betraying her trust if I tried to, you know...?

I found myself laughing at my thoughts. I was completely inexperienced in that area and was not sure what I would do if I did get into her bed. What if I tried and it was not what she was expecting? How embarrassing would that be? Would she be willing to talk to me after that? Would she be willing to talk to me if I did not go to her as she might have been expecting? It was all so confusing and I spent most of the night holding on to my manhood which seemed to have a mind of its own at this point! Eventually, I found myself doing what I had sworn to myself that I would never do again! The relief that resulted was only tempered by the thoughts that I may have left tell-tale signs that Rumbie might be able to detect when she came to unmake my bed. So I decided that I would wake up before her and unmake my own bed before she came. Those were the last thoughts that I remember.

"Wakey, wakey!" Rumbie woke me up as she opened the curtains and let in a flood of light. I sat up quickly and nearly threw the blankets off me until I realised, just in time, that I was in my underwear – and that my underpants were below my knees! The sight of Rumbie standing at the window with the light behind her did not help my situation. She was dressed in a flimsy night dress that left very little to the imagination! Once again, my manhood seemed to behave independently of me and I pulled the blanket even tighter, worrying that she may have been able to see what was happening under the blanket!

"Did you wet the bed?" she teased, I think, "You are holding on to that blanket as if you think…"

"I'm naked under the blanket," I interrupted wanting her to understand the reason for my behaviour.

"So you think I might rape you?" Crikey! Did she know what she was doing to me? Once again the thoughts that I had been having during the night came back. Were these the clues that my friends always talked about? The thought of being '*raped* 'by a woman created even more turmoil in my naked loins. I would have been the willing victim of rape at this time. Would it still be rape? I asked myself.

“No! no,” I said, my mouth feeling unusually dry, “it’s just that I’ve always slept naked and I was worried that I may not be fully covered.”

For a few moments, Rumbie stood watching me – examining me really – and I had the distinct feeling that she was considering whether to come into my bed or not.

“I’ll leave you to it then,” she said as she left the room.

I quickly got up and folded the blanket, making sure that there were no ‘tell-tale spillages’ that could have been detected from my nocturnal activities.

Disappointingly, she came back into the room dressed in a pair of jeans and a loose fitting t-shirt. They still showed off her figure rather well, but it was nothing like what she had had on before.

“Did you sleep well?” she asked.

“Yes I did,” I lied, “You?”

“I was very tired, and in some pain in my jaw, but I slept really well for the most part. I’ve been awake for a while, though.”

I did not immediately ask her why she had been awake for some time, mainly because I was trying to decide whether she may have been having the same thoughts that I had had during the night!

“I was thinking about our conversation yesterday,” Rumbie went on, “I’d like to introduce you to my uncle, Tobias…”

She wants to introduce me to her family!

“He was in the war in Mozambique and yet he seems to have no respect for the leaders of that war. I think that you may find that what you perceive as a tribal conflict between the Shonas and Ndebeles is really the continuation of power consolidation by people who want absolute power. My uncle has some rather harrowing stories about happenings in Mozambique."

The immediate effect of her statement was the calming of the fires that were raging in my body. I found myself getting angry. How dare she want to minimise the suffering of my people by claiming that we were not specifically targeted? Her voice and her manner suggested that she was genuine in what she was saying. I was equally convinced that she was wrong.

"But for now," she said, looking directly into my face, "I think that you need to go home and see your people. I can only imagine what your mother has gone through over the last ten years, and I know she will be so happy to see you."

CHAPTER FOUR

Two hours into the bus journey from Johannesburg, I was regretting the decision that I had made to take the Zimbabwean made AVM bus instead of a coach.

"They are a lot cheaper," George had told me. "The coaches are a lot more expensive but, you'll still get home!"

George and the others of course went home regularly even though, like me, none of them had passports. It was them that had connected me to the conductor who was going to *'facilitate'* my crossing into Zimbabwe. We had left Park Station in Johannesburg just after sunset and it was now quite dark. The well-lit sprawling conurbation of Johannesburg and Pretoria was behind us and we were trudging along in the bus whose seats were the most uncomfortable that I had ever sat on. Every so often, we were overtaken by a coach in which the passengers looked more relaxed and comfortable, only reminding me how miserable my own bus ride was. The rather large woman that sat to my left, took most of the two-sitter seat, leaving me squashed against the cold metal of the bus wall. I wondered why I continued to listen to George! None of his advice had ever been sound.

I consoled myself with the thought that I was only going as far as Beit Bridge, which we would reach in the early hours of the morning, and then it would be a short journey to Maramani! I was imagining all sorts of reactions when my mother, MaMpofu and the others saw me. I had been given more money than I had ever seen in my life by Mr Van and I had bought gifts for everyone. I still had a fair amount on me even though my facilitator had asked for a significant proportion of what I had.

The woman next to me had been eating nonstop since we left Joburg and kept offering me some of her faire which consisted mainly of crisps, biscuits, doughnuts, more crisps and, when we stopped at a service station for a toilet and refreshments break, chicken and chips. I was so nervous that I could not eat anything, let alone her particular mixture so I kept politely declining her offers.

"Don't you eat anything?" I gathered that that was her question from her manner and tone. I still understood very little Shona in spite of the time I was spending with Rumbidzai. I indicated to her that I did not understand Shona but also that I had eaten just before getting on the bus.

"*Festi* time to Zimbabwe?" She must have assumed that because I did not speak her language, I was not Zimbabwean.

"I'm from Zimbabwe," I told her.

Her whole body shook as she laughed, although I '*felt*' more than saw the shaking.

"You don't speak Shona and you're from Zimbabwe? Oh," she seemed to reach some realisation, "*Mundevere?*"

"I am actually *Venda* but I do speak isiNdebele, yes." I had never identified myself as Venda before, preferring to accept the widely held view that everyone from our part of the country was Ndebele.

"But Venda's are from South Africa," my ample friend insisted.

"Not all of them. People in the Beit Bridge and surrounding area are Venda."

"I did not know."

We rode in silence for a while and I was grateful that my discomfort was not being compounded by having to talk to this woman who was not unpleasant – apart from her eating habits - but I was much happier with my own thoughts which oscillated between worrying about the approaching border and my last conversation with Rumbie.

She had arrived at the station unexpectedly, never having indicated that she would come to see me off. I was pleasantly surprised, of course, and could not believe how happy I was to see her -having all along thought that we had said our final goodbyes at work and I would only see her again on my return from Zimbabwe. She looked really lovely and, it seemed to me, she had made a special effort to dress up for the occasion!

"You thought you'd got rid of me for a few weeks, hey, but here I am!" she spoke casually but her body language was anything but casual. Strangely, this made me happy because I thought that it was her sadness at our parting that caused her apparent nervousness. We made small talk for the few minutes before the bus was due to depart and I was not even sure why she had come because we seemed to run out of conversation every few sentences. Finally, as the driver started the bus and everyone was taking their seats, Rumbie produced a parcel from her bag. 'A parting gift,' I thought excitedly!

"When you get to Beit Bridge, a cousin of mine who works for immigration will pick up this parcel from you." She seemed to hesitate, then, as if she wanted to get it out as quickly as possible; "These are a few items of clothing for my daughter."

"YOU have a daughter?" I was stunned. How dare she string me along like that? I had almost convinced myself that, even though we had not actually said anything to each other, I was going to tell MaMpofu at least, that I had this Shona girlfriend that reminded me very much of her. Well, girlfriend does not necessarily mean that she is my lover, after all! But, she had a daughter!

"Yes," she sounded defiant. "I have a six year old daughter. So, now you know," she sounded concerned but relieved. "Well," she said as she patted me playfully on the cheek, "time for you to go. I hope to see you when you get back." She shook my hand and I felt something that she passed on to me. It was a two hundred Rand note. "Buy yourself something to eat on the way." She made as if she was going to give me a hug, then changed her mind. "Have a safe trip and please come back," she said softly.

I realised then that I still had the note that she had given me in my hand. Her daughter was six, and she had told me that she was twenty two! 'She's been doing it since she was sixteen!' I said to myself. I was still a virgin at twenty-six of course and I had been respecting her. Even when she clearly offered herself to me, I had not seen it because I had assumed that she was as innocent as I was! She had told me that the bodies of all adults make certain demands on them and I had not realised that she was telling me that HER body was making those demands. She only wanted sex with me and I had been stupid enough to think that we could be more than just sexual partners. I was not interested in just a sexual partner! I had kept myself pure for this long and I had almost given it away to a Shona with a history! I put the note in my shirt pocket and tried to forget about the bitch called Rumbie.

But I could not. All I could see was her sad, teary face as she waved good bye at the station; her infectious smile that always seemed to cheer me up; her laughter that permeated my many thoughts. I really enjoyed being near her, spending time with her. Did it matter that she had a child?

On the other hand, how many men had bedded her in the last six years? She probably had a boyfriend even now. This Uncle Tobias that she was going to introduce to me was probably her boyfriend…

"Hey *wena*!" the voice was virtually in my ear, "wake up! We are almost at the border."

In spite of my discomfort, I had fallen asleep! The nervousness that I had kept hidden behind a calm exterior came to the fore. In spite of the many assurances that I had received from my work colleagues and from the bus conductor, I was still worried. I was truly anxious. What if the authorities refused to let me through; worse still, what if they decided to put me in jail? It would mean that I would not be seeing my mother on the next day. I would not be seeing MaMpofu and the others. And how long would it be before I went back to Rumbie? Would she worry about me or would she just move on and find another lover? After all, she already knew what to do with men! I felt a shiver run down my spine. She was probably sleeping with another man right then with me now out of the way. Then again, I really did not know that she did not sleep with other men even when I was in Johannesburg. She had only let me into a flat a few days earlier when I went to visit her- that is after I hit her at work! I remembered how casual she had been about me spending the night in her flat. 'She's obviously used to men sleeping in her flat', I concluded as another shiver ran up my spine.

"Are you cold?" The large woman besides me asked, laughter in her voice, incredibly, she was chewing!

"No!" I said, realising how warm it was even that early in the morning. Why would she think I was cold?

"You seem to be shivering. Are you nervous?"

Was I that obvious? How would I react if I was questioned by an officer…?

I need not have worried. The money that I had paid the conductor turned out to have been well spent. On the South African side, he told me to get off the bus and just mingle with the others until it was time to board. There were many other buses and I could easily get lost in the crowds. So lost in fact that I nearly missed my bus and had to be found by the conductor, who was not pleased with me for causing the delay. On the Zimbabwean side, he told me to stay on the bus and not do anything stupid. Of course he did not define *stupid* so I was not sure what I could, or could not do. After what seemed like ages sitting in the bus in which the temperature seemed to rise by the minute and the clothes that I had worn for the night chill were now inappropriate, a female officer came onto the bus and slowly walked up the isle towards me. My heart was pounding as I, once again, imagined what fate would befall me once I was in the hands of the authorities. 'What if they decided that I was a returning dissident?' I asked myself thinking of how my homeland had been like ten years earlier.

She stopped next to my seat. I did not dare look at her fearing that this might be construed as stupid. It was very hot. Sweat ran down my face and my back. My palms felt like my hands had been dipped in warm water.

"Sipho?"

"Yes'" I tried to say but no sound came out, at least none that I heard.

"Hello," she said offering her hand, "I'm Chipo."

Why was she telling me her name, and wasn't her name the Shona equivalent of my own. How ironic would that be; being arrested by my namesake!

"I'm Rumbie's cousin." I could have hugged her, but was not sure whether that might be a stupid thing to do. But my relief was unbelievable.

"Did you think I had come to arrest you?" She laughed a laughter that sounded so much like Rumbie that I looked up into her face. She looked nothing like Rumbie, her face looking almost hostile. But she was smiling although her smile was not as pretty as Rumbie's. Why was I comparing her with Rumbie?

"How are you, Chipo?" My voice sounded strange even to me. It must have been the reduction of adrenalin as I realised that I was almost safe.

"You're better looking than Rumbie said. She always gets the nice men." The joy at hearing that Rumbie had talked about me to her cousin and described me as good looking was dampened by the second part of her statement. So, it was true, I thought, she had had many men!

"I mean, she is always being chased by nice men," she tried to correct her statement. "From when we were young, we could be admiring the same guy but they went for her and not for me," there was a note of regret in her voice. "But I love her dearly. You have a parcel for me?"

"Oh yes." I said reaching under the seat of the bus and bringing out the plastic carrier bag that Rumbie had given me at the bus station. "How is her daughter?" I found myself asking.

"Well, I think she's okay. I'm only going to see her next week when I go home to Rusape."

I found myself wanting to give Chipo something and I reached into my shirt pocket, bringing out the note that Rumbie had given me. Something fell out and Chipo went to pick it up.

"Well, you guys must be serious. This is a nice photo of my cousin. She clearly doesn't want you to forget her when you meet your old girlfriends..."

"I have no..." I started to say, "It's been ten years and I have lost contact with any girls back home," I did not want her knowing that Rumbie was my first girlfriend. Well, Chipo clearly thought that Rumbie was my girlfriend even though I was not sure. I took the picture off Chipo and looked at it. It was a particularly beautiful picture and seeing her face took my breath away, even though it was only a picture!

A few hours later, I stood outside the Moyo Trading Store at the township that had been the main centre of attraction in my childhood. It had been an uneventful ride on the bus although it had been even more uncomfortable than the bus ride from Jo'burg, mainly because, unlike the earlier ride where the bigger items of luggage had gone onto the carrier on the roof of the bus, I had had to sit with most of my purchases, which were quite substantial, inside the bus as the carrier was full mainly of agricultural inputs – bags of seeds, fertilisers, ox-drawn ploughs, and even an ox-drawn cart - as people were preparing for the coming rainy season. It had reminded me of the drought years before I left home and I had wondered whether the rainfall in our home area had improved.

Anyway, now I stood outside the Moyo Trading Store with all my goods around me and wondered why the store looked so much smaller than I remembered. As the dust settled after the departure of the bus, I also noticed how deserted the place looked. I remembered it always as being a hive of activity and it was the one place that I looked forward to being sent to when I was growing up. Where was everybody?

"Do you need help with that, young man?" said a voice from the store.

I recognised Mr Moyo immediately although he looked a lot older than I remembered him. There was a certain tiredness in his eyes that I had not noticed before and he clearly did not recognise me because when I greeted him enthusiastically and called him by name, he peered at me, holding his hand up to shield his eyes from the sun.

"Do I know you?" Even his voice sounded tired.

"Yes, Mr Moyo," I said, unable to contain my excitement at seeing a face that had been so much part of my childhood. "It's Sipho!" I was almost shouting and pumping his hand up and down, "Sipho Dube..."

I felt his hand stiffen in mine, and then he pulled away and walked unsteadily to a stool on his shop veranda. He looked very old indeed.

"Sipho?" He did not sound convinced, "Son of Solomon? Are you alive?" His voice sounded incredulous. "It has been such a long time that we all thought you had, you know..." He seemed unable to finish the sentence.

"Died?" I finished it for him. "No, I'm very much alive, as you can see."

"Your friends came back, a few months after you left and said that you were the only one that had managed to cross, having just been missed by the flash flood that discouraged them."

"How come it took them a few months to get back?"

"They got picked up by the soldiers and they were accused of being dissidents coming in from South Africa. Super ZAPU, they called them." He paused and looked into the distance. He looked very troubled. "Once the soldiers decided you were a dissident, you were lucky to come out of there alive!"

"But they had no weapons. How could they have been dissidents?"

"They were accused of having hidden them and were tortured, beaten and force marched into the bush to show the soldiers where they had hidden their weapons. Of course they did not have any weapons but it seems that the harder they denied this, the more they were tortured." Mr Moyo spoke in an even, measured voice, but I could detect that there was real anger beneath the calm exterior. It was almost funny to me that my erstwhile friends could have been accused of being dissidents. They were innocent rural boys who had just tried to go and find their imagined fortunes in South Africa!

"Anyway, you are in luck." Mr Moyo sounded flippant, "Here comes Zenzo now."

I looked in the direction that Mr Moyo was looking and saw what looked like an old man slowly limping towards us. His gait looked very strange indeed and I could not equate that figure to the young man that I had, for nearly a week, walked with in the bush on our way to the Limpopo; the young man who had been the main instigator of the many fist fights that were a necessary part of our cattle herding days.

It took him a long while to get to us while Mr Moyo and I watched in silence. When he got close enough, he looked up and when the initial shock of seeing me had passed, he broke into a toothless grin and came at a surprisingly brisk pace, and hugged me. He was not the cleanest person who had ever hugged me but I was so happy to see him that I did not mind.

Whatever happened to him in the years that had passed since our excursion into the unknown must have been very hard on him. He broke down and cried like a baby.

"Sipho, Sipho…." was all he seemed able to say. I felt like crying, but somehow thought that it would be unfair for me to cry under such circumstances. Clearly he had real cause to cry. What could I cry for? We stood like that for a long while, hardly moving, even though the odour coming from Zenzo was beginning to get to me. It was a mixture of sweat, urine, unwashed clothes and an unbathed body! Mr Moyo seemed to have found reason to sweep his shop front thoroughly.

Gradually, I extricated myself from Zenzo's clutches and busied myself moving my luggage from the side of the road onto Mr Moyo's shop veranda. Zenzo found himself an old wooden soft drinks crate on which he perched himself. I could not imagine what circumstances would have reduced my friend to the sorry state that he now was in.

"How did you survive?" Zenzo seemed to have recovered from the initial shock of seeing me. "We thought you had drowned…"

"Drowned?" Mr Moyo sounded very surprised, "you guys said that Sipho had managed to cross and that you had been held back by a sudden flood! Now you say that you thought he drowned?"

"Well," Zenzo was looking slightly embarrassed, "clearly he did not drown as you can see but yes, in all these years, we thought he had drowned. However, when we saw the hope in his mother's eyes at our appearance, we could not bring ourselves to tell her the truth, especially after hearing that her husband had never been found."

"He was never found?" I asked in surprise. I had long assumed that my father had been killed but this was the first time that my worst fears had been confirmed.

"No, he was not," Mr Moyo was looking very pensive and seemed unable to carry on for a while. "Gukurahundi was not a joke, you know. It left many widows in this area," he looked across at Zenzo, "and many crippled young people who have lost all hope." Mr Moyo was speaking in a monotone, and I could sense that this was a subject he did not enjoy talking about. "Can I offer you a cool drink?" He asked suddenly, almost as if he wanted to change the subject, "well, it's not exactly cool as our gas fridge is not functional because we cannot find any gas!"

I accepted the warm drink he offered because I was very thirsty in the stifling heat but also because I felt like rejecting it would cause him more pain on top of that which was already etched on his face.

"We hear of bodies being found down disused mine shafts and some mass graves have been discovered, but there is no way of telling whose the bodies they find are," he seemed close to tears. "And our government," he went on, "does not seem to understand, or care, that the pain of not knowing is worse than that of grieving and burying your dead."

"Why should they care? We are not Shona." Zenzo sounded flippant but there was real anger behind that voice. I found myself, in the middle of this, thinking about Rumbie. Would she support what had happened here? I decided that she would not.

"As for your mother," Mr Moyo looked directly at me, "She gave up," my heart skipped a beat, "after many years of waiting and hoping, she finally left. I understand that she is working in Beit Bridge." I was not sure if I imagined it but Mr Moyo and Zenzo seemed to exchange looks that suggested there was something more that they could not tell me.

"You mean I left my mother in Beit Bridge? So who is here, then? MaMpofu?" I asked, feeling rather confused.

"Things have changed a lot since you've been away," Mr Moyo sounded very tired, "Many young people have left the area since…" he seemed unable to carry on for a few seconds,"…since the troubles. Your uncle Peter took his wife and they now live in Harare; in fact most people have moved to the cities, mainly to Harare, but also to Bulawayo although I understand that opportunities are scarce as most of the industries have closed or moved to Harare and indeed many have gone to Botswana and South Africa."

"We, the damaged, are left in this dust bowl." Zenzo sounded like he wanted to laugh, yet at the same time, sounded like he was close to tears.

"The damaged?" I did not know what else to say.

"Look at me. Do I look like the Zenzo you left behind on the banks of the Limpopo? Our encounter with the Shona soldiers was …," he shifted in his seat as if to make himself more comfortable, "they took us to a place where we found that many other young people – and some not so young – were imprisoned. For many weeks or months, we lived in this camp where our daily routine started with long hours of humiliation which ranged from severe beatings, to interrogations that seemed to go on for hours on end." Zenzo looked into the distance and carried on in a mechanical voice, "The three of us, of course got special attention as they wanted us to admit that we were dissidents trained in South Africa. They wanted to know where the training bases were and where we had hidden our weapons. We did not know enough about South Africa to even lie about where we had been trained."

'They trained you well for interrogation,' they would say, 'but we have ways to break you.'

"So, they broke us, literally. My legs have almost healed now, but this one," he indicated his left leg, "was broken and for a time, I dragged it around until a doctor, I think, came to the camp and tried to fix it. It has never been properly fixed."

Mr Moyo took down a dusty bottle of a cheap brandy that seemed to have been on the shelf for a long time and poured some into three tin mugs. He kept one and offered the others to Zenzo and me.

"I don't drink," I said as I pushed the drink back to Mr Moyo. Zenzo gulped his thirstily and grabbed the one I had refused.

"I'll have it. You, Mr Moyo, are a life saver. We had some *thothotho* yesterday and I have such a hangover!"

Zenzo now drank thothotho! Thothotho was an illicit drink that, in my childhood, had been associated with very poor people with nothing better to do with their lives. Looking at Zenzo, he fitted that description well.

"Well," Zenzo seemed to want to tell his story, "they seemed determined to prove that we were dissidents and nothing we said would convince them that we were not. So the torture got worse. We had wires attached to our..." he indicated his crotch area, "... engines and they put electricity through them," he flinched as he remembered, "I have never felt so much pain. It induced involuntary erections that seemed to amuse the soldiers so much that they were unaware of the pain they were causing. In fact, there was one that would, after this all this, take us away and ..." he hesitated and then went on quickly, "he said that he wanted to show us that all Ndebele were women and so he would make us his women."

"You mean, have sex with you?" I had, in my many years in South Africa, come across people who were said to engage in such sex acts but had never associated such activities with my countrymen. "Was he a homosexual?" I asked incredulously.

Zenzo looked at me blankly and I quickly realised that he had never heard the word before.

"You know that there are men who prefer sex with other man, right?"

"Why would... come to think of it, he seemed to enjoy it. It was the only time he seemed to treat us with any gentleness. I had always assumed that he was doing it to humiliate us, but he would actually finish inside and pour his 'stuff' inside us!"

I could not think of anything more disgusting.

"Anyway, now I cannot be with any woman."

"You mean you now enjoy men?" I asked innocently.

"No!" Zenzo looked shocked, "they damaged my engine," he again indicated his crotch area, "and I cannot get it up!"

"So now drink is his woman," Mr Moyo said quietly.

"Well," Zenzo was looking at his cup rather intently, "she doesn't, complain, doesn't need my support and certainly has no expectations of me…"

"She expects to be bought!" Mr Moyo said, refilling Zenzo's cup.

"Yes, but thankfully, I have friends who are businessmen!"

I looked at the two of them and thought how different they seemed. The businessman in his crumpled shirt and tie looking to maintain a certain image in spite of the empty shelves in his shop and the apparent down and out with no image to preserve whatsoever; yet there seemed a genuine warmth and camaraderie between them.

"What about the others?" I asked, "Samson and Philani?"

"Philani's family originally came from the Chipinge area in Manicaland and I believe they moved back there," Mr Moyo explained. "As for Samson…"

"He was the lucky one," Zenzo interrupted.

"He has done rather well then?" I asked hopefully.

"You could say that," Mr Moyo seemed unsure how to answer my question, "He…"

"He spends his days running around like a madman!" Zenzo finished Mr Moyo's sentence for him.

"He is mad!" Mr Moyo countered.

"What do you mean, he is *mad*?" I did not understand what they were talking about.

"He is mad," Zenzo insisted, "as in..." he made a circular motion with his finger pointing towards his head in a familiar gesture that indicated mental instability. I was shocked.

"You mean he is mad, mad, not angry mad?"

"Perhaps it's his anger that made him mad," Mr Moyo offered an explanation.

"He was very angry when we were picked up by the army and because he continued to argue with them, he got beaten more than the rest of us. But it seemed that the harder they tried to break him, the more he argued. It was as if he was daring them to kill him!"

"What did you mean then that he was the lucky one?"

Zenzo looked at me for a long moment and seemed unsure whether he could really make me understand how difficult things were in that camp. It occurred to me, in that moment, that no one who had not been in the camp could even begin to understand the conditions in it.

"Well," Zenzo said at length, "Samson leaves in a world in which he does not seem to remember anything of what happened in the camp. In his more lucid moments, he will talk about our trek in the bush and will even mention your name..."

"My name?" I was astounded.

"Come to think of it," Mr Moyo seemed to have recalled something, "Samson did mention something about a drowning when you guys first came back! But no one took him seriously. He was mad, after all."

"He mentioned you, just the other day, in fact." Zenzo had not mentioned this to anyone. "He came running towards me and as I made way for him to pass, he stopped in front of me looking somewhat excited; 'Do you think Sipho made it to South Africa?' he asked, then his face became less animated and he carried on running."

"He must have felt it in his bones that you were on your way," Mr Moyo said, to laughter from Zenzo and I.

"Anyway, how is South Africa? Are you back for good? How come you are alone? I would have thought that there is a Mrs Dube by now. You know, one of those Xhosa girls with the big, you know," he extended his arms backwards to indicate a large derriere.

"South Africa is different, you know. It's a lot more developed and I have really got used to life there. I work for the white man whose son found me on the bank of the Limpopo." Briefly, I told them about how I had escaped drowning and what my life had been like since. The only small detail I left out was that I had a Shona girlfriend – in the sense that she was a girl who was my friend of course!

"So there is no Xhosa girl?" They seemed more interested in that than in anything else.

"No, there isn't," I answered honestly.

"Not even a Zulu?" Mr Moyo persisted.

"No." I answered again feeling as if I was being cross examined.

"You must have someone, surely?" Zenzo was almost salivating at the prospect, I assumed, of me having a girlfriend that I had sex with.

"There is someone, but she is not South African," I said tentatively.

"I knew it!" Zenzo slapped his thigh with excitement. "Where is she from? Botswana?"

"No, she is Zimbabwean."

“Oh.” Zenzo sounded disappointed. “You had to go to South Africa to find a Ndebele girl?”

“Yes,” I lied.

I felt my excitement rise as we approached the homestead. The first thing that I noticed, though, was that the big Mopani tree was gone. It left the landscape looking a lot more barren than I remembered. The huts looked somewhat smaller than my memory had suggested and the grain store in which I had hidden many times as a child and had been the one that had to go in to take out the grain, being the smallest, was no longer there; and only the rocks that it used to stand on remained to indicate where it used to be. I shuddered as I remembered how terrified I had been as I passed the grain out of the dark and dusty place. I always imagined that a snake could have been missed by the cursory inspection – by candlelight – that always preceded my entrance, and the odd rat that scurried past my feet would cause such panic in me that one day I had peed onto the grain. It meant, of course that I had had to be slow in bringing the grain out in order to dry out before I re-emerged.

As Mr Moyo’s young employee, who had been asked to ferry my not inconsiderable purchases by donkey cart form the township – as the collection of derelict and mostly empty shops was still called – to my home, brought the cart to a halt, a skinny dog came towards us wagging its tail as if to welcome us. Clearly it was happy to see us as there seemed to be no one else around. The place looked desolate and uninhabited. There was an eerie ghostly silence that was only exacerbated by the rickety buildings that looked like they needed repair – or complete replacement. I noticed that there had been an attempt to rethatch one of the huts, but whoever had done it was not very good. The only thing that looked alive, apart from the dog, was the mulberry tree that was laden with fruit. But even here, there seemed no sign that anyone was eating the fruit and there was a virtual carpet of fresh and rotting mulberries on the ground underneath the tree. I picked one of the fruits from a low hanging branch and put it in my mouth. It was as sweet and juicy as I remembered.

The tree itself brought back mixed memories; we had got into trouble for breaking it when it was small because we had played a game of high jump over it and not all of us were able to clear it. Later, it had become a convenient and ready source of the 'punishment sticks' that the adults would make us wait under the Mopani tree with. It was hard to believe that this was the same tree.

"Khulu does not like people eating his mulberries."

I had forgotten that I had someone with me.

"Khulu?"

"Yes," the young man seemed frightened even to talk about this, "he lives alone and I understand that he chased away or killed his family members."

It was definitely not the homecoming I had so looked forward to and I started to worry about where I was going to spend the night, it being quite late in the day.

"Ekuhle!" I said in the traditional salutation when one approaches a homestead, even though this particular homestead seemed completely deserted.

"Who is it?" The faint voice startled me. It came out of the newly rethatched hut and when the door opened, an old man, walking with considerable difficulty with the help of a crooked walking stick, came out. I could understand why the young man would have been frightened of him. Elderly men – or women for that matter – who looked like that were generally considered to be witches or, in this case, wizards! But he did not frighten me because I recognised him immediately. It was Khulu, my grandfather's younger brother who lived some kilometres away but was always visiting, as he clearly was, then.

"Khulu!" I was so relieved to see a familiar face that I ran to him to shake his hand. But he refused to extend his hand and peered at me suspiciously.

"Ulisotsha?" he asked, looking and sounding hostile.

"No, Khulu, I'm not a soldier. It's Sipho!"

"Sipho? Sipho from where?"

"Your grandson, Sipho…"

"I have no grandson called Sipho!"

"Well, you're older brother's grandson then. I went to South Africa many years ago and…"

Khulu looked like he had seen a ghost. He held my arm with his boney hand and peered into my face suspiciously. I could not tell whether he believed me or not; whether there was any recognition at all on his part. Still holding on to my arm with his right hand while his left hand supported him on his walking stick, he led me towards a stool in the shade provided by the mulberry tree. When he was finally comfortable, he let go of my arm and peered at me again and then seemed to notice the other young man with me.

"And who are you?" He asked, squinting his eyes as if he was trying to focus.

"Gift," the young man still sounded frightened, "Mr Moyo's grandson."

"Mr Moyo from where?"

"The businessman, khulu. The one who has the store at the township."

"Jokoniya has a grandson?"

"It's not his real grandson. . I think it's an orphaned youngster that he is looking after."

"How old is he?"

"I don't know, Khulu," I said honestly, thinking that he must have known Mr Moyo as a young man and still saw him as such.

"And who are you? A soldier?"

"No, Khulu, its Sipho. Your grandson who went to South Africa."

"Didn't you die?"

"No I did not die. I am here."

"The others came back without you." He did remember, I thought happily.

"What do you want?" I had celebrated too soon.

"I've come home. Where is everyone?"

It was a most frustrating conversation. Khulu seemed to drift in and out of reality and I could not get any clear answers from him. One minute it seemed like he knew what he was talking about, and the next, he was completely incomprehensible. Gift had left as soon as he could after offloading my luggage and for a few hours, there were just the two of us and the conversation soon died as Khulu seemed to retreat into a world that only he knew; so I took a closer look at the homestead that bore no resemblance to the one that I had left all those years ago. I could not imagine what could have happened to reduce my childhood home into this collection of ramshackle huts that looked totally abandoned – apart, of course from Khulu's hut. A stray donkey startled me as it sauntered across where MaMpofu had once kept her patch of vegetables, watered by any water thrown out of the kitchen. For a few minutes, the sights and sounds of my childhood came back to me. I saw the girls playing under the big mulberry tree with a long rope which two of them held at either end while the others took turns to go in and 'skip'. 'Fish, fish, spell you name; F I S H…'.I wondered where this clearly English game had come from and how it had been introduced into our village. I was standing under the big mango tree – looking a lot bigger than I remembered – I smiled to myself as I remembered the beating I had suffered under the Mopani tree because I had been caught stealing partially ripe fruit from the mango tree. We were all supposed to wait until there was enough ripe fruit for everyone to share. It had been a long while since I had actually enjoyed fruit picked from a tree, I thought.

I considered my position. I had come home laden with presents for people whose whereabouts I now did not know, and Khulu was not being much help; my dear mother was working in Beit Bridge – although I could not imagine as what – and I had gone past her believing that she was at the village; MaMpofu, my next favourite person was now leaving in faraway Harare with her husband, my uncle Peter. Clearly, I had to go back to Beit Bridge but what was I going to do with all the goods I had brought? More immediately, where was I going to sleep as the bus that had brought me from Beit Bridge would only return on the next day? Perhaps if I went back to the township and spoke to Mr Moyo. I found myself wishing I could talk to Rumbie. She would have had something to say about this situation – probably a joke. But there was nothing funny about where I found myself, having been so looking forward to getting home! Perhaps I should have taken the new-fangled cellular phones more seriously; I imagined myself with a cell phone and being able to call Rumbie at that very moment. I did not know at the time about network and the need to be in an area of coverage!

“Those things are for rich people”, I said out loud.

“Sipho!” the aged face with the toothless smile did not immediately register. But she clearly knew me and seemed really pleased. She looked like she wanted to hug me but her hands were full of some wild fruit that she had picked and something wrapped in her head scarf that I could not see. Her hair, which would have normally been covered by the head scarf, looked like it had not been combed – or washed – for many days.

“Why are you speaking to yourself? Have you caught khulu’s disease?” there was something vaguely familiar about that voice! Then I remembered, but the image that came to mind was the one I had seen as I squatted behind the bush near the well. I looked away, feeling slightly embarrassed. But how had she aged this much in ten years?

"MaTshuma!" I was really pleased to see a somewhat familiar face, "Here, let me help you with that," I offered to take the head scarf from her. She hesitated, then handed me the package. It was lighter than I had anticipated.

"It's just some wild leaves that I picked for relish," she explained, looking and sounding embarrassed. "Things are really tough here, and the drought hasn't helped." The hardships were clearly etched on her wrinkled face. "I was just passing to see how Khulu is," she went on. "Poor thing, his own home was burnt by the soldiers, you know, so he came to stay temporarily and has ended up with the whole place." There was no bitterness in her voice. She was just stating a fact.

"Why would they do that?" I was horrified.

"You know how stubborn these old people are. He kept telling them that Joshua Nkomo was his President! Completely refused to acknowledge Robert Mugabe."

"But he is an old man! Surely they could have made allowances for that!"

MaTshuma shrugged her shoulders resignedly, "Clearly they did not."

"And where did you spring from? I thought..." she hesitated, seemingly unsure how to proceed, "well, so many of our people have disappeared into South Africa and have never come back."

"I always wanted to come back," I explained, "but things were difficult to start with and then I wanted to come back with something for the family, for my mother." I felt a pain in my chest as I realised that my mother had had to go to work in Beit Bridge because I was not there to support her. "How is my mother?"

"Well," MaTshuma seemed to pick her words carefully. "Your mother has not been home for a few months, but the last I heard, she was alright. Life has not been kind to your mother." The lump in my throat grew even bigger. If MaTshuma, in her condition as I saw it, could see the difficulties that my mother had had, how bad was it? "For a long time," MaTshuma went on, "Your mother held on in the hope that you and your father would come back. She would not accept that your father may have been killed. In fact, she travelled to the mine to see what she could find out, but no one knew anything. The company told her that without his death certificate, he was considered as having left work without giving notice and was therefore not entitled to anything."

I felt numb. How callous were my father's employers? Surely they could have made an exception knowing the circumstances of my father's disappearance. He had, after all, given them many years of loyal service and the least they could have done would have been to help out his widow.

"Many women whose husbands disappeared are in that position," MaTshuma interrupted my thoughts, "even wives of people who worked for the government got nothing."

"Why did they not just go to the relevant offices and explain their situations?" I asked incredulously.

MaTshuma chuckled, "they wanted proof", her shoulders drooped as an indication of her exasperation, "they wanted the women to show how and where their husbands had died, but how could they?"

It struck me then that I had come home to nothing. The home that I had imagined all these years no longer existed. The people I knew and had so looked forward to seeing had all moved on and those who were left had nothing. No hope, no future, no food; nothing. It was a sobering moment. The only one who was of any consequence, it seemed to me, was my mother. But even she had had to leave this desolate-looking place to seek a better future elsewhere. For as long as I could remember, people had been leaving Maramani; but the community had seemed to continue to exist. Now, the exodus seemed almost total! For a brief moment, I wondered what Rumbie would have made of all this.

"What if I had brought her as my bride," I said out loud to myself.

"What are you going to do?"

I had almost forgotten that MaTshuma was standing next to me.

"Go back to Beit Bridge, of course," I said, sounding more confident than I felt. "I have to see my mother."

"What about your things?" She was looking at the collection of things that I had brought with me that still sat on the ground near the mulberry tree. They did not seem so important now.

CHAPTER FIVE

I slept most of the way on the bus to Beit Bridge the next morning, having had two consecutive sleepless nights – the first because the bus ride from Johannesburg was particularly uncomfortable, and the second because I had ended up sleeping in MaTshuma's rat infested kitchen, khulu having completely refused to share his room with me. It had not helped that I had shared the kitchen with MaTshuma's bed wetting grand children whose blankets stunk up the whole place. So I had left at first light, glad to be out of that place but also not wanting to miss the bus.

I had left most of the grocery to MaTshuma, with instructions that she could keep some of it, but use the rest towards khulu. Although I was not confident that khulu would get much of the food, I felt that as she was the only one that seemed to have any interest in khulu's welfare, she deserved whatever she could get. I had left the other suitcase, which had the presents for other members of the family, to be passed on to MaMpofu on her next visit, which I had been told was imminent.

"We were expecting her last weekend," MaMpofu had told me, "I'm not sure why they did not come. They might be coming this weekend." It reminded me how difficult it was to communicate to this part of the world.

The farewell had been brief that morning and she had hugged me at length to show her gratitude. Somehow, I found myself feeling embarrassed as I, again remembered that image from my squat in the bush. I had considered waking khulu up but felt that I would only get more of the frustrating conversation that would not add much to my home visit experience.

So, I left, carrying my much lighter luggage comprising mainly of a suitcase which had the clothes and trinkets that I had bought for my mother. My own few items of clothing that I had brought were in a separate bag that hung over my shoulder. I had had a brief conversation with Mr Moyo, who I had found already up and sweeping around his shop. There was not much to sweep, but this was his morning ritual that he had done for as long as I could remember.

"Good morning Mr Moyo, there doesn't seem to be much to sweep there."

Mr Moyo had straightened his back – with some difficulty, I noticed – and chuckled as he swung his arm expansively towards his shop.

"Well," his eyes were full of humour, "I need to get the place clean before the first customer arrives," he paused and looked at me almost pleadingly, "If the first customer arrives."

"What have you got that I can buy," I had asked feeling like I needed to help him out.

"Well, I've got some matches, bicycle spares, some towels that I ordered a while back and have not been able to sell, the usual sweets and biscuits…" he trailed off as if he could not remember what else he had in his shop. There was nothing else so I bought a couple of towels that I did not need and a packet of 'Choice Assorted' biscuits, remembering how much of a treat those had been on the odd occasion that my mother would bring a packet home. It had been a while since I'd had such a 'treat'.

"And why are you up so earl… don't tell me you're off already?" he seemed to notice my luggage for the first time, "What happened to all the things you brought home?"

"I left most of them with MaTshuma, who seems to look after khulu. No point in lugging them back, is there?"

"So, you're off to see your mother?"

"Yes," I had replied. "Just as well I did not know that my mother was in Beit Bridge. I probably would have not come home at all."

"Well, it is good that you came. You now know what your home has been reduced to by our independence. Life is tough in this part of the world," he seemed to hesitate, "don't judge your mother too harshly."

As I stood on the dusty pavement of the Beit Bridge bus terminus, I wondered about Mr Moyo's last comment. What was there to judge my mother for? Many women went out to work and it was not unusual to me that she had decided to get herself a job. My only regret was that she had had to go out and work, because I was not there to support her. It was early in the day but it was already very hot, although most of the people that scurried about seemed oblivious to the heat. I approached a group of young men that seemed to be doing nothing in particular and asked for directions to the Beit Bridge Tavern.

"You want to go to the Tavern?" one of them, with a cigarette dangling from his young lips, asked nonchalantly as he pulled his hand out of the pocket and looked at his watch , "It's a bit early…"

"The Tavern doesn't open until much later," his friend jumped into the conversation, "In fact, it has only just closed. You'll have to come back later in the day. The people will be sleeping now."

"Well," I felt the need to explain my predicament, "I live in Johannesburg and I had come home to Maramani but was told that my mother now lives in Beit Bridge and works at the Tavern."

"Your mother works at the Tavern?" the second young man sounded incredulous, which I found irritating. What was so surprising about my mother going to work? "Is she a wow…!" he was unable to finish his sentence as the first young man seemed to kick him in the sheen.

"Tell you what," the cigarette smoking youngster, who seemed to be the leader of the group pulled me aside, "the

Tavern is a sort of night club which opens in the late afternoon and generally does not close much before midnight but usually opens until the early hours of the morning. They will probably be sleeping now. Why don't you find somewhere to spend time until about three in the afternoon?"

"I'm tired and I need some sleep. Surely there must be a way of contacting my mother. I have not seen her in ten years!"

"The Beit Bridge Inn will, for a few Rands, give you a bed for a few hours. I can show you where it is."

It was too good an offer to refuse and the group led me to the front of the Beit Bridge Inn, a dingy-looking building that looked like it needed a facelift. Inside, it was dark in spite of a single light bulb that hung from the ceiling. It therefore took me some time to see that there was a reception in the far corner, behind which an elderly man regarded me with an expressionless face.

"Want a room?" he said as he turned to pick a key from the board behind him, "One hour? Its two dollars per person per hour, so, ten dollars."

"But there's only me." I said.

"Only you?" he sounded surprised, "well then it's fifteen dollars."

"But, I thought you said ten dollars per person per night…"

"They are double rooms," he interrupted me. "Do you want the room or not?"

"But I only need it for a few hours…"

"We charge per night, even during the day."

I handed over the required amount, desperate to put my head down and get some rest.

"What will you be doing in there on your own?" He asked me as he handed over the keys to my room which he told me was on the first floor.

"Resting," I answered, surprised at the question.

"Most people who come to rest for a few hours come with partners. One of these young ladies," he nodded towards a woman who was mopping the floor in the passage, "can help you to rest."

The penny dropped then. I had heard of such establishments where men – usually married men – could go for a few hours of illicit sex with women who were not their wives. I felt quite annoyed that he could place me in that category of men.

"No, thank you," I said tersely.

I could not sleep, partly because the room was not particularly clean and the sheets looked like they had been on the bed for quite a few 'rest' sessions, and I decided to sit in the only chair in the room, but mostly because of the noise. There was constant movement in the corridor and the noises from the rooms adjacent to mine left little to the imagination. In spite of myself, I was listening to the different noises that the different sets of 'resters' made and decided that not much resting was taking place. I was not resting either and my manhood, being what it is, responded to what I was hearing! Thinking of Rumbie and the flesh that I had seen when I visited her when she was recuperating from her dislocated jaw, I did what I had to do; hard, imagining that I was taking out all my anger at her for lying to me about being a virgin. She had, of course never told me that she was a virgin; I had assumed it. But it served my purpose at the time to imagine that I was revenging! Afterwards, I wondered whether Rumbie would even come into an establishment like that.

I woke up to an eerie silence and for a few moments, I did not remember where I was, surprised that I was sitting in an awkward position in an uncomfortable chair. Gradually, I became more aware of my surroundings and I remembered where I was.

I needed to pee and I got up and out of the room to go and find a toilet. As soon as I left the room I found my way to the one toilet on that floor by following the smell, which was inevitable as I soon found out that there was no running water! It was just as well I had not eaten anything on that day. I wanted to get out of this hotel as quickly as I could. I went back to my room and tried to clean myself up as best I could under the circumstances. The man at the front desk raised a quizzical eyebrow when I asked for directions to the Beit Bridge Tavern but did not comment. He just gave me the directions in a monotone that suggested that he probably gave these directions to many a visitor to his establishment.

I found myself sneaking out of the Beit Bridge Hotel as a thought had just occurred to me that someone – Rumbie's cousin Chipo for example – might see me walking out of that place. What would she think I was doing there? What would she tell Rumbie? I felt a strong urge to talk to Rumbie and tried to find a public call box. All the ones I came across were broken and I finally gave up and went looking for The Tavern, which I found without too much difficulty because of the directions I had been given. The blaring music that came from within was also a dead giveaway. I'm not sure what I had expected of the Tavern but this certainly was not it. The first thing I noticed inside the high brick wall was what looked like a once-thriving flower garden with lawn; but the flowers had long withered and died and there were patches of lawn that hinted at its past glories. Scattered around the garden were metal tables and chairs that used to be white but were now mostly rust. Several, mostly male, patrons sat in small groups or as singles at some of the tables. A group of young men was chattering excitedly around a mini soccer table – commonly known as 'slug' in Zimbabwe. A smaller group was standing around a pool table with two of them holding cues and taking turns to play. The others watched in fascinated silence.

I did not venture inside mainly because of the loud music but also because I was a bit apprehensive about meeting my mother. What was she doing in a place like this? I chose an unoccupied table in the corner furthest from the tavern entrance but with a clear view of all the activity in the garden. I needed to understand why my mother would be working in such a place and what sort of work she did.

In spite of the heavy makeup and tarty dress, I recognised MaNcube immediately. She came out carrying a tray with several drinks on it. I was surprised at how short her dress was and thought that she was showing too much of her breasts. She walked with a suggestive swing to her hips which reminded me of some of the girls I had seen in the shebeens in Joburg. But what was an old woman like MaNcube doing dressed and walking like that.

"Hello MaNcu'," one of the patrons at the table she was approaching said, "You look nice today."

"She always looks nice," another one of the patrons said as he playfully slapped her on the buttocks. "Today you are coming with me!"

"What about my husband?" She asked, holding her hips in mock indignation.
The group around the table erupted in laughter.

"Your husband?" The first man said, blowing his nose with a handkerchief he had taken out of his pocket and wiping his eyes with the back of his hand.

"Let me be your husband tonight," he said, pulling her by the waist onto his lap. She pushed him away gently and bent over to clear the table. I looked away in embarrassment as she exposed more of her upper thigh than I wanted to see. Somehow, given her reputation back home, I was not surprised that she appeared to have joined the oldest profession.

"What can I do for you young man?" I looked up to be confronted by MaNcube's bosom, which was virtually in my face. Then our eyes met and I could have sworn that the colour drained from her face.

"Sipho?" She was whispering. "Sipho," she said again as if she thought I had not heard her the first time. Then she turned and ran.

"MaMguni, MaMguni," she shouted as she ran, "look who is here!"

"Who?" I recognised my mother's voice from within, "I hope it's not that Congolese truck driver from last week. He was…"

"No! No MaMguni, come quickly!"

A woman dressed exactly like MaNcube came running out of the bar, but it was not until she was a few paces away that I recognised my mother! I was confused. What was my mother doing dressed like that in public? She looked like a prostitute! Before I had time to process what I was looking at, she was all over me. I had never realised how strong my mother was but she held me in a bear hug and lifted me up almost as easily as I remembered her doing when I was a child. I could feel her kisses all over my face and neck and I did not know what to do, never having experienced so much affection from my mother before. So I just stood there, arms dangling on my sides while I looked over my mother's shoulder at the surprised looks of many of the patrons.

"Sipho, Sipho, Sipho, my son; my baby boy, my baby boy," she said over and over again. Not having thought of myself as a baby boy for many years, I sought to correct her.

"Mother," I said gently trying to extricate myself from her grip, "I am not a baby, and I am not a boy…"

"You'll always be my baby boy!" She insisted. "I thought I'd never see you again, and here you are." She loosened her grip to look at me in the face without letting go of me, then she tightened her grip again.

"My son; my baby boy…"I clearly was not going to win that argument.

"She told me that she had no children," one of the man that I could see over my mother's shoulder said, looking genuinely confused.

"Oh Shut up you fool," MaNcube's tone was sneering and severe.

"I wanted to marry her…" the man insisted but then wilted under MaNcube's stare.

"*Wena Nkomo Ngizakutshaya,*" MaNcube was walking menacingly towards the man.

"Leave the man alone MaNcu," one of the other man said as the group was breaking up and people were walking back to their tables, "He has problems speaking to decent girls and you whores are all he has."

I felt my mother stiffen, then she let go of me.

"Let's get out of here," she said to me picking up my suitcase which had been sitting on the ground besides the table that I had been sitting at. She took off her apron, threw it on the table and started to walk out. Then she stopped and turned to look at the gathered group.

"This is Sipho, my son," she declared. There was no mistaking the pride in her voice. "He was dead, and now he is alive again."

I remembered hearing that in a sermon on one of my rare visits to church, at Rumbie's invitation. The story of the prodigal Son was one that I had always identified with even though I, unlike the son in the bible, had left home with nothing but had hoped to come home a different person. In my imagination I had always seen myself driving back home in my own car but I had not been able to buy one yet although I had obtained a driver's licence and had left some money back in South Africa that would make a nice deposit for a decent second hand car. Was that why it had taken me so long to come back home? I wanted to come home to impress, and had left my mother in such desperation that she had to… I remembered Mr Moyo's words then; *'Do not judge your mother too harshly'.*

"None of you," I heard my mother say, "will ever be even half of the man that he is." To be honest, I don't know why she said that.

Her 'home' was not too far from her work place. I was pleasantly surprised at the big house into whose gate we entered, with its well-tended garden and colourful flowers, although by this time it was too dark for me to fully appreciate the beauty.

"Nice house," I commented.

"Yes, it is. But we live at the back."

"We?" I was surprised at the reference to more than one person.

"You and me, of course. The main house is for government officials, immigration and customs."

She had a two roomed cottage at the back of the house and she let us into a sparsely but beautifully furnished sitting room which, for some reason, reminded me of Rumbie's flat.

"Have you had anything to eat? Let me cook a nice home meal for you. There is not much here but I can go and buy nice groceries tomorrow.."

I regretted having left the bulk of the groceries with MaTshuma but did not feel that this was the time to mention that to my mother, so I took out the few grocery items that I had managed to carry in my shoulder bag – some rice, baked beans, canned sausages and a few other bits and pieces. She quickly got to work making an onion and tomato gravy which she spiced and added to the baked beans and sausage. I had not realised how hungry I was and I ate the food with such relish that my mother commented, "You poor thing, do you not eat enough in that South Africa of yours?"

"Of course I eat enough…"

"Is there a *malokazana* to cook for you?"

"I can cook for myself, mother."

"I know. But is there a daughter-in law for me; to look after me in my old age?"

"Well," I hesitated. Could I tell my mother about Rumbie who after all was not even my girlfriend? "There is someone but…"

"I knew it. Tell me more about her. Is she a nice Ndebele girl?"

"What has her tribe got to do with anything? I though you would be more interested in what kind of person she is and whether we love each other."

"So she is not Ndebele. What is she? Zulu? Tswana? What?"

"There'll be plenty of time to talk about that, mother," this was happening all too fast. I needed time to ease her into understanding what Rumbie meant to me, even though I did not quite understand if I meant anything to her. "We have a lot of catching up to do."

She looked puzzled for a moment but seemed to decide not to pursue the subject.

"So, what have you been up to, mother?" I asked the question even though I did not really want to know the answer.

"Let us pray."

Given what I had witnessed at her place of work, I was a bit surprised by this. I did not do much praying myself so I was not sure what to do; whether to kneel or just bow. Clearly my mother was also not sure what to do and seemed to look to me for her cue. We both bowed our heads to a prayer that was comically honest.

"Dear God in Heaven… I mean, dear father in heaven," she was quiet for a while then she touched my hand and asked, "Is it dear God or dear father?"

"I think they both work," I answered honestly.

"Okay. Dear father God, The Pastor at the church says that you are faithful. I did not believe him. Today I believe the Pastor because I have prayed to you many times about my son, Sipho, that you should bring him back to me. Thank you so much God. I mean dear God. The Pastor also said that you will hear me even though I am a sinner; he says that I should confess my sins to you. I confess god, I mean dear God all my sins although I cannot tell you what they are because my son is here. But Pastor also said that you know everything, including what is in my heart. AMEN."

I was surprised. I had never known my mother to pray and after what I had seen of her 'profession', prayer was the last thing that I had expected her to do. I looked around her room. It was clean. Very clean although the furniture was sparse. For a few minutes, we sat in awkward silence, not quite sure what to say to each other. My mind was in turmoil. I was very happy to see my mother of course, but I was not sure what to make of her life style and living conditions. I felt angry although I was not sure why or with who I was angry – my mother for being… I could not bring myself to think of what to call my mother. Or was I angry with myself for abandoning her all those years ago – after she had been abandoned by my father? I should have known that I had a responsibility to her. I should have come home sooner. I even began to wonder whether it would be right for me to go back to South Africa and leave her like this.

I became aware that my mother was sobbing. I was not sure what to do so I sat there and let her cry. Quiet sobs at first that gradually grew into a fully-fledged wail. I sat across the room and watched her. It occurred to me that throughout my childhood, I had never seen my mother in such distress, although her husband's prolonged absence must have been a source of much pain.

"I'm sorry my son," she was wiping her face with her apron. "I had given up on ever seeing you again, although there was never any doubt in my mind that you were alive."

"No mother," I responded, "I'm the one who should be sorry. I should have come home sooner and..."

"NO!" I was shocked by the vehemence in her voice. "Many men; many young men were killed. I was happy that you were out of the way. I just prayed that God would keep you safe and that one day you would come back to me."

I had never once prayed for my mother's safety, I thought.

"I know you are surprised and disappointed by finding out what I do for a living."

I was not ready for this, so I tried to protest.

"It doesn't matter mother..."

"It matters to me Sipho. I am a prostitute. A whore. But today, I am a proud mother. I have a son who has been away for this many years and he has come back. I want the whole world to know. I want to parade you in front of everyone so that they can see that I am the mother of a fine boy. But people will not let me forget who they think I am. They will want to make me continue to feel worthless; make you feel that your mother is worthless. So, yes Sipho. It is important to me that even if no one else understands, I want you to understand; that sometimes, people do things out of desperation, out of necessity."

She spoke with such passion and intensity that I had no choice but to listen. She had, after all, spoken very openly about her life style. I had been worrying in the short time that I had been with her, how I was going to face her every morning knowing what she did for a living. For a moment, I wondered how Rumbie would take the news of my mother's 'profession', at the same time, wondering if it would be necessary to tell her, given that she was not really my girlfriend. But I was hoping...

"Sipho," my mother interrupted my thoughts, "have you ever been hungry, really hungry without knowing where your next meal is coming from?"

I did not answer her but I knew that in all my life, even in my childhood, there had always been food. The only time that I could say I was hungry for any length of time was during the trek to South Africa but that lasted a few days and there was always some wild fruit, a locust, some bird eggs and some such morsels to be had.

"Well, I have," she clearly was not expecting an answer from me. "I have been so hungry that I started to look at the lizards, spiders and other crawling things around our home as possible food. I cooked leaves of trees that I have never known to be eaten and tried to eat them. Few of them were somewhat palatable, but most, I threw away. There were days when I sat and waited for death to overtake me, but the thought that you might come back and find me not there stopped me from doing anything stupid."

For a few minutes, we sat next to each other in silence. I think that my mother was not sure how to continue the conversation she had started. I was so happy to see my mother again but really did not want to continue talking about her.

"You, my son, are a very handsome boy," she said quietly after a while. "You remind me of your father. He was a good looking man, your father."

"I hardly remember him. I think he was very tall."

"To your young eyes he might have seemed tall, but he was about average height. Anyway, we were very happy when we first got married. He was a good husband and when you came along, we became the happiest couple in the village. But your coming also meant that he needed to go out and work. I was so excited when he got the job at the mine. Those were THE jobs that everyone in the area aspired to in those days. Every month end, he would come home with parcels of food and clothing for us, some toys for you and he would leave enough money to last until his next visit. We were the envy of the neighbourhood!"

"I remember having lots of toys, which I would take with me when I went out with the other boys to herd cattle..."

"You sneaked them out because I would not let you take them and invariably, they did not come back!"

"Yes. I was very careless with things and I always seemed to lose my nice toys."

"Your friends stole your toys; you did not lose them!"

I had never thought that my friends would steal from me and the realisation came as a complete surprise.

"Anyway," my mother looked very pensive, "the visits got fewer with time and your father told me that the cost of coming every month was proving too much for our young family. In any case, it was during the war of liberation and it was not safe to travel too often so I understood. Stories started to come through about him having another woman but I ignored them because on those rare occasions when he came, we would be so happy – and he always denied having another wife. I believed him."

She was close to tears again, so she said nothing for a few minutes. I watched her, thinking how handsome she still looked for her age. She was in her forties and to my mind, forty year olds did not look like that!

"Then of course after independence, there were the problems with the so called dissidents and the army came in. I was surprised to hear that he had been taken away by the soldiers but at first, I did not worry because your father had never really been political and I was sure that they would soon realise that he was innocent. But it seems that there was no interest in whether you were guilty or innocent. If you could not speak Shona, you were a dissident or a dissident sympathiser!"

"Surely they could not believe that everyone supported the dissidents because of the language they spoke? Did you see any dissidents yourself?"

"To be honest, it was all very confusing. Most people in our area had believed that Joshua Nkomo was going to win the elections at independence in 1980 and there was a general belief that he had been cheated! So there was disgruntlement and anger at the new government, which was seen as being for Shona people. We did hear stories of some of the soldiers from Matabeleland leaving the army because they felt that they were being treated unfairly. Some of them, I understand, did try to go back to the bush to fight but most just left the country and went to Botswana or South Africa. I am not sure whether these then regrouped in South Africa to form Super ZAPU, because these appeared to be a different group from the ones that were operating from within Zimbabwe. They were, I was told by those who know about guns, better equipped and better organised. There was some talk that these were being trained and equipped by the South African government but no one really knew and to the soldiers who came, they were all dissidents and we were supporting them because we were Ndebele!"

It was as if my mother was having to dredge some very painful memories from deep within her subconscious mind.

"Anyway, in all that confusion, your father managed to get himself taken away by the army and has never been seen since. Eventually, I came to accept not only that he had had another family but also that he had been killed. Of course I went to see your father's employers in the hope that they would give me some money to help my situation – you had left for South Africa and we had not heard from you – but they wanted proof that your father had died and not just walked out of his job. I tried to explain to them how my husband loved his job and would never walk out of it and of the stories that he had been taken by the army.

'Men change,' one of the officers in the personnel department told me, 'and many people in this area supported or became dissidents so, for all we know, he walked out of his job to join whatever cause he thought he was fighting. Without a death certificate, we cannot do anything.'

It did not help that the man who was telling me this was Shona and had to speak to me in English through an interpreter!"

She stood and went to the window where she stood for a good few minutes. I had an idea she was hiding her face from me probably because she was crying. There was no sound or movement from her for what seemed like an age, then she seemed to gather her wits and came back to her seat. She held my hand and looked at me directly.

"What did you do?" I asked the question only because I felt I had to say something.

"What could I do? I went back to Maramani, but here too, things had changed."

"How?"

"Well, to start with, we had had a few years of drought so food was in short supply. Many people had left the area because of the dissidents – and soldiers, who seemed to … well, if you were seen as being familiar with the soldiers, the dissidents did not like it and you were a sell out that needed to be dealt with. On the other hand, if you were thought to be sympathising with the dissidents, then the soldiers would come for you. Of course in a situation where people are hungry, there is bound to be those who will do whatever it takes to ensure that they get food."

"And by 'whatever it takes' you mean…"

"Look, soldiers had food and if you gave them information about dissidents, real or imagined – sometimes people used the soldiers to get back at people that they had vendettas with – you could eat for a few days. And if you were a woman," she hesitated, which made me wonder whether that was how her new lifestyle had started – "I'm sure you are old enough to know what happens."

For a few minutes we sat side by side, holding hands, but each one of us was deep in thought. I could not imagine what my mother might have been thinking. I was trying not to think about what my mother might have had to do in order to eat. Once again I felt guilty. It was my fault that my mother had had to sell herself in order to survive.

"For a long time I resisted," she cut into my thoughts. "We had some food still in the caves but with successive droughts, it was bound to run out. Your uncle Peter had taken his wife, MaMpofu, back to Harare with him, and many of the men had had to move into the cities to try and find work. At this point, the boys you left with appeared and told us that you were the only one who had crossed before the flood and they had decided to come back, only to meet the soldiers and be taken for dissidents coming in from South Africa. I was so excited that you had crossed and were alive, but after not hearing from you for a while, I started to worry. You were so young and the older people that I had trusted to look after you had come back without you! How were you going to survive in the notorious South African cities? I decided then that God was punishing me for something very bad that I had done. To add to all that, khulu had his homestead burnt by the soldiers and he had to come and stay with me!"

She was quiet for a while then smiled ruefully, almost to herself then carried on.

"When MaNcube, who had spent some time in Beit Bridge came dressed up in the latest fashions telling me there was work to be had in Beit Bridge, I jumped at the chance. I had reservations about being a waitress in a bar, but that could not be any worse than my situation then. She did not tell me the whole truth, of course but by the time I realised what was expected of me, it did not really matter. I am so sorry my son," she said and it felt like she had concluded her story.

I was angry, although I could not say who I was angry with. I could not be angry with my mother. She had done what she had had to do to survive. But she was my mother! How did she expect me to relate to the people that I had known most of my life knowing that they knew what she did for a leaving? I remembered what Mr Moyo had said, which had not made much sense at the time. “Don't judge your mother too harshly”, he had said. So he knew what my mother did. Who else knew? I wondered. I felt sorry for my mother but, was that the only thing she could do?

“Did you ever try being a vendor?” I asked without realising how judgemental I was being.

“Of course I thought about it. But I would have had to have some money to start with. In fact, when I started doing ...” she could not finish that sentence, “I thought it would be for a few weeks until I had enough money to buy things to sell. But after paying rent and food and sending some money home for khulu, there was never enough! In any case, many of the vendors I know also do what we do to increase their income.” It was as if she was justifying her line of work!

I did not quite know what to say, so I told her my story; about how I nearly drowned and was found by the boys who took me to their parents and everything else that had happened to me in the preceding ten years. I told her about Mr Van der Merwe and how good he had been to me; I told her about my job and how well I was doing and how I had convinced Mr Van to open a bakery that I one day hoped to manage. Finally, I told her about the Shona girl who had got me suspended because I had punched her when she ruined my surprise for Mr Van.

She listened without interrupting, although she cried with me when I talked about the near drowning; smiled when I related my experiences at the senior Van's farm; laughed with me when I told her of my first experiences in Joburg, having never been to a city before. I even told her of my neighbour, Mr Mlambo whose Zimbabwean origin I had only discovered after five years of being his neighbour!

It was well after midnight when I finished telling my story. My mother stood and yawned, made a bed for me on the floor and asked casually, “this Rumbidzayi, is she your girlfriend?”

“Why would you say that mother? I never said she was my girlfriend! I punched her...”

"Yes, yes you said that. But do you know that when you talk about her, you change? You remind me of how you used to talk about MaMpofu as a child. Your face gets brighter and, well, sometimes I would even feel a little jealous because you seemed to like her more than me. Anyway, it sounds like even the punch was full of passion."

"That was anger, mother, not passion!"

"Sometimes, you cannot tell the difference between anger and passionate love," there was a naughty glint in my mother's eye. "Well…?"

"Well what?"

"Is she? Your girlfriend I mean."

"Mother, she is Shona."

"So?"

I was running out of excuses, but felt some relief that my mother did not seem to mind. But then again, Rumbie was not exactly my girlfriend – and she had lied to me!

"Well," I said, choosing my words carefully, "she's not exactly my girlfriend…"

"Oh," my mother sounded disappointed. "Is she just someone you sleep with from time to time then?"

"Mother!" I was shocked, "I don't sleep with her…!"

"What are you waiting for?" This conversation was getting out of control.

"Rumbie is a work colleague and a very good friend. I don't have the kind of relationship with her that you seem to think I have…"

"There you go again," my mother interrupted, "I can't quite describe it but when you mention her name, your face, I don't know, looks so happy. Have you told her how you feel?"

"No, mother. I don't, I mean, I haven't said anything to her and anyway, she has a six year old daughter and she lied to me about it."

"She told you she was a virgin?" Why was my mother being so difficult?

"Well, no! We never discussed that."

"So, if it was never discussed, when did she lie to you?"

"She did not tell me that she had a baby!"
"Did you ask her?"

"No."

"She told me..."

"I thought you said that she did not tell you?"

"She only told me at the bus stop when I was coming here!"

"Had you asked her?"

"No. She just handed me a parcel to give to her cousin who works at the border, then told me it was for her daughter!"

"My son," my mother sat down again, "do you know that she was worried about telling you because she was afraid that you would react exactly as you are reacting? She probably believes that you are a nice guy but thought that if she told you about her baby too early, you might just walk away and she would never have the opportunity to show you what a nice person she is."

"But how many men has she slept with over the last six years?"

"In the time that you've known her, Sipho, have you seen other men around her? Has she given you any reason to believe that she is 'easy'?

"No, but..."

"No buts!" My mother seemed to be taking her side. I found myself getting angry with her. She was, after all, a prostitute! What did she know about morals? She seemed to read my mind.

"Sipho," she said quietly, "I know that you probably don't approve of my lifestyle and are wondering whether I am in any position to give you any advice. The truth is, I have gone into this profession out of necessity. I don't know what circumstances led to her having the baby, but I have seen many young girls end up in our profession out of necessity. They have been rejected by the fathers of their babies and then rejected by their families. Out of necessity, they end up on the street, because they – and their babies have to eat. Rumbidzayi sounds like someone who has learnt her lesson and is ambitious. Don't leave her because she somehow does not measure up to a moral standard that hardly exists these days!"

The prostitute seemed to be making sense, I thought.

I woke up to find that I was still sitting on the chair, the bed that my mother had so lovingly made for me unused. I could not remember how the conversation with my mother had ended but assumed I must have dozed off at some point during the discussion. I was surprised at how refreshed I felt having slept on a chair, but soon realised it must have been the relief and comfort of finally seeing my mother after so many years. The house was very quiet and I assumed it was because my mother was still asleep. But when I got up and checked her room, it was empty and her bed was made. After about half an hours waiting, I decided to explore the surroundings and I went outside where I came face to face with Chipo, Rumbie's cousin. She was hanging clothes on the laundry line and at first did not seem to recognise me, although I sensed that she was making an effort not to look in my direction.

"Good morning Chipo. Is this where you live?"

She looked up, surprised that whoever it was had recognised her.

"Hello. Do I know you?" She peered at me again, "Sipho? What are you doing here?"

"I'll be living here for the next few days at least," I said indicating my mother's backyard cottage.

Chipo looked very surprised and looked at me pitifully, "what do you mean you'll be living there? Are you that desperate?"

"Well," I said innocently, "where else can I live?"

"Rumbie told me you were such a gentleman – that you had never even... In fact, she's been phoning and asking if I'd seen you. If only she knew."

"Knew what? That I'm living with my mother?" I felt myself getting angry at my mother. Was this how everyone was going to see me? Did everyone at the bar last night realise that she was my mother or did some of them think I had been picked up?

"Look, Sipho," Chipo sounded like she wanted to make peace, "for what it's worth, we all only assume that she is – you know – but if the truth be told, none of us have ever seen her, you know; she certainly never brings any men home, and that is why I was surprised to see you – I didn't recognise you at first, but I was surprised and embarrassed that she had actually brought a man home."

Did that make it any better? I wondered. Was she somehow purer because she was discreet? Surely every patron of the Tavern knew who she was and what she did!

"She is my mother and I love her very much," I said although I was not sure if I was talking to Chipo or to myself.

"I'm sure you do. She is a very nice person and sometimes gives us very good advice. On her days off, she spends a lot of time in the garden..."

"She's got vegetables?" I asked relieved that she at least was growing some of her own food.

"No. I mean yes she does have a small vegetable patch at the back of her cottage, but what I'm talking about is the flower garden. She can spend hours in our garden tending the flowers. She is the reason our garden looks so good!"

I looked across the hedge that separated my mother's cottage from the main yard. What I had seen the night before had not done her justice. The garden was a veritable oasis in the Beit Bridge dryness all around it. Flowers of every description and colour were all around us and the lawn was immaculate.

"We've often speculated over how she ended up, you know," Chipo hesitated, "doing what she does."

There was an awkward silence as I thought about my mother and the position she must have found herself in. I could not believe that there was nothing else she could have done, although no alternative immediately came to mind. Could she not have offered herself as a gardener to someone who could pay her a decent wage? She clearly had skills in that regard. But 'garden boys' – as domestic gardeners were called – were usually male and were not particularly well paid. They were not recognised as having any skills in their field of expertise! Of course, many of them only carried out instructions from their employers, but I had known some who were quite passionate about their work – as my mother clearly was about her hobby. Yet they remained unrecognised and unrewarded.

"Rumbie phoned last night. I wish I had known..."

"Rumbie? How is she?" I was surprised at how pleasant and exciting that sounded.

"She wanted to know if you had delivered the parcel. I told her you had, but that I had not seen you since the border. She seemed disappointed that I had no further news of you." Chipo looked directly at me as though she was expecting me to comment on her last statement, but what could I say? I had gone to Maramani and so Chipo could not have seen me.

"Are you two an item?" the question was not exactly unexpected, yet it took me by surprise.

"No!" I said somewhat too loudly, "I mean, well, we are good friends…"

"I think that she sees you as more than that," Chipo interrupted.

"Did she tell you that?"

"No, but there was just something in her tone that suggested to me that she is very fond of you. In fact when I told her how handsome I thought you were, she told me, in no uncertain terms, to 'keep my dirty hands off you'!"

So, I thought to myself, Chipo thought I was handsome? This was probably the first time that any woman, besides MaMpofu and my mother of course, had told me that I was handsome. She was not what I would call pretty, but I found myself liking this girl. She could be the one that told Rumbie just how I felt about her. But maybe not. I should be able to tell her myself…

"Have you told her?" Chipo asked unexpectedly.

"Told her what?"

"That you love her."

Why was everyone making that assumption? First my mother and now…

"Hello you two," my mother, in a bright floral dress that made her look somewhat younger than her forty six years, stopped and put the many parcels that she carried on the ground. "Do you know each other?'

"No," I said as Chipo simultaneously said "yes".

We both burst out laughing, to the obvious bemusement of my mother.

"This is Rumbidzayi's cousin, Chipo," I explained. "We met only the other day when I arrived from Joburg with a parcel from Rumbie..."

"So now you know why I've always called you *malokazana* hey, Chipo?" My mother addressed Chipo in a manner that suggested that there was good rapport between them.

"That's because you always promised that when your son comes back from South Africa, he would marry me! But now he is taken – by none other than my cousin!" There two were clearly at ease with each other.

"But my son denies that there is anything between him and Rumbie, even though his whole body when he mentions her name tells me otherwise. You be careful *malokazana.* He is probably wanting to try his luck with you while he is away from Rumbie. You know how these men are."

"Mother, please! I'm not like that. I would never..."

"Take advantage of a woman?" my mother interrupted me again, "are you not your father's child?"

The betrayal by my father obviously still bothered her and the easy going persona seemed to desert her for a moment.

"I should be so lucky," Chipo sounded regretful, "perhaps I should go to South Africa to find myself a nice decent Zimbabwean man!"

My protestations that there was nothing between Rumbie and I were clearly not making an impression with these two.

"Look at the time!" Chipo exclaimed, "I have to go and get ready for work. When I get back, after your mother has breast fed you of course, perhaps you could come over and we can phone Rumbie together." She spoke over her shoulder as she rushed into the house.

"Nice girl," my mother said as she started to pick up her parcels. I took some of them and together we went into her cottage.

It was probably one of the most pleasant days that I remember. My mother had gone shopping and she made a large greasy breakfast of fried eggs, sausages, minced beef and mushrooms. It was all too much for me and she was disappointed that I could not finish it!

"Never mind," she said pleasantly, "you'll have it for lunch. I spent my whole weeks earnings on a celebratory breakfast and you only nibbled at it!"

She stood and went into the other parcels that she had brought. There was a nice looking pair of shoes that were not quite my taste but looked pleasant enough.

"I checked your shoe size while you slept this morning," she explained.

The brown suit didn't quite fit but as my mother explained, "we can go and change it." There were a couple of shirts and a tie to complete the outfit. It had been many years since I had had anything bought for me and I shed tears as I hugged my mother. We held each other for a few minutes then she pushed me back and held me at arm's length.

"My son has come back to me," tears were running down her face. She wiped them off and then went on, "I spoke to you uncle Peter this morning…"

"Is he here in Beit Bridge?" The excitement was too much. If uncle 'Ncane was here, that meant MaMpofu was also here…

"No, he is in Harare, but I spoke to him on the phone. He has bought himself one of those cell phones that everyone seems excited about. Sold one of his cows to buy it..."

"A whole cow for a phone! That's stupid. In any case cell phones don't cost that much, surely?"

"They do here, but I agree that it is stupid to sell a cow in order to buy a telephone. I can always phone from my work place."

"How is he though?"

"He is very well. MaMpofu was not close to him so I could not speak to her but I am sure she will be as excited to hear that you are home."

"Will I get to see them at all?" I was resigned to the fact that I would not be able to see all the people from my childhood as everyone seemed to be scattered all over the place.

"We have agreed to contact as many people as possible and have a big get together next weekend. Not this one that's coming. The one after that."

This was the most exciting news that I had heard since coming home.

"I hope MaMpofu can come," I could not contain my excitement.

"Don't worry about that son," my mother reassured me. "It was your uncle's idea and he will come with MaMpofu, I'm sure of that."

I spent the rest of the day following my mother around while she did her chores around her home. We could not stop talking about what had happened since I left. I noticed that the subject of the soldiers during the so called Gukurahundi was one that made my mother uncomfortable so, as far as possible, I stayed clear of it. But it did come up from time to time.

"I have lived so many years wondering what happened to you; wondering if the others had told the truth about you crossing over without them. But when I see what happened to them when they tried to come back, I feel so lucky; so blessed that you were not part of their experience. And now that you've come back, I know it was God's will that things happened the way they did; and that my suffering all these years was not in vain."

I did not quite know what to say. My experience with religion was almost non-existent and I could not see how this could have been part of some plan by God. Still, I was grateful that I had survived the flash flood and everything else that had happened and was now back with my mother.

"It was pure luck," I said, not sure what else to say.

More than once, the subject of Rumbidzayi came up and it was clear that my mother wanted me to confirm that she was my 'significant other', but how could I? The subject had never even come up! Of course I missed her terribly but that did not necessarily mean that she missed me.

"Rumbie is a very nice person, mother," I said to her, "but right now, I'm not sure what the state of our relationship is. I punched her quite hard, remember? And then I found out at the last moment that she has a six year old child. She is also Shona, of course…"

"Of course she is Shona!" My mother seemed to lose patience with me, "the question is, do you love her?"

"I like her…"

"That's not what I asked you. I asked if you love her! Having a child is not a crime. After all, you are not a virgin yourself, surely?"

"Actually, I am," I said quietly.

I could not tell whether my mother wanted to laugh or cry. She stood up suddenly and wiped her brow apparently keeping her face away from me. She was suddenly very busy although I could not see what exactly she was doing.

"Well," my mother said after a few minutes, "at least you'll have a readymade family." She came and sat next to me. "I'm sorry, I should not have said that last bit. But my son, relationships are very complicated. Remember that at some point, you will want someone that will be your partner for life and I cannot think of a better partner than one who is your friend. I envy you finding someone that you seem to get along with so well. Your father and I..." she hesitated, "were never really friends. We were young and were probably drawn to each other physically but we never had the kind of heart to heart discussions that you seem to have with Rumbie."

There was an awkward silence during which I thought about my mother's statement about being drawn physically to my father. Although I had no personal experience, I had seen some films where man and women did some things that I could not imagine my mother and father doing.

"As for her being Shona," she interrupted my thoughts, "I have seen enough of the world to know that people are people, wherever they come from."

"And by 'the world' you mean Maramani and Beit Bridge?" I said, laughing.

"You'll be amazed how much of the world we see here in Beit Bridge. All I'm saying son is, the world is a lot smaller than we think. And there is more that we have in common as humanity than our differences. Look how happy your uncle Peter and MaMpofu are..."

"And yet, there was Gukurahundi," I said, feeling that I had to counter the logic that she seemed so confident about.

"Yes," she said quietly, "there was Gukurahundi. Yet when I see how people interact with each other... look, I know that there is an element of animosity between the different tribes in our country, but it seems to me that when people get to know each other – like you and Rumbie seem to have – the so called differences fall away. Who ever thought that in Zimbabwe, white men would marry black women and vice versa. Yet it is happening fairly regularly."

Whatever had happened in the ten years since I left home, I had come home to a different culture to the one I left all those years ago to seek my fortune in South Africa. I had come home to a different mother!

CHAPTER SIX

The excitement had been building up for days and the whole village had been transformed. From my vantage point on a rock just outside the village, I watched the activity below. The smoke to my right and the accompanying aroma of roasted meat told me that the slaughterers of the ox that had been selected for the occasion – from my mother's small herd – had almost completed their task and were now enjoying some of the spoils in the form of *"amantshontsho"* – bits of liver and other choice meats that would have been "stolen" by those with the dubious privilege of killing and skinning the animal. The village itself was a hive of activity as a stream of young girls who carried pots of water – obtained from several kilometres away – on their heads, were emptying their precious cargo into whatever receptacle could be found. The older ones seemed to be going back for more water. Women, under the strict supervision of MaMpofu were busy on several fires cooking large three legged pots of rice and some *"isitshwala" - the* staple maize meal dish; although I could see MaMpofu cooking what I presumed would be a 'special' pot of some small grain (I could not tell which small grain) isitshwala. In the absence of the big Mopani tree that had been the meeting point for several decades, men sat under a smaller tree that offered precious little shade and enjoyed some home brewed traditional beer and some of the meat that had come from the ox. Their conversation, which I could not hear, was animated and boisterous.

'Some things never change,' I said to myself as I watched the scene below. The men seemed to do little yet enjoyed more of the faire while the women laboured over fires in thirty plus degree heat. They would only get to eat after everyone else was fed – although of course I knew MaMpofu would probably have made sure that food was stashed away for them. To my right, at the entrance to our homestead, someone had found some paper lettering in different colours which read, “We come Home Sipho” because, as uncle Peter had explained, “we could not find the letter L”. I wondered if anyone else had noticed the discrepancy! Khulu sat on his own in the shade of his hut and appeared to be dozing. The younger boys were playing football with a ball made of bits of plastic tied with string, the game being interrupted often as one or other of the boys was sent off on some errand.

The whole scene resembled preparations for a wedding feast and I found myself thinking about Rumbie. It had been several days since my last telephone conversation with her. In the week or so that I had been at my mother’s, Rumbie had become a regular caller on Chipo’s phone – actually, it was shared by the civil servants that lived in the house but I liked to call it Chipo’s phone. I smiled to myself as I remembered how much time I had spent on the phone with her. In the end, Chipo’s colleagues had complained!

“The others are complaining about the amount of time you spend on the phone. They will also be expecting calls you know!”

I had apologised of course but in fact there had really been nothing of any substance that we had been discussing. We had talked mainly about work and how everyone was doing. It was as if we were each waiting for the other to say something personal – of course it was up to me to do that but the opportunity never seemed to arise.

“Mr Van really misses you,” was how she often ended the conversation, to which I would respond with, “well it was his decision to suspend me!”

Only in our last conversation, when I told her that I was going to the village for a week or so did she say something that could have been personal.

“A whole week!” she had said emphatically, “What about your passport?”

I had told her that Chipo was going to try and arrange that I get a passport so that I could try and regularise my stay in South Africa. I had had to fork out a significant amount of Rands to Chipo's contact who was facilitating the issuing of the passport.

"I'll only be a week," I had reassured her. "And after that, I'll be able to visit home more regularly."

This did not seem to please her as much as I had hoped.

"Why would you need to visit home more regularly? I'm here in Joburg aren't I?"

I had mumbled something about my mother needing me, but was surprised at her question.

"I'm not likely to hear from Chipo's contact for another two weeks anyway," I said in response to her question about the passport, "so there will be time for me to visit the village. They are planning a bit of a homecoming party. Nothing too big, just family and friends."

"Of course, Sipho," she had said sounding regretful, "you've been away for so long they are bound to want to do something. You'll probably meet your childhood sweetheart there." Had she sounded jealous?

As I surveyed the scene below me, I thought about what I had said to Rumbie about the function being 'nothing too big'. This was one that, as MaMpofu had put it, "they will talk about for years!"

The reunion with MaMpofu had been more emotional than I had anticipated, and somewhat comical. She and Uncle Peter had found us waiting for them at the Beit Bridge bus rank when they got off their bus from Harare. She had come off the bus in some haste, having seen me from within the bus before I saw her. She came at me like a steam train – and she is not a small woman. She had meant to hug me but, because I was not expecting such a powerful show of emotion, she hit me with unexpected force and we both fell over! It must have been quite a sight and some people thought we were fighting. We got up and as I tried to dust myself off, she hugged me again and kissed me on the cheek.

“Sipho, Sipho!” she said lifting me up with ease, “How could you do this to MaMbofu?” her Shona accent was more pronounced than I remembered.

When I looked into her face, tears were running down her cheeks.

“I never said this to your mother, but I was sure you were dead! Your friends had told me the truth of what happened and made me promise not to tell your mother. ‘It will be better for her if she believes that he just disappeared into South Africa like so many have done in the past. She’ll just think that ‘*watshona*’ into South Africa and keep hoping’. They were right as it turns out, but it was a secret that I’ve had to keep all these years from your mother and from my husband.”

“Welcome home young man.” Uncle Peter gave me a very firm but warm handshake, “and what is the secret you’ve kept from me all these years?” he turned to his wife, looking at her rather fondly.

“Never mind, Peter. We’ll miss the bus to the village.” She had lifted the bags she had brought down from the bus and walked hurriedly towards the Maramani bus rank, shouting back to her husband, “get the rest of the luggage from the bus carrier, hurry, Peter.”

“If you’re not already married young man,” ’Ncane Peter said in a low voice, shaking his head, “don’t marry a Shona. They are so bossy!” Somehow, he did not sound like he meant that. There was clearly something special between those two, as I was going to find out during this visit.

The few days since had been hectic. Preparations for the party were in full swing although as the ‘special guest’, I was not allowed to participate. Every time I tried to do something, someone else would come to tell me that they had been tasked with it .So I took long walks to visit my old school – which had not changed much except that I did not recognise any of the teachers – and to visit our old haunts like the stream we used to fish in; mostly silted over as the effects of stream bank cultivation, necessitated by the villagers need to be close to water, given the persistent drought of the last few years! It was on one such walk that I met Bridget. I did not recognise her at first as the last mental picture of her was of a chubby, overconfident five year old with a runny nose.

"Hello, Sipho, my husband," she said cheerily although of course I had no idea what she was talking about. "I heard that you were back!"

"Hello," I replied politely, "do I know you?"

"Sipho! How can you be so proud! We were going to get married, remember?"

I was sixteen when I left and certainly had no plans to marry anyone. I had just about begun to discover my own sexuality but I did not have a girlfriend! Rumbie had said something about a childhood sweetheart and I had laughed it off. Was I about to find out that I had one after all? How come I did not remember her?

"It's Bridget!" She said cheerfully, "Bridget Nkala. I always told you that you and I were going to get married. I got tired of waiting, so I married someone else as you were not coming back."

"Bridget!" I shouted, relieved. "How are you?"

She was right of course. She had upset me those years ago by always claiming that she was going to be my wife. She had grown into a pretty young lady but she could not have been much more than fifteen!

"Married?" I asked incredulously, "How old are you again? I mean you were five or six when I left so you can't be more than fifteen..."

"I'm sixteen next month, actually. And my daughter is nearly a year old."

"And you are married?"

"Yes. To Promise, your old friend. He was the next best thing after you!"

"Promise was never my friend," I said remembering the many fist fights between Promise and I, instigated by the older boys who would tell either one of us that the other had said something about the other's mother. All they had to say was something like 'Promise says your mother is a whore', and we would go at each other! There was never a clear winner and it took me years to realise that this was all for the entertainment of the older boys.

"He respects you a lot though. Always going on about how he wishes he had joined you."

"He may be luckier than he realises," I said remembering what had happened to my fellow travellers. "So, when did you two get married?" I tried to get away from the subject of our trek to the border.

"Well, when I say 'married' I mean that, well, I got pregnant and, well, what else could I do?"

"Had you finished school?"

"Of course not! I was expelled from school for being pregnant!"

She looked down to the ground with what could have been embarrassment. I would not have expected her to know about things that made people pregnant at her age!

"Did he rape you?" I was not sure why I asked that question.

"No! Why would you think that?"

"Well, from what I heard, you were quite bright and great things were expected of you…"

"I was going to be a pilot," she said quietly.

"So? What happened to that dream?"

"Sipho, Sipho," it sounded as though she was pitying me, "I slept with Promise, just once. You don't seem to understand, just like my father, how strong the urge is at a certain age – and the temptation. It was a mistake and it was over before I even knew it had happened."

I did not quite know what to say. Could this have happened to Rumbie? Was it a momentary lapse when she succumbed to the 'strong urge' that Bridget had just mentioned? Had she enjoyed it? What had happened to the guy…?

"For that moment of insanity," I heard Bridget say, "I was called a whore, a loose girl who would only end up working as a prostitute! I felt lucky that Promise did not deny responsibility and agreed to take me in."

"So you married him."

"You could say that. It was one less mouth to fed for my parents. So, we live together at his parents' home and as he does not work and spends his days at the Township, I spend my days caring for his parents and for my baby."

It seemed so unfair. That a life so full of promise could be ruined so totally by a moment of childish indiscretion…

"Of course now when he comes home drunk, smelling of traditional brew, tobacco and sweat as he does not like to bath, he demands sex because I am his wife even though he has not paid a single cent of *amalobolo* for me!" Tears were streaming down her cheeks and I felt very sorry for her so I hugged her to comfort her. It was only for a moment but someone must have seen us because a few days later, I had met Promise at Mr Moyo's shop.

"So, the hero has returned," he was obviously drunk and swayed from side to side.

"Promise, my friend, it's so good to see you!" I felt a genuine affinity to my erstwhile fist fight foe.

"Did you hear that?" Promise addressed the others around him. "He just called me his friend! The hero from *Joza,* who wants to steal my wife just called me his friend!"

"He thinks that his Rands can buy him women," one of his companions said.

"She is my wife. I have sex with her any time I want and you come with your fancy clothes and Adidas tekkies" he indicated my clothes with his arm, "and you think you can take her away from me?"

"I have no intention of taking your wife from you," I protested, thinking how unfortunate Bridget had been to end up with a bum like him.

"You were seen!" he was almost shouting. "In broad daylight too. You were seen kissing my wife by the river!"

It all made sense then. Someone must have seen me hug Bridget to comfort her and reached the only logical conclusion that people in these parts could have reached.

"I did not kiss you wife and ..."

"Are you calling me a liar? Themba here saw you," he pointed at a young boy who I had never seen before. "Are you calling him a liar too?"

"No, I'm not calling him a liar. He probably mistook..."

"Themba," Promised advanced towards me menacingly, "did you or did you not see this man kissing my wife?"

"I saw him. He put his arms around her..."

"So, you think that you can come back and steal my woman?"

It had been a while since my last fist fight and I was in no mood to get into one then. But Promise clearly wanted a fist fight. He probably had told his comrades that he was going to teach me a lesson and could not afford to lose face by not going ahead and doing just that. But as much out of practice as I was, Promise was in a worse condition and was drunk. I tried to walk out of the shop but one of his mates blocked my way. They clearly were going to have some fun with me. There were too many of them and I would not have a chance if they all decided to join in. I decided that surprise would be my best weapon.

I turned round, grabbed Promise by the collar before he realised what was happening, dragged him towards me and head butted him. Before he could recover, I kicked him in the crotch and punched him in the face so hard that blood came squirting out of his nose. All his friends scattered and fled.

"I told you Promise," I heard one of them say, "These guys from Joza are bad. He's probably carrying a knife!"

"I was just playing with you." Promise slurred.

"Sure," I had my face so close to his that could smell his bad breath, "so was I. But if I wanted your wife, I could have her at any time. But I did not kiss your wife."

"I was just playing with you," he said again.

It was one of the most satisfying moments of my visit thus far.

But now it was time to join the others, and for the party to begin in earnest.

The conversation under the tree was loud and boisterous, probably because of the traditional brew that was flowing freely, although I noticed a few bottles of lager and one or two small bottles of cheap brandy. I had just walked the gauntlet of mothers by the cooking fires trying to remind me that they had pretty daughters and young girls giggling their admiration of the man from *Egoli* that they'd heard so much about! I felt rather important if somewhat embarrassed by the attention.

"Sipho!" MaNcube shouted as she looked up from the dish in which I could see goat's offal that she was preparing by tying the intestines round the tripe before boiling in the large three legged cast iron pot that stood beside her, ready for the purpose. It had been many years since I had had that particular dish, one of my childhood favourites. "Your mother tells me you have a Shona girlfriend."

As if on cue, everyone stopped what they were doing and all attention was focused on me. My mother, who had been cutting some cabbage for the inevitable coleslaw that seemed to grace every important feast stared incredulously at her friend looking as though she could have strangled her.

"Oops,I was not supposed to say that. Sorry magee, you seemed so…"

"I did not say any such thing MaNcu! What I said was.,.." she seemed unable to go on and I felt that I had to come to her rescue.

"I do have a friend who is Shona and is a girl," I said calmly although inside I was seething. The last thing I needed right then was people making jokes about Rumbie in the same way that they had done about MaMpofu all those years ago. "So, yes you could say that I have a Shona girlfriend."

"What is it about these Shona women that attracts our young men?" A woman I did not recognise said as she took a break from whatever chore she had been engaged in.

"We are beautiful," MaMpofu stood in the middle of the homestead with her hands on her hips, "and hardworking and," she wiggled her hips, "we know how to please men."

Everyone burst out laughing. MaMpofu was one of the most respected members of the family and people had even forgotten that she was Shona.

"You're not really Shona MaMpofu." MaNcube said, "You are one of us!"

"Exactly! Now unless you want your husbands to get even drunker on hungry stomachs, you ladies better get back to work!"

I wish I could say that that was the end of it. But it was not, because the men had overheard the women's exchanges with me.

"So, young man, you want to follow the footsteps of your uncle Peter?" Mr Moyo, looking rather splendid in his black suit, white shirt and matching black tie looked and sounded soberer than the rest. The hat that sat on his knee completed the initial impression that this was indeed a successful businessman. But for the shoes that were in need of some polish and threadbare suit that, on closer inspection had seen better days, he would have looked completely out of place among the motley collection of villagers in their various states of 'unwash'!

"The footsteps of uncle Peter?" I feigned ignorance.

"You want to marry a Shona?"

"Oh that. No, Mr Moyo. I have no plans to marry anyone at the moment. Who told you that I..."

"No one told me. I heard the women just now." Mr Moyo was a very affable man and he was not going to pursue the subject but another men who had just been relieving himself behind a guava tree that did very little to conceal him joined in as he was going back to his seat.

"Marrying a Shona is like, like ... who wants to marry a Shona anyway? They are very strange people."

He walked on, still putting away his manhood, much to the delight of the young boys whose soccer game had just been interrupted again. I was left wondering what his understanding of 'strange' was. Rumble's behavior was certainly more normal than other behaviors that I had been witnessing.

"Hello, my friend." The rather surprising salutation was from Promise. He looked as unkempt as the rest of the men although, being younger, his state of dishevelment appeared more pronounced. He also looked like he was quite drunk, which may have explained his over friendly greeting. Instinctively, I turned to look for Bridget, who I had not noticed to this point. I spotted her among a group of younger women who appeared to be sorting out the different plates that had come from the various surrounding homes to cater for the larger than normal gathering. I made a mental note to go and greet her later.

"We were class mates you know!" Promise was telling the others. "Same class throughout primary school. In fact we sat side by side for most of the time."

I did not remember ever sitting next to Promise in class but I was not going to argue the point.

"What happened to you?" The youngster who asked the question was not immediately visible to Promise, who was trying to identify him for future retribution. "You beat up your teachers didn't you? You see what happens to those who listen to their teachers? If I were you Promise, I would not mention being in the same class..."

"Ngizakumukula"! Promise had spotted the young man and was making strides towards him. But the boy was much too quick and got away before Promise got anywhere near him. It was all in good fun – although that may not have been quite how Promised would have seen it – and everyone had a good laugh. This was something I had always noticed about these parties and functions; while the women were still slaving at the pots enduring the heat and the smoke, the party had already started for the men. At the end, the men would stagger home and leave

the women to clean up – but probably still expect *isitshwala* for the evening when the women got home!

I accepted a soft drink that was offered to me and found a piece of cut log that served as a stool. From my vantage point, I could watch the goings on almost as if I was not part of it, which was strange because this was all for me. For the moment though, I seemed irrelevant to the whole shindig! It all felt rather surreal. I had been so looking forward to seeing these people and yet it seemed like I had very little in common with them. These were, most of them, the people I grew up around; the people who raised me in fact because children were raised by the community. But somehow, by me being away from here and experiencing a different life, I felt like I was among strangers. It got me thinking about the tribal divisions that we were so obsessed with. Living in South Africa had got me in touch with people from many parts of Africa – particularly the Southern African sub region. One of the things I had noticed was that the languages of the sub region were very similar. Similar sentence structures, similar phrases and idioms and indeed many common words. Was it not possible that as people drifted apart over the centuries the different experiences they encountered meant that they redefined their languages and customs to suit particular conditions? After all, at some point, there were no borders and Africa was just one huge land mass, controlled by the various Kingdoms that existed then but not really owned by anyone. When Mzilikazi, as we were taught in history, left what we now know as Zululand, did he think he was moving to another country? It seemed to me that he was moving away from without any thought of where he was moving to! How many other groups of people did the same? It was unfortunate, I thought, that our history as taught in schools was based on the thoughts and assumptions of strangers whose experience of Africa was limited to whatever encounters they had had with some, but not all Africans. The Venda people, my people, are the same people as the Venda people of Northern South Africa who speak a language that if not listened to properly could pass for Shona. The Khalangas on Zimbabwe's Western border are the same as the Khalangas on Botswana's Eastern border – and the language they speak has elements of Shona in it. Yet, because they are in a region defined as Matebeleland (by whom?)are defined as *Mandevere,* who are different from Shona!

"There you are, Sipho, I've been looking for you everywhere!" I was startled. I had been so deep in thought that I had been unaware that everyone else was eating!

"You obviously did not look here because I've been here for quite some time," I accepted he plate of food that Bridget offered, "so you can't have looked 'everywhere' as you just said."

"No, not everywhere but, you know what I mean!"

"Anyway, thanks for finding me but this is way too much food for me. Can you get me another plate so I can reduce the portion?"

"This is a special plate prepared especially for you by MaMpofu and your mother. I don't think it's a good idea for you to take some of it off. They will feel that you did not enjoy their cooking. Eat what you can and leave the rest. The dogs will have a feast today!"

"It's such a waste," I said thinking what little forethought there was. In a few days, some of the people here would be starving, but for today, we'll eat until we throw food away!

There was rice, *um'nqhutshu,* huge chunks of beef, some goat meat and goat offal's, *amacimbi*, roast chicken and, of course, coleslaw. Yet as I watched, a fire was being prepared on which to roast some more meat! Somehow, I seemed to lose my appetite just seeing all this food. If anyone else noticed, they were not showing it.

The food was surprisingly tasty, even though I only ate part of it. I had all the goat's offal's and some of the beef, which was very tender. Then I tried the chicken and had some amacimbi. I could not do much more so I found a youngster whom I offered my plate to and told him to share with the other children. He clearly did not hear the last part because he quietly disappeared behind khulu's hut. When he emerged about twenty minutes later, his stomach reminded me of how we used to feed the puppies until they were literally dragging their stomachs on the ground. The belief (mistaken as it turned out) was that the puppies would not need to eat for a couple of days which meant that we would not have to cook for them. The young fellow would find out on the next day that he'd still need to eat! In fact he might wish he had shared the food sooner than he realised. Still, for today, he had enjoyed a very good meal.

*"Sifakeleni u stekete!" (*play stekete for us). The request from Promise seemed very popular and I was curious to hear this popular choice that I had not heard before. It turned out that 'stekete' was the Ndebele mispronunciation of a very popular song – Chitekete – by a Shona artist called Leonard Dembo. The music had been going for a while but now it got louder. Virtually everyone, including the women who momentarily abandoned their pots, took to the dance floor. Embarrassingly, my mother joined in with a dance that I can only describe as inappropriate! And she was pulling me to join her on the dance floor! Reluctantly, I got up and joined her. The song was very danceable to –although I cannot , by any stretch of the imagination, call myself a dancer – and I found myself swaying to the beat and lost in the music. I could not understand any of the lyrics although everyone else seemed to make up Sindebele approximations of the Shona words. Everyone sang the title bit of the song so that every few seconds a very loud ,"teketeeee" would be heard. It was indeed a fun home coming party.

"Not bad for a Shona song hey?" MaMpofu was standing next to me watching the revelry.

"It's a very good song," I agreed. "I wish I could understand what he's saying though."

"Never mind," MaMpofu linked arms with me and pulled me away from the dancing. No one, not even my mother who was 'getting down' with one of the unwashed, seemed to notice. We walked away from the noise and in a few minutes could hardly hear the music although we did here the very loud shouting of "encore"! when the music stopped.

"Tell me about this Shona girlfriend of yours," MaMpofu said rather unexpectedly.

"She's not my girlfriend!"

"I know, but you wish she were, right?"

"Why do you say that?"

"Because that's what your mother told me and mothers know these things."

"My mother is the last person I'd expect to have anything to say about this..."

"Why? Because she's a prostitute?"

I was stunned. Everyone had treated my mother with such respect that I was convinced that no one knew of her other life in Beit Bridge.

"You know? Who else knows?" How could my mother have done this to me? Was everyone pretending to my face and calling me the son of a whore behind my back?

"Don't worry," MaMpofu reassured me. "I don't think many people in the village know, or care what she does. They respect her a lot for the way she has pulled herself up after she lost everything, including her only son."

"Was there nothing else she could have done?"

"Have you looked around you? Have you seen how different things are from the time you left? You were very young, of course and probably cannot see the difference. But life in Zimbabwe is tough for everyone. The promise of independence has never been fulfilled and, well, people have had to do what they have had to do in order to survive. It is not easy for someone coming in from a normal economy to understand just how bad things are in our beloved country."

We walked in silence for a few minutes. I was conflicted. I loved my mother dearly and could understand how the loss of everyone you loved may lead to decisions based on 'nothing to lose'. But prostitution was the kind of 'profession' that meant a complete loss of dignity. How could I love and respect a mother that slept with men for money?

"Our jobs in Harare are at risk." I stopped walking suddenly, not sure that I had heard her right. Uncle Peter had always had a job and...

"Surely you will get other jobs?" I said hopefully.

"Not in this economy." MaMpofu said simply. "We keep hearing that the factory is relocating to Botswana or Zambia and we are not sure what will happen if it does close. Factories are closing everywhere and there are no jobs to be had."

"But I've heard people say that all the jobs are in Harare How can you be saying that there are no jobs?"

"I suppose when you are away from Harare, it may seem like that. I think that some companies may have done that in the beginning, you know, to try and cut costs by consolidating their businesses but I can tell you that a lot of companies are closing, even in Harare. It got worse since the so called ESAP that our government has embarked on..."

"ESAP?" I had not heard the term before.

"I am not sure what it stands for but our rulers tell us that they had to do it at the behest of the World Bank or something and now it is supposedly responsible for our problems!"

"So, why did they embark on it if it is creating problems for us." None of it made any sense.

"I am not a politician, Sipho. All I know is that our country is not what it used to be! Of course there is also the tribal politics," she went on with a sigh, sounding as though she was tired of it all.

I was not sure what she meant so I decided to keep quiet until I knew where this was going.

"Do you know that there are members of my family who still have not forgiven me for marrying outside the tribe? In fact to hear some of them speak, you'd think my husband comes from another country altogether!"

This was the first time I was hearing this. I had always assumed that she struggled to fit into our family, but that uncle Peter had always been accepted by hers.

"I knew that your uncle really loved me because of what he went through to get my family to accept that he was the one I wanted to marry. In fact, even accepting his proposal took me some time because, firstly my friends laughed at me for being wanted by a *Mundevere*, but I also knew my family's attitude towards them. Lesser men would have given up; not Peter." She smiled sweetly at what must have been pleasant recollections of a difficult courtship.

"Then, of course came the bigger obstacle – my family. My grandmother, who for years had been telling us stories of how cruel the *Madzviti* had been to the Shona people was absolutely horrified.

'Did you say Sekai wants to marry a Mudzviti?' she would ask regularly as if she had forgotten what she had been told before. 'Over my dead body. I will not allow this home; my family to be desecrated by one of those usurpers!'

At the time I said nothing but would shut myself away and cry for hours. My mother did try to support me but she really had no say in the matter, being a *mutorwa.* She was, in fact being told that she had to speak some sense into me. My father refused to speak to me for months on end and I felt completely alone."

All this information was completely new to me and I was not sure how to respond to someone that I had always looked up to as a pillar of strength. For the first time in my life, I saw MaMpofu as vulnerable and human. I wondered whether she had, in fact, ever told anyone about this.

"It was your uncles' strength and resilience that got me through that period. He told me about the battles he was having with his own family and I realised I was the one who was letting the side down. So I went and confronted my father during one of my visits from town.

'Father' I said to him quietly and respectfully, 'I know that you do not like Peter and his people. However, I want to tell you that Peter is the man I am going to marry. It would be nice to have your blessing but if I don't get it, I will move in with him and we will live as man and wife. I have been a good daughter; I have listened to everything you taught me. I have not slept with a man out of wedlock, but you are making life very difficult for me and for Peter, whom I love very much' I closed my eyes and waited for the inevitable barrage that would come. To my surprise, he stood up and came and hugged me and without a word, walked out of the room."

"What did you do?" I asked although I was somewhat disappointed that the confrontation that I had anticipated had not taken place.

"Nothing. I was disappointed that he had not had the guts to answer me. There was so much more that I had wanted to tell him. But not long after that word was sent out that Peter's family would be welcome to come and traditionally formalise our union. It turned out that one of my older cousins my father's eldest sister's son, who had a good relationship with his uncles, told them in rather graphic terms that unless they were prepared to sleep with me themselves, they had better let me marry Peter! 'Would you rather,' he apparently asked them, 'allow your daughter to marry someone whom she loves even if he speaks a different language, or would you rather she marries one of the local lads whose main activity is drinking *Chibuku* that he cannot afford and has to bum off the likes of Peter, simply because he speaks the same language as you?'

It would seem they had no answer to that one!"

"And your grandmother?"

"She died a disappointed woman, although Peter being Peter, I think he had won her over and only her pride stopped her from openly saying so. She often boasted to her neighbours about her Mundevere grandson who seemed to be the only one that remembered that she needed warm shoes for the winter and also always brought her the sweet things she liked whenever he visited!

'If only he had been one of us,' she would always end her praises. She had expected me to carry on the hate that she had for the Madzviti who caused so much pain in her childhood, but what kind of world would we live in if we never forgot the wrongs done to us?"

"Are you saying then that the people of this region should just forget what happened to them? Much as I hardly knew my father, should I just forget that he ever existed?" I asked, somewhat confused.

"I don't know, Sipho. In fact I am not so sure that it was the soldiers' own wishes. Many of them were too young to know what happened all those years ago. But it's not up to me what you think. All I'm saying is what does continually talking about it change? Who benefits from such talk except the politicians who get supported, not because of their policies but simply because of their tribal affiliations? So, even if they fail, like ours seem to be, they continue to get support because their tribal grouping happens to have the numbers." She paused, as if she wanted me to say something; I had nothing to say.

"You still have not told me much of this Rumbie that I hear so much about," MaMpofu took my hand and steered me round to indicate that we were going back.

“And where have you ‘heard so much’ about Rumbie...?”

“From your mother, of course. Where else? She seems to think that you are in love with this girl.”

“I wonder where she gets that notion.”

“Are you?” MaMpofu was looking very serious, “in love with her I mean?”

“I like her very much, but...”

“She’s a Shona?”

“NO! Well, yes there’s that but that can be overcome...”

“I’d not be so sure of that, but go on.”

“She has a six year old child that she had never told me about...”

“Then how did you know she has a child?” I wished she wouldn’t keep interrupting me and I told her so.

“She told me...”

“I thought you just said she never told you.”

“MAMPOFU!” I had never raised my voice to her before and I immediately regretted it, but she was not letting me say what I wanted to say! She got the idea.

“Anyway,” I said after a few minutes’ silence, “I like her very much... in fact I think she likes me too but we’ve never really talked about what we feel for each other. We’ve been more like very good friends.”

I began to regret raising my voice because I now wanted MaMpofu to comment and she said nothing. We walked in silence for a couple of hundred metres until the silence became unbearable for me.

"She's a very nice girl but..."

"She's a Shona with a child, you already said that." I was relieved that she was talking to me. "You say that you have not told her how you feel?"

"I have not told her but I think that she realises..."

"Then find yourself a nice Ndebele virgin girl to get married to."

"MaMpofu!" I had raised my voice again with less intensity, though, "How can you, of all people, say that."

"Of all people," she mimicked me, "I'm the only one qualified to tell you that. Now listen. Marrying a Shona, means bringing into your home, someone from a different culture, with different customs and probably different expectations from one that is from within your own culture. You will have to always be on the lookout for her to make sure she is comfortable because, if they laugh too loudly having spoken in a language she does not understand, she will think they are laughing at her or about her. When you speak to your own people in your own language, she will feel left out and abandoned and of course she will be made to feel very unwelcome by your family and neighbours!"

"But my mother sounds like she would welcome her..."

"Your mother?" she interrupted again. "In our culture, your mother is not your relative, which I've always found strange because she is the only one who can vouch for who your father is!" She chuckled, "In our Shona culture, your mother is what we call a *mutorwa* – one who has been taken in or brought into the family. She will have very little say on the matter. Right now, no one is saying much because you have not confirmed that you want to marry this girl. Once you confirm it, their true colours will come out. Remember that not everyone in your family wishes you the best, so their motives may not necessarily be tribal, but tribalism is the easiest to blame."

What MaMpofu was saying made sense without making sense to me.

"But you MaMpofu have lasted. Are you saying you went through this?"

"Worse! Your uncle and I nearly divorced because he thought I was making false accusations about his family. These things will not be said to your face. To you they will say what a nice person she is and how lovely it is that you followed your heart and all that nonsense. It is her that they will target. Think about that!

Of course, at this point, you don't know what her family's attitude will be towards you being from another country..."

"I'm not from another country..."

"You might as well be. Look, the countries as we know them now were demarcated by Europeans for their own purposes. Tribes were split into different countries because it suited them; and tribes that were somewhat different were put together in the same countries because it suited the Europeans. The borders could have been anywhere and there is no logic, at least to us as Africans, as to why they are where they are."

"So, what happens to Rumbie will happen to me in reverse. Her people may target me in the same way that my people may target Rumbie?"

"Not necessarily. They may take a genuine liking to you and you will live happily ever after. Somehow, I doubt it." She stopped and looked directly into my face. "The baby." MaMpofu seemed not quite sure how to go on. "Now, if you thought you had problems, the baby brings a whole new dimension into the mix!"

"She lives with her grandparents..."

"Oh yes she does. For now. Do you think that she will continue to live with her grandparents after you guys are married and her mother is settled down? Do you think that Rumbie is working so hard so that she can find a husband who will abandon her child? In any case, what happens when her parents die?"

"Look, MaMpofu," I found myself retreating, "I have not said that I want to marry this girl. I only said that we are very good friends."

"Yes, Sipho, you did. But from what you say, she could be the best thing that has ever happened to you!"

The woman was completely mad!

"I only say these things because I know how you are feeling now. That thing in your pants is telling you that she is the only woman in the world for you." Was a mother supposed to talk to a son like that? "Otherwise you would have been chasing all the young girls in the village who will do anything to snare you so you can take them to Joza with you; the ones whose mothers keep sending you bowls of traditional meals because word has got round that you have missed some of your childhood faire. What I am saying to you is that you need to interrogate all these things before you commit!"

"Oh Okay." I could not think of anything else to say.

"How did she get pregnant?"

"I only found out about the baby at the bus station. I mean, I know how people get pregnant..."

"I don't mean that Sipho. Was she raped, for example? Was she in love with the guy who then denied responsibility? Might she still be in love with him? Why are there no other men around her?"

Perhaps, I thought to myself, I should find myself one of these girls from the village after all. There were some quite pretty ones that I had seen. Suddenly, I found myself thinking about Bridget and getting angry at Promise. How come I was still a virgin, yet a bum like Promise had sex with a pretty young woman any time he wanted?

"Look, Sipho, you may have many more challenges than the language your intended speaks. If there were no children in your marriage for example, and she has already proven that she can have babies, do you know the temptations that she will have?"

"What temptations?" The woman was not making sense.

"Your uncle and I have no children and I know the kinds of temptations that that can bring. Generally, it is the woman that gets blamed, right? Men like to think of themselves as not only virile but fertile. So the pressure was on for him to find himself another woman – preferably Ndebele – who could give him an heir; and for a while, he succumbed, which is why I spent so much time here at the village. It was to give Peter a chance to find someone else..."

"And you agreed?"

"Of course not! It was not put quite like that. I had to learn his language for the sake of our children and his parents were getting old and needed constant care, so my coming to Maramani had a double benefit – at the time I was not aware of the third benefit that Peter would have a chance to find a woman who could bear children."

"How did you find out about..."

"Oh, Peter admitted it to me afterwards. He had had a relationship with a woman who, like your Rumbie, had a child of her own, who also spoke the same language, of course, but not only did that affair not produce children, he found out that he loved me too much to continue with the affair – at least that's what he says," MaMpofu finished with a chuckle.

"So, you guys were good after that?"

"I had to perform of course!"

"Perform?"

"Well, I was not exactly innocent myself."

"You cheated on Uncle?" This was getting embarrassingly complicated.

"NO! But there was a lot of pressure from my family – female members of my family – to try elsewhere and see if I was as barren as my husband and his family were suggesting." She smiled ruefully as she remembered. "'That is how to keep your marriage intact,' they told me. 'Women will always be blamed but clever ones just go and find themselves another man to get them pregnant. The husband is happy because he believes the child is his and the marriage is saved.' Apparently, this happens all the time and sometimes, a couple can have several children in this way. And as long as the husband does not find out..."

The world was proving to be a lot stranger than I had ever realised.

"There is a saying in our Shona culture," MaMpofu went on, apparently warming to her subject, *'Gomba harina mwana.'* It simply means that the clandestine lover of a married woman can have no claim to any children born as a result of the illicit affair."

"In other words," I was beginning to understand, "you could have gone and found yourself a lover and I would have had cousins that are not really my cousins?"

"I could have; I very nearly did, especially after I found out about your uncle's own affair. Strangely enough, there were man in my husband's family willing to assist – and try out a Shona, I bet. But I did not go through with it; so out of my own guilt, I had to perform at your uncle. I threatened to leave him and, in one of my least proud moments, teased him about his lack of 'success' with the other woman!"

"Poor uncle Peter," I said really feeling sorry for the man.

"Hey, I'm the one that got cheated on! But you are right. In the end, he was so miserable at the thought of losing me and I could see that he really did not want our marriage to break up, so I relented, but on the one condition that we seek medical help, which proved that he was the one with the problem."

Shit! I thought to myself, if Rumbie got pregnant, how sure could I be that I was responsible. MaMpofu seemed to read my thoughts.

"Of course you can never be sure under any circumstances but the fact that she already has a baby will put extra pressure on you."

"So, do you think that I should try to prove myself before I marry Rumbie?"

"I thought you said she was not your girlfriend?"

"She's not, but let's just say, in the event that I decide to marry her."

"It's not just your decision, of course. She may have other ideas."

"MaMpofu, I am asking with the assumption that she will have agreed."

"Well, how do you propose to go about proving your fertility then, young man?"

"I can find a young lady that I can make pregnant..."

"And how sure will you be that you are responsible?"

She could be so exasperating. "I'll find myself a virgin!" I said triumphantly.

"Ah! That settles it then. You know, of course how to identify a virgin by looking at one?"

"Surely among all the young girls in the village there must be a few virgins...?"

"The world has changed my son. Even during our teenage years, girls were getting sexually active quite early. Now, after the experiences of the war of liberation and 'Gukurahundi' sexual intercourse for young girls is not such a rare thing. In any case, traditionally, girls were sometimes married off at twelve and thirteen years old, so it may not be as new as we think. But good luck with your virgin search!"

My relationship with MaMpofu had always been good, but I felt as if our discussion that afternoon had moved it up to another level. Her candour on the subject of the challenges that her marriage had had got me thinking hard for the first time about what sort of woman I would like to marry. By many of the criteria I set, Rumbie always came tops. Then again, how much experience had I had with girls. I determined to spend the last two weeks of my holidays getting some experience, and hopefully, finding a virgin!

When we got back to the party, the dancing and gyrating was indicative of the revellers' state of sobriety! Khulu sat in exactly the same position that we had left him, except he seemed to be in a deep sleep with a half-finished bottle of lager dangling dangerously from his hand; Mr Moyo looked somewhat less regal, dust on his not-so-new suit suggesting a close encounter with the earth at some point. Promise was holding onto Bridget in a somewhat uncoordinated 'lover's dance' and my mother, having given up on the unwashed, was dancing with MaNcube and singing along rather loudly to a Brenda Facie tune. It looked as if a rather painful form of fun was being had by all. Even some of the young girls that I had thought might be virgins were looking less innocent; and less sober! That night, in the somewhat uncomfortable grain store, on a bag of sorghum, I had my very first sexual encounter.

"Are you finished already?" The innocent looking girl looked and sounded angry and disappointed. I had, of course, released my load before entering her innermost, "I thought you guys from

Joza were .." She quickly pulled down her dress and pulled up her underwear. "Can I have some Rands for a Coca-Cola."

I gave her a ten rand note that was in my pocket and she seemed very happy.

"We can try again if you want," she said looking as though she was about to take her pants down

"No, thank you," I said tersely, feeling embarrassed not only because I had succumbed to 'the thing in my pants', as MaMpofu had put it, but also because I had failed to even...

I cleaned myself as best I could and furtively left my hiding place trying to re-join the now much quieter scene without being noticed

"I'm not good enough for your party, hey?"

I turned round to see Zenzo sitting against the wall of the room I had just come from He had a plate full of meat on his lap and another one on his side. I felt a lump in my throat because I had totally forgotten about Zenzo – and Samson.

"I'm so sorry Zenzo. I completely forgot..."

"It's alright," he said simply, "I'd forget me too."

"Not like that, Zenzo. I was so busy visiting people and I was not really responsible for inviting..."

"It's alright, I said. I found out at the last minute and I came. Look how much meat I have," he indicated the plate on his lap, "and I've got another plate for Samson," he said pointing at the plate on his side.

"Oh, is Samson coming?"

"Of course not! He doesn't know, but I'll eat for him!" He looked really happy. "And there is more meat in the plates that the people have discarded..."

"You mean that you did not get your own plate. Let me speak to my mother..."

"It's alright, Sipho. If I don't eat what the others are throwing away, it will only go to waste."

His 'logic' did not make it any more palatable. I still felt awkward that he was being a scavenger at my party. One of the people that were responsible for my being in a different place; a place that was clearly doing better than my home country, was now nothing but a scavenger..."

"I see you've just done Sifiso." He changed the subject without warning.

"Sifiso?" was that her name?

"Yes. The girl who came out of the room just before you," my embarrassment was complete. "Don't worry," Zenzo went on, "that one, she gives everybody. Even me, if my engine was working, she would give me"

I was not sure whether he thought he was telling me some good news – his toothless grin seemed to suggest so, but I wanted the ground to swallow me. My virgin search had started really badly!

CHAPTER SEVEN

The final two weeks of my holiday went by very quickly. The days just seemed to get faster and faster as my departure date approached. Indeed the party was still being talked about in the area in glowing terms. In spite of Sifiso's obvious overtures, we never 'tried again'. But I did try a few other girls, none of whom were as innocent as they looked. In fact, after my encounter with Sifiso and the 'good news' from Zenzo, I had taken the extra precaution of going to Mr Moyo's shop and buying condoms.

"I had assumed you had brought some better quality ones from South," Mr Moyo said without even flinching. I, on the other hand was totally embarrassed by having to make such a purchase and had in fact been waiting outside his shop until I was sure there was no other customer coming.

"They finished." It was the only thing I could think to say.

"Been a busy boy, I see," Mr Moyo went on clearly wanting me to keep him company for as long as possible. "It's a wise thing you do though. The Shona soldiers killed many of our young people, but they also brought AIDS, which continues to kill our young people long after they went"

"But Mr Moyo, AIDS is everywhere, even in South Africa," I tried to correct the obvious misconception, but Mr Moyo was having none of it.

"Are there no Shonas in South Africa?"

"There are but..."

"You see, they have spread it everywhere," he seemed excited to have been proved right.

"Mr Moyo," I said, "AIDS is currently killing people all over the world. All over Africa and beyond. Even in America and parts of Europe..."

"These Shonas go everywhere!"

"It is not the Shonas who spread the disease. In fact even though they are now saying it came from Africa, the first cases were found in America..."

"Condoms hey?" Sifiso had walked into the shop without either of us noticing and I was still holding the batch of condoms that I had just purchased. It was a very embarrassing moment for me and I walked out of the shop without another word.

"Come and see me later," I heard Sifiso shout after me.

"He's not for the likes of you," Mr Moyo admonished gently.

"But he is my boyfriend." I had walked on, not wanting to hear any more of their conversation.

The several brief encounters almost included Bridget who seemed willing enough and had, in fact agreed to a rendezvous by the river. At the last minute though, the thought of proving Promise right by stealing his woman stopped me, much to her anger.

"So, its true what Promise says that you are afraid of him; that he always beat you at fist fights in school," she said when we met at the township on the day before I was due to leave for Beit Bridge. "So afraid in fact that you will not touch me even though there was no chance that he would find out?" She was speaking in low tones so that she would not be heard, but the venom in her voice was frightening, almost.

"It's the principle," I tried to explain to her, "You are married to Promise and..."

"And these other girls that you've been, err, fucking?" It was clearly not a word she was used to saying, but in her anger, she had wanted to make me feel cheap – and she did. "In any case I'm told you are not that good anyway!" Was the whole village aware of my shortcomings? I smiled suddenly as I thought of the word 'shortcomings'. That was what I had been experiencing; short comings!

"I'll tell Promise that the girls say that you can't even get it up," she stormed off in a huff, having probably interpreted my smile as me mocking her.

The farewells had been going on for a few days. Uncle Peter and MaMpofu had left for Harare a few days earlier and the parting with my aunt had been, if anything, more emotional than when I first left.

"Don't stay away too long this time," she had said, the quiver in her voice giving away the emotions that she was trying so hard to hide "You'll kill your mother," she added, trying to make it sound like it was not about her.

"I won't," I had promised sincerely, "I'll try to be home for Christmas."

"And bring that Rumbie with you. We need another party!"

There was a silence that suggested that the name was not new to everyone around and I realised then that she must have been a subject of much discussion.

"Nothing is decided yet," my mother tried to make light of the situation, "But, yes, bring us a *malokazana* next time."

My mother left a day later with her friend MaNcube saying that she had to get back to work. I wondered whether she actually enjoyed her work and I started to think of ways to get her out of that profession.

"I'll see you when you come to Beit Bridge. I'll have made some money then and can give you something to remember me by. I can even buy a present for my malokazana." She was sounding very excited, but I was thinking about how many men she would have had to sleep with to make the money.

"It's not necessary, mother," I said somewhat tersely.

"Not necessary? My only son is going away, may be for another ten years and he says it's not necessary for me to get him a present. I will do anything..."

"MOTHER!"

She must have realised then how uncomfortable what she was saying was making me. She quietly hugged me and walked away without another word.

In spite of my misgivings, the weeks with Khulu had been quite interesting – in the times when he was lucid, anyway. He would suddenly start talking about the second World War as if it had happened just the other day. Then he could retreat into some dark place that no one could get to.

"So, you want to marry a Shona?" he had asked suddenly when I had gone in to say my farewells. I was stunned, not having realised that he had been aware of anything that was being said around him.

"They are witches you know." I was not sure what to say in response, so I said nothing.

"When we came back from the war," Khulu had gone on, "I met this Shona girl in Salisbury (*eSozibeli,* as he called it). What a woman! If it was not that she was Shona, I would have married her." He sounded as if he regretted not marrying her. "She was good," Khulu had gone on, "for a Shona" Did everyone have to make that assertion. People are people, I thought to myself.

"Do you remember her name?" I had asked.

"Who?"

"The Shona girl!"

"You want to marry her? You'll bring a witch into our home!" I wondered if Khulu just went into these dark places in order to avoid uncomfortable conversations.

"I was talking about your Shona girl," I tried again.

"I don't have a Shona girl. You have." He clearly was not going to talk about his girl from Salisbury again. Not this time anyway.

In all the time, my own excitement at seeing Rumbie again was building up. The brief liaisons that I had had had done nothing to quench my hunger for her. I knew then that whatever the future held for Rumbie and I, I wanted to make love to her, at least once. I smiled to myself as I thought about the phrase I had just used in my mind for sex with Rumbie. I wanted to 'make love' to her, not to f..."

"Sipho, my friend," Promise had interrupted my thoughts, "I thought I had missed you. I just wanted to wish you good lucky."

"Oh thank you, Promise," I was feeling guilty about my thoughts about his wife and what I had almost done.

"Please organise a job for me when you get to Joza. I need to work and look after my family. In fact, Bridget was telling me how nice it would be if we were to come and be near you in Joza." I wondered about Bridget's motivation.

"Yes," I said, "that would be very nice."

All these thoughts went through my mind as I waited for the bus that would take me to Beit Bridge from where I would take a coach back to Johannesburg, and Rumbidzai. Chipo had confirmed that my passport was ready – by a letter that came on the bus - but that I could not use it because I would still need to get a Visa, which would take long to organise, so I would have to 'border jump' again which I was not looking forward to. But it had to be done if I was to get back to Rumbie!

"You are off, I see," Mr Moyo was sweeping outside his shop again. That was all he seemed to do.

"Yes, Mr Moyo. I have to get back to work."

"It was good that you came home. But I also understand why you have to go back. There is nothing here for young people. I would have left if I were younger."

It was one of the depressing experiences that I had had. Many of the young people that I had looked forward to seeing were not there, having either disappeared during 'the disturbances' as some people called Gukurahundi, moved to the cities or other mining towns or left the country altogether. Those that were left displayed a hopelessness that was palpable and that one could feel almost physically. The men got drunk at the township and the girls? I sighed.

'The girls look forward to finding a husband, any husband, and if they can't? They will find what comfort they can from the stolen moments that they will from time to time enjoy with the Promises of this world.' For a few weeks I had been one of the comforters; each one of my 'conquests' probably thought that I just might be their ticket out of the grinding poverty, dreariness and hopelessness that my home had become. How long would it be before I came back this time? Apart from my mother, there seemed little reason for me to want to come back. What had happened to the country of my birth? What future did it offer its people?

I was so happy to see Chipo when I got back to Beit Bridge. She seemed genuinely happy to see me and appeared to have made a special effort to look her best when she came to meet me at the bus rank. That may just have been my imagination, of course,

"Welcome back!" she said, giving me a warm hug that may have given me ideas, if she had not been Rumble's cousin. Or was it my new found sexual prowess that had my imagination running wild.

"It's good to see you, Chipo. It's good to be back in some civilisation after Maramani!"

"I don't know," she said with a naughty glint in her eyes, "Rumbie and I are convinced that your found your childhood sweetheart and forgot about us!"

"Would I do that...?"

"Yes, of course! You are a man!"

Indeed, I thought. Like every other man, I had taken advantage of the vulnerability of the young girls who saw me as more than just a brief encounter in the woods.

"You did, didn't you? Your face said it all then!" Was I that obvious?

"No, Chipo," I said out loud, "I don't know what you saw in my face but I was really thinking about the desperation of some of the girls in the rural areas. They'll do almost anything to find a way out of there. And, for most of them, sex is their apparent ticket, until they find out that men will just use them and leave them; by which time it is too late. They've lost their innocence and are left with the responsibility of bringing up a child on their own!"

"And you claim that you did not take advantage yourself?"

I wanted the conversation to move on. "Let us just say that the temptation was very strong, but, you know how it is with AIDS and all that. I would not want to take that back to Rumbie," I immediately regretted saying that. I was not sure how much Rumbie had told her cousin about our relationship and whether she knew that we had not actually had any sexual intercourse. I was not even sure that we would have sex when I got back to

Joburg. She probably had men sleeping with her from the day I left! I felt a certain constriction in my chest at that thought. Chipo regarded me for a long while as if she was trying to make her mind up about my activities during my stay at Maramani.

"Is it true," she hesitated, "that you and Rumbie have never, you know...?" WHAT WAS WRONG WITH WOMEN?!

"Do you talk about every man you sleep with to your cousin?" That ought to shut her up, I thought.

"First of all, I do not sleep with many men! But yes, for that special someone, we do talk about it; in great detail too!" She seemed to enjoy telling me that.

"Perhaps then I'm not her special someone."

"Sipho, if you were not her special someone, we would have been laughing at you for not... Well, she has such a high regard for the fact that you have not tried to sleep with her even when all you would have had to do is ask!"

That easy. I could have had Rumbie just by asking and I did not think to ask!

"She told you that?"

"Not in so many words," what relief, "but she says that she has not been with a man since , you know, her baby's father and sometimes her body 's needs can be overwhelming."

"So she didn't actually tell you that she would have..."

"Girls know girls, Sipho. She may not have said it out loud, but she said it in other ways." Chipo was being coy. I was relieved of course because although Chipo seemed pretty sure of herself, Rumbie had not actually said to her, 'I have not slept with Sipho even though I wish he had asked.'

"Are you guys telling me that you have no secrets from each other whatsoever?"

"Pretty much, so far," I sensed some doubt in her voice. "Of course we've been apart for a while and maybe things are different."

By this time we were approaching the gate to Chipo's house and I was excited at the thought that Rumbie had not had a man since.. wait a minute. Was that because she was still in love with the man? What were the circumstances of her getting pregnant? Maybe this was even their plan; throw that into a conversation so that I believe that Rumbie is more innocent than she actually is!

"How did Rumbie get pregnant?" the question seemed to catch Chipo off guard.

"Well she..." she stammered, "she hasn't told you?"

"No, she has not."

"Then I think it's best I let her tell you herself."

By the time we parted as I went to my mother's cottage, I was still asking myself why she would not tell me about Rumble's pregnancy. She, in fact seemed to close up after the mention of her cousin's pregnancy and I could sense that I was not going to get anything out of her about that. I decided then that I was going to ask Rumbie herself as soon as I saw her! But how? It was not as if I could just walk up to her and say, 'Hello, Rumbie. How did you get pregnant?'

That thought got me thinking about what it was going to be like seeing Rumbie. Was she coming to meet me at the station? She probably would be at work and I would only see her on the following morning when I reported for work. That was depressing. Perhaps I would have to find an excuse to go to her flat?

"I know!" I said out loud to myself, "I'll get Chipo to give me something for her; a letter or even a present!"

"Talking to yourself, I see!" My mother had walked in without me realising. She looked fresh and smelt of some cheap perfume, which made me wonder where she was coming from to have been so freshly bathed as she seemed to be.

"I was singing, mother," I tried to lie.

She burst out laughing. "Then, You may not be my or your father's child because we were both very good singers and would not call what you did then, singing!"

"Is that possible?' I asked my mother, a horrifying thought coming to my mind.

"Is what possible?" She was looking mystified.

"That I'm not my father's child."

She put down the parcels she was carrying and came to sit next to me.

"Sipho," she looked quite angry, "Never think like that again. I have not always been what I am today. Before your father went away, I had not known any other man. You came out of a loving and honest relationship between your father and I. The biggest mistake we made in our young marriage was to live apart. Your grandmother, God rest her soul, tried to warn us but we would not hear of it. All we saw was the riches that would come as a result of your father going to work for the gold mining company." She looked and sounded very sad about that part of her life.

"'It is not good,' my mother in law tried to tell us, 'for such young people who are married to live apart. At your age, you need to be together and be there for each other physically, or one or both of you will be overcome by temptation'. We had laughed of course. We were so in love that the thought of cheating on each other – certainly the thought of me cheating on your father – had never crossed my mind, and your father had always told me that I was the only woman for him." She seemed to not want to carry on with the conversation and tried to change the subject.

"I could not think of anything that might please my malokazana, so I bought her some 'tie and die' fabric. Do you think she will like it?"

"I'm sure she will," I answered without any commitment. "So, at what point did either of you start cheating?" I was not going to let it rest.

"I don't know son," my mother sounded very genuine. "When I first heard rumours that your father had another woman at the mine, I refused to believe it and I thought it was people just being jealous of our happy marriage. But the rumours persisted, and your father's visits home became less frequent. You, of course, were born during this period- in fact I was pregnant before your father even left for the mine, so you are definitely your father's child."

"Did you cheat on my father?"

"Not at first. I held on in the belief that whatever was happening at the mine was because he needed, you know, some release and that we would get back to where we were. He was a good provider and I'm sure you remember how well catered for you were"

"That is true," I agreed with my mother, "I remember how excited I would be when he came home with presents for us..."

"For you mostly," my mother corrected, "yes, there was the odd dress for me, but most of what he brought, even the groceries , was about what his son liked."

"So you decided to cheat too?"

"No! Well, maybe a little bit..."

"What is a 'little bit' of cheating?"

"I meant that my physical needs had a little bit to do with my cheating. It was more the situation. Persistent droughts and of course the arrival of the Shona soldiers and the food embargo. We found ourselves in a situation where we had to do unsavoury things to ensure food on the table for us and our children."

"Did MaMpofu cheat on uncle Peter?"

"I don't know. No one spoke about what they had to do, and no one asked, even when it was obvious, because everyone benefitted from the food that our activities brought. MaMpofu, of course spoke their language so we don't know what she might have had to do. There were stories that she may have been giving them information, but I don't know that for sure."

"Was that where you got the taste for" I felt that I had to ask the question, "what you do now?'

She broke down then She had been holding out and seemed to be in control, but when I asked her that question, it seemed to break her, she sobbed like a little child and for a while, she could neither speak nor move. She sat there and sobbed uncontrollably. I was at a loss as to what to say or how to comfort her. So I just sat there watching my mother cry without any shame, her make up streaming down her face with the tears and other bodily fluids coming out of her nose. Was it regret for what she had done? Was it her shame at being in the oldest profession?

"You, my son, don't seem to understand how difficult my life has been. I lived most of my relatively short married life alone with my in laws. You do not seem to understand what difficulties that poses for a young woman. Relationships with in laws are not easy at the best of times, but when your husband is not there to offer some protection and comfort, they can be impossible. I then had the responsibility of making sure my son had food at a time when food was difficult to come by. Would you rather I let you starve?" Was she blaming me? "I chose to ensure that you had food, because that is what mothers do. You can judge me all you want, but I do not regret doing what I did then. You then disappeared into South Africa! If you can tell me what you would have done in the same situation that was purer, please tell me. What I know is that, while my methods may have been questionable, my motives were the purest."

She stood up and looked directly at me with her hands on her hips. It was a defiant stance.

"And if you think that I enjoy what I do now, then you have no knowledge of the human condition. I feel sorry for that Rumbidzai if indeed she is going to marry you. Sexual intercourse is one of the purest enjoyments that we got as a gift from God – in the right circumstances. Being denied it, as I was by your father, is one of the cruellest punishments a woman can endure. When the Shona soldiers came, there was an element of enjoyment because I felt as if I was effecting some revenge on your father – in circumstances where my passions had been dormant for some time! What I do now is purely business; a way to survive; a reason to go on living in the hope that one day, I would see my only son."

It was a strange way to end the last day of my visit back to my homeland.

CHAPTER EIGHT

Apart from my pounding heart as Chipo took me across the Zimbabwe side of the border and I melted into the melee on the South African side which allowed me to cheat customs and immigration, the trip back was fairly uneventful. The coach was a lot more comfortable than the bus that I had come up on and I slept much of the way. When I was awake, my thought oscillated between reviews of my first visit to my homeland for the first time in ten years, thoughts of my reunion with Rumbidzai, and how I was going to cope with being at work again. It struck me then that although I was Zimbabwean, I knew very little of my homeland. I had never been to any of the major cities, for example and I made a mental note that on my next visit, whenever that would be, I would go to Bulawayo, at least, although by all accounts, Harare sounded more interesting. I was not sure what I felt about this particular visit. Certainly my home village was a lot different from the one I had left and the people were changed. I could not quite decide whether it was the naivety of my childhood that made it seem as though it had been more leisurely and easy going than what I found on my return. My mother had certainly changed. She seemed a lot more cynical of the world and her new profession seemed to have hardened her somewhat, although sometimes it felt as though she was putting on an act.

"I'm sorry that I was so hard on you last night," she had said that morning as she helped me pack. "Perhaps it's the thought of losing you again that is making me nervous – and sad."

"But, mother, you are not losing me. We've just found each other!"

“How long before you come back this time?”

“I have said that I’ll try to be home for Christmas,” I said without much conviction. It was the tradition of most Zimbabweans to come home for Christmas and although I had never done it, it seemed the natural thing to do.

“Please try, my baby,” she was pleading, and sounded as though she was close to tears. I felt tears welling up in my eyes as I remembered my mother, what she had become and how difficult it must have been for her to let me go again. I had wanted to promise her that I would organise for her to come and join me in South Africa, but I was an illegal and it would be difficult. Perhaps when I married Rumbie...

“Now you are letting your mind run wild,” I said out loud to myself.

“Sorry?” The pretty young lady sitting next to me had been reading a novel and not said anything to me since we left the border.

“Sorry,” I responded, “I’ve just been thinking and I must have spoken out loud.”

“Penny for your thoughts?”

I was not sure what that meant, so I said nothing.

“First time to Joburg?’ she seemed to want to carry on the conversation.

“No, I...” I wanted to tell her that I was resident in Johannesburg but remembered at the last moment that I had to be careful who I tell about my status.

“I come hear all the time.”

“What do you do? When you come down?”

"This and that. I am looking at opening up a bakery." It was the first thing that came to mind.

"In Zimbabwe? I believe that the economy of that country is in free fall. Why would you want to open a business there?"

"You believe..."

"Yes. I'm from Malawi myself," I could not have guessed that from her accent, "and we have always thought that Zimbabwe was going to go places, but somehow it seems to have stagnated. What is happening in your country?"

Did I even know what was happening? The only thing I knew for sure was that the people of my home area felt neglected; even abandoned. But I did not know what was happening in the rest of the country!

"I's not that bad," I could not think of anything else to say.

"Not that bad? Well, I suppose it's your country and you nave to keep an optimistic view. I never used to travel all this way before. iI used to get all that I needed for my business in Salisbury – Harare now of course – and I can tell you, your country is deteriorating at a faster rate than anything I have heard about before. In fact I did my tertiary education at a college in Sal, Harare and I used to wish I didn't have to go back to Malawi! Now, well, perhaps you should consider setting up your bakery in Malawi. It is not as developed as Zimbabwe is, but the way things are going..."

"Well, I'll think about it." I was hurt that someone from Malawi, of all places thought that my country was in such a poor state. And yet, when I thought about it, was that not what everyone in my village had been saying? Even Rumbidzai had shown little inclination towards going back to Zimbabwe.

"There is nothing for young people to do back home," she had said on one of the few occasions we had discussed our common homeland, which, come to think of it, did not seem so common. She was from Mashonaland – Manicaland, she always told me but I did not know the difference – and I was from Matabeleland. Her people, from what I had heard, were responsible for much of the misery that I had witnessed. My mother was where she was because of her people....

I woke up to realise we were almost in Joburg. We were on a motor way and I started to recognise some of the landmarks. The last time I had been awake was at Louis Trichardt where the coach had stopped briefly for a refreshments and toilet break. I had got off with my new friend from Malawi although the conversation was becoming difficult as I had to keep remembering my lie about being a Zimbabwean businessman. Eventually I had had to tell her that I was based in Beit Bridge and knew very little about Harare as she kept asking me about places in Harare.

She was really rather good looking and I started to wonder if she had a baby and what my prospects would be with her. But she was from Malawi and I had heard some stories about cross border trading women. Their reputations were not good at all, but she did not look like the kind who would do things that I had heard about – like sleep with any man who might be able to provide free accommodation – and some Rands of course.

"Can I get you anything?' She had asked unexpectedly as I was still getting over the realisation of how much cheaper things were in South Africa compared to Zimbabwe.

"No, let me get you something," I retorted.

"You are not a chauvinist, are you? I had you marked as a gentleman." There was laughter in her eyes, "I can afford it you know."

"No, I just thought it was better..."

"If you, as the man bought?'

"Is that wrong?"

"Look, Sipho," she had said, "I run a successful business in Malawi – not that I need to because my husband is a senior civil servant – but I do this because I don't want to be just a housewife. To be honest I make more money than my husband now, although I make sure that he comes in to the business from time to time so that he feels that he is part of the business and therefore we make the money together. You look to me as though you are just starting out and I'm sure you could use all the Rands you can get. So, let me treat you, this time."

Was I that obvious? She sounded like she did not buy my story of being a businessman and although I felt slightly offended, she was so pleasant about it that I accepted the burger and cool drink she offered.

"Why don't you fly then?" I had asked.

"I do sometimes," she answered almost flippantly, "but you don't make money by spending unnecessarily. Besides, some of the things I'm going to buy will need to come accompanied by road, otherwise they may get stolen on the way and it costs too much to fly them."

I must have slept rather heavily after that because I had not heard her get off at Pretoria as she had indicated that a friend was meeting her there. I realised then that I had not even asked her for her name, although she knew mine.

The sight of Rumbie standing beside the coach took my breath away. She was dressed in a pair of blue jeans that hugged her legs and buttocks so tightly that I wondered how she could even get them off! Perhaps that was the idea, I thought. There was no chance that I could get those off without her consent, which I was not sure would be forthcoming. The loose fitting top she wore gave the impression that she had nothing holding her breasts under it! So obsessed was I with her body that I hardly noticed the beaming smile and the outstretched arms.

She virtually dragged me off the coach and hugged me so tightly that I just stood there, my arms caught in her embrace and unable to embrace her back.

"It is sooo good to see you, Sipho," she still had me in her tight grip, "I thought that you would never come back!"

I was surprised – and embarrassed – at the uninhibited show of emotion, although Rumbie did not seem bothered by it; not even when we got some rather disapproving looks from some of the passers-by. Despite that, I could not extricate myself from her because for some reason, the 'thing in my pants' as MaMpofu had put it, had decided to respond to her embrace in a very obvious and visible manner!

"It's good to see you too Rumbie," I said, my voice sounding husky.

"I did not think that I would miss you this much," she tried to pull away, but for reasons that she may not have understood, I kept pulling her back. "Work has been so boring without you there for some intelligent conversations. I'm sure Mr Van misses you too; he keeps asking me when you are coming back!

'How should I know Mr Van' I ask him. 'When did you say that he should come back. I'm sure he will want to stay with his family for as long as possible'. Sometimes it felt like I was saying this to myself rather than to Mr Van."

We could not stay in that position for ever and with a rather strange gait, one hand in the pocket trying to reposition my misbehaving manhood – the sight must have been comical if anyone had looked but, thankfully many were busy with their own reunions – I went to look for my one piece of luggage which I found having already been offloaded. Without a word, I reached for Rumble's hand and we walked out of Park station looking, to all intense and purposes, like a love struck couple of teenagers.

To my surprise, she hired a cab in which she chatted rather excitedly all the way while I struggled to keep the raging fires in my loins in check. All the way to her flat? She was obviously expecting me to carry on with the cab to my own place perhaps I should invite her to come with me. She had never been to my residence after all and as she seemed so happy to see me – as happy as I was to see her at least- we could not part just yet!

"Come on," she said, looking radiant, "we're here!"

"Here?" Was she asking me in?

"Don't tell me you've forgotten where I live already. It's only been a few weeks." She was inviting me in!

"Yes of course. I thought..."

"You think too much Sipho Dube!" She led the way towards her flat.

"Hey! My money." the cab driver had been forgotten and Rumbie seemed to notice my funny gait as I came back from paying the driver.

"You Ok?" She was looking somewhat concerned.

"I'm fine," I said again trying to reposition the offending member.

"You didn't bring back any... thing funny from those girls from home, did you?"

"Anything like what? What do you mean 'girls from...'" The penny dropped. So did the fire that had been raging. Could I have brought something?

Rumbie burst out laughing. "You should see your face. I'm only teasing you! You didn't, did you?"

"Did I what?" I was genuinely puzzled.

"Sleep around of course. You men are all the same."

"No. NO!" I denied, too vehemently, I thought, then immediately felt guilty. I had sort of slept around after all. "Well, not that the temptation was not there, but you know, every time I thought of you..."

By this time we had reached her door and she was unlocking it.

"You could not touch those pretty Ndebele girls because you thought of me? Mr Dube, I hope you did not. But just in case, we'll use protection."

"I didn't bring any!" I was thinking about how I had thrown away whatever I had not used because I did not want Rumbie thinking that I had, you know. Even though I had.

"Don't worry, I have some." She keeps condoms! The bitch.

"No, Sipho, it's not what you are thinking," how did she know what I was thinking, "I spoke to Chipo and she told me that I should be careful that I do not lose you because 'he is a good man'. I decided that, well, in case you wanted to..." she looked embarrassed, not quite sure how to finish the sentence, "well, Mr Dube," she straightened her back almost as if she was showing her defiance, "to have sex with me, I should be careful that I don't catch anything. I have a daughter to think about you know!"

Although there was a part of me that still questioned her morals, the fire in my belly was going to be extinguished by only one thing. What did it matter that she had taken the lead? She was not a virgin, after all and was clearly more experienced. Without too much else being said, she led me into her bedroom helped me put the protection on – my hands were shaking so much that I was having trouble – and we made the most passionate love that I had ever experienced in my very short stint of sowing wild oats.

I must have said many things to her during our most passionate moments because afterwards, as we lay side by side, panting away our exhaustion - I had not known it to be so tiring –

or satisfying before – she turned to me and asked, "Did you mean all that?"

"All what, exactly...?"

"That you love me; you want to marry me and that you don't care that I'm not a virgin?"

I remembered thinking those things but had not realised that I had said them out loud.

"I must have.." I said, somewhat confused.

"You don't know?" She propped herself up on one elbow and looked directly into my ace, I felt her warm nipple press into my chest, and felt even more confused.

"Well, for as long as I have known you, I have always assumed that you were, you know..."

"Innocent? A virgin?"

"Well, yes," I answered timidly.

"Why?"

"Why what?"

"Why did you assume that I was a virgin. I made no such assumptions about you!"

'I am a man' I wanted to say to her, but that made no sense even to me. It was almost funny. I had been a virgin until a few days ago and had assumed that she was too. She had not been a virgin for at least six years and had assumed that I was not one either. So what was this? She wanted me just for sex and I had told her that I wanted to marry her! I got up to go to the toilet. I needed time to think. I wished for a moment that I smoked cigarettes, and would have lit one up like I had seen in the movies. I spent a long time in the toilet trying to clear my mind, but the love making had been so good that I could not think. It was as if all my energies and thought processes had gone down to that area of my body that had been so satisfied for the first time in my life.

When I came back into the bedroom, I was fully dressed while Rumbie was lying on the bed totally naked. The light coming through the window as the sun sunk deep into the horizon made her skin look a golden brown, making it impossible to ignore. Every part of me, well the one part particularly was telling me to undress and go and lie besides her, but I needed to understand some things first.

"What took you so long?" She asked before I said anything, "Were you masturbating in there? Didn't I satisfy you, then?" Why was she being so ... bitchy?

"I don't do such things," I said tersely.

"You don't? I do." She burst out laughing "Don't look so shocked Sipho. I have not had a man in my life for so long and, you know, a woman has needs. In fact I had not felt like that for a long time until the night of the Christmas party at work when I felt you..." She laughed again. I was not sure if she was making fun of me or if she was embarrassed by what she was saying. "I was vulnerable that night, but I respected the fact that you did not take advantage. In fact I'm pretty sure that if you had, our relationship would have not gone much beyond that. But I have fantasised about you since!"

"How long has it been since you've had a man?" I was still not sure what her motives were.

She got up, put on her dressing gown and sat on the edge of the bed. I could not help myself looking at her upper thigh, which was exposed,

"How long has it been?" she seemed to be talking to herself. "I've never really had a man."

What kind of idiot did she think I was? “You have a six year old daughter and you say that you have never had a man? Don’t tell me. It was the Holy...”

“I was raped!”

She burst into tears then. The controlled, calm Rumbidzai that I had known was transformed into a helpless little girl who sobbed inconsolably and for what seemed like an age, I sat and watched her, not quite sure what to do or say. She was twenty-two, she had told me, and her daughter was six, so she must have been fifteen when she was raped. The same age that Bridget was when she had her moment of weakness. Had Rumbie been raped or did she also have her moment. She had already admitted to her body sometimes taking control to the extent that she would masturbate, so perhaps during one of her weak moments some man had taken advantage. Would that be rape?

She seemed more in control; got up and went into the bathroom. When she came back, she had cleaned herself up and looked almost back to her best. She seemed embarrassed that she had let me see her in her weakest and most vulnerable of moments.

“Sorry about that,” she said quietly, “I’ve not thought or spoken about that part of my life for a long time.”

“When you say you were raped...”

“It was one of my teachers – well, one of the many temporary teachers that the government were employing as they sought to expand educational opportunities in the early years of independence. I was in form three and was considered one of the brightest students. I was something of a teacher’s pet and he was always getting me to run errands for him. I felt important of course and although there were some rumours about this particular teacher and some girls, I ignored them, thinking that they were jealous of my special relationship with Mr Gondo.” She smiled ruefully, “Well, it was special,” she was quiet for a while.

"When he asked me to bring the class's books to his house for marking I thought nothing of it. After all, it was in broad daylight and within the school grounds. In fact I never even thought of the possibility that something like that could happen to me. So I walked into his trap in complete innocence."

She stood and went to the window. "Knowing what I know now, I realise that he had been preparing me for a long time. Always complimenting me on how well I dressed, although, like everyone else, I was in uniform, sending me on errands that other students would not be asked to do and so on." She was rubbing her left arm with her right hand although she seemed completely unaware of what she was doing. Somehow, it made her look like a little girl.

"So," she went on, her voice sounding mechanical and detached, "when he put his arm around my shoulder, I did not resist because he had done so many times before. I was so stupid!" She was quiet for a long time while she looked out of the window. It was clear that she was not looking at the children playing outside or the traffic on the road. She had been transferred to the teacher's house.

"It was only when I felt his finger on my nipple that I started to worry but initially thought it was an accident because the finger only bushed my nipple momentarily. But then he got bolder, put his arms around my waist and started to rub my breasts with both hands and lick the back of my neck. I tried to push him away, at first not believing that my favourite teacher could be trying to," She turned round to look at me. The pain and hurt in her eyes was very clear; but there was something else. Her eyes were pleading to me, asking me to understand that this had nothing to do with her. I am still not sure what I felt at that moment. Part of me was accusing. 'She must have wanted it,' I thought. Surely any girl would have known that it was dangerous to be alone with a man, in his house! Part of me wanted to go and hug her and tell her that it was alright, this happened a long time ago. Most of me wanted to kill the teacher. I just sat there, looking at Rumbie in a state of paralysis, mentally strangling Mr Gondo.

"I just remember this searing pain as he," she broke off and looked away, "he forced himself on me and, just like that, he was done. I looked down to see blood running down my leg as he tried to wipe it off with some rag .

'You wanted it, didn't you?' he was saying to me over and over again, 'you wanted it you little bitch...'

'No, sir, I only came to...'

'You always say that you little whores! Did you think that I was your brother or something?'

I was stunned at the callousness of the man! I must have been some sight. My pants were down by my ankles and one shoe was off. I was still leaning against the table on which he had just violated me, I was sobbing as I felt him button up my school uniform blouse which, I later found out, had a button missing.

'Pull yourself together,' he said. 'Go and clean yourself up in the outside toilet!'

I was in a daze as I went outside, feeling as if the whole world was watching me. I don't really remember much else that day. I did not go back to class but went straight home. I wanted to hide from the whole world. It did not help, of course that home meant the daily chores that had to be done, after a lengthy inquisition on why I was home so early. All I wanted to do was curl up and die."

Rumbie appeared to have finished her story as she was quiet for a long time after this. I could not believe that any man, let alone a teacher could behave so badly, yet part of me was still questioning her motives for going to the teacher's house in the first place!

"For the next few days, I kept much to myself, not wanting to risk something slipping out in conversation. Mr Gondo hardly looked at me and the errands stopped.

'He's done it to you, hasn't he?' Rachel was not a particularly friendly girl who was in my class. I had never really warmed to her and she always seemed proud and distant, so the question from her was completely unexpected.

'Sorry?'

'I can tell,' Rachel said. 'He's done it to me, and a few other girls. I see the signs. He is very friendly to you and makes you feel important, then when he's done with you, well, it's as if you don't exist..'

'I don't know what you are talking about', I said to her curtly.

'Look,' she said, 'did he not tell you afterwards that he would take care of you? That as long as you did not tell anyone he would make sure that your marks were good and he would help you revise? Yet, has he spoken to you since?'

She was right, of course. Mr Gondo had not spoken to me since and whenever I tried, he was always rushing off somewhere.

'Just pray that you are not pregnant', Rachel had said. Of course I did not believe that I could be pregnant after one extremely brief encounter, but I was wrong!"

She came and sat next to me and held my hand. I let her, without holding her back

"After a couple of months, during which time Rachel had become my only friend, it became clear that I was pregnant. When I told Mr Gondo, his response was that he did not believe that he was the first to sleep with me, in spite all the evidence that of course only he and I had seen. He then disappeared from the school."

"Disappeared?" How does one just disappear, I was thinking.

"He was a *MuVhitori,* from Masvingo – formerly Fort Victoria – and it was thought that he had gone back there."

“He was not Shona , then?” I really did not understand.

“Sipho, how much do you know of your home country? The term Shona refers to a group of dialects. The languages we speak are similar, with marked differences.”

“Like most of Southern Africa?”

“No. Yes, in a way. Like isiNdebele and isiZulu or SiTswana and Sisotho. They are similar but with marked differences”

“But they are virtually the same language!”

“You could say that. Sipho, are you going to let me finish this story or not? I have since heard that he went to study abroad. He’s never been in touch and to tell you the truth, I really don’t care. But I love my little girl.” For the first time in a while, she actually smiled. “She is what kept me going, after having got to the point of thinking about suicide.”

I felt a strange pain in my chest thinking that had she committed suicide, I would not have met her. But I also felt really angry with Mr Gondo for having her before me!

“My family were kind of understanding but bitterly disappointed. Somehow, I got the sense that the male members of the family were not quite convinced of my innocence in the whole situation and I was determined to prove them wrong.” She looked at me again, almost as if she was asking me if I believed her. I was not sure and I still had more questions but I said,

“How could they not believe you? You must have imagined it.”

She was quiet for a few minutes, then she went on.

“Anyway, I had always told them that I was going to be the first doctor from our family, and I could have made it, I know that” She said with conviction. “I was determined that I would make something of my life. I was going to show that Mr Gondo that he was not going to destroy my dream. As soon as the baby was born, I enrolled with a distance learning College and I studied hard, not easy when you have a baby to look after. Within three years, I had done my 'A' levels, but had not done the subjects I needed for me to study medicine, because they were difficult to do through distance learning. So I enrolled for a CIS and as opportunities were getting scarce in Zimbabwe, I decided to come to South Africa and have been fortunate to land a job with Mr Van, who helped me get my papers."

I found myself looking at Rumbie with a new respect, although there was still the feeling that she may have led Mr Gondo on. Perhaps she had had a childish crush on him and he had taken advantage!

"Have you ever heard from Mr Gondo?" I asked, wanting to reassure myself that they had not communicated at all.

"No. He went away and has never been in touch. He was not from our area so no one knew anything about his family. I don't think that I ever want to see him again. In fact, for many years, I wanted nothing to do with men in general. Then you, Mr Dube, came along. I realised after spending time with you at work that, unlike many men that I had interacted with, you would never take advantage of the vulnerability of a woman!"

If only she'd known about my recent activities back in Zimbabwe!

"I just had a lot of respect for you," I said.

"And now you don't? I knew I should never have allowed you into my inner sanctum!"

We talked, we laughed, we cried and we made love. Time, it seemed did not matter. I told her all about my trip back home in great detail, leaving out only those bits that may have been embarrassing – like my mother's profession – and the bits that may have created tension – like my philandering. She listened with very little comment but there was no doubt that she was hanging onto my every word. By the time I finished, it was the early hours of the morning.

"Look at the time," Rumbie said looking at her watch and getting out of bed to go to the toilet, "it's nearly four AM!"

"We'll never get up in time for work!"

"I don't think you are expected at work today," Rumbie said, "I asked for the afternoon off to go and meet you and Mr Van said that both of us should take the day off. 'He'll be tired from his travels and you guys have a lot of catching up to do,' he said with a suggestive wink. He seems to have understood us more than we understood ourselves!"

I woke up to find Rumbie dressed in the shirt that I'd been wearing the day before and ironing my clothes that she had taken out of my travel bag. I watched her for a while before she realised that I was awake. She was indeed very beautiful and I could not imagine how anyone could have violated anything so delicate in the manner that she had described Mr Gondo as having done.

"What time is it?' I asked sleepily.

"Oh, you're awake. It's after ten, but you looked so peaceful – and contented – that I did not have the heart to wake you. I am impressed, Mr Dube. No snoring!"

Had she slept with other men that snored then?

"My father was a snorer! We all used to wonder how my mother managed to sleep in the same bed with him. He sometimes kept the rest of us awake!"

She bent over to pick something out of my bag and she had nothing on under the shirt!

"By the way," she said straightening up, much to my disappointment, "I found this in your bag?" She lifted out the tie and die fabric that my mother had bought for her.

"Oh, I forgot, that's a present from my mother to you."

"To me? How does she know about me? What does she know about me?"

"Well, as you know, she lives on the same premises as your cousin, Chipo and she wondered how Chipo and I knew each other."

"Then she bought me a present?"

"I told her that you and I were very good friends..."

"You often sleep with your very good friends?"

"Well," I was not sure what to say, "I think she realised that there was more to our relationship than mere friendship..."

"Was there? I mean, until I seduced you last night, we were just friends weren't we?"

"You did not seduce me!" I protested, "you raped me!"

"Sipho, please do not joke about rape. It is not a funny subject, under any circumstances."

I had to apologise for my insensitivity. It was still a subject that clearly, she was not comfortable with. The light hearted banter seemed to die out then and for a while, we said nothing to each other. But the subject of my mother had also brought painful thoughts to me.

"Did Chipo say anything to you about my mother?" I asked, thinking that she must have known of my mother's 'profession'.

"Only that she works in a bar, and that she is something of a gardener who looks after their flower garden very well."

"She is a prostitute," I said, wanting to get that out of the way as quickly as possible. Rumbie stopped what she was doing and came to sit next to me, leaving the still hot iron on one of my best shirts! I had to jump out of bed quickly to stop it being burnt.

When I turned round in my nakedness, I expected her to make some rude comment about my erect member, but she seemed to have been looking past me.

"Sipho, I had no idea," she looked and sounded genuinely concerned. "Does Chipo know?"

"Yes," I said.

"She never said anything to me!"

"Would that have made a difference?" I was so disappointed.

"Gosh no, Sipho. You are such a gentleman and...."

"She has not always been a prostitute and she brought me up in a loving home where she taught me to respect women. But life has a way of changing our best laid plans. It certainly has not been kind to my mother."

That opened up all the painful memories of my home visit that I had kept from her thus far. I told her about my childhood home and how abandoned it looked. I told her how people had suffered when the Shona soldiers came to fight the so called dissidents; the food embargoes, the successive droughts; my father's mysterious disappearance. Finally, I told her about my erstwhile comrades who had never made it into South Africa but found themselves being accused of being dissidents.

"My mother," I went on, "found herself without a husband, without her only son, without any way of sustaining herself. My father's former employers would not even give her anything because they needed a death certificate to prove that he had died!"

"My God! That could have been me!" Rumbie was not making any sense. "Many of my childhood friends have become prostitutes because there is nothing else to do! I had a fatherless child to look after. Imagine what I would have had to do had I not come to South Africa. Imagine what would have happened had I not had the ability and discipline to study as I did."

She and my mother appeared to be speaking the same language. I thought of MaTshuma and how much older she looked when I saw her coming from picking wild leaves for relish! She was not much older than my mother, yet she looked twenty years older. But I was also surprised at what Rumbie was saying. I had thought that the new government of Zimbabwe was for Shona people; that they had jobs and did not suffer like us. 'All the jobs are in Harare', everyone had told me during my visit.

"So, Gukurahundi is real?" Rumbie interrupted my thoughts. What a strange question!

"Did you think that people made it up?" She could be so irritating!

"No," She recoiled at the aggressiveness of my question, "it was talked about but I was too young to understand it all. What I remember is that there had been problems in Matabeleland with people who were fighting the government and the army had had to go in to quell the problems. Most of the adults seemed to think that it had nothing to do with us and that the government had a responsibility to protect ordinary people from the dissident trouble makers." She held my hand and moved closer to me, "honestly, I had no idea that it was as bad as you describe, but I really had never bothered to find out more...you know," she looked quite excited, as if she had remembered something very important, "my uncle Tobias has been saying to me for a while that the troubles in Matabeleland is a blot on our country's independence that will take a long time to erase. I never really bothered me because I sometimes think that uncle Toby's time in the bush had affected him, you know, mentally!"

"Uncle Tobias is your real uncle?" the conversation was getting uncomfortable and the thought that this very pretty girl who had given me so much pleasure was part of a people that meant my people so much harm was not sitting well with me.

"Of course he's my uncle! My mum's brother's son. Can he get any more real than that?"

"Then he is your cousin, not your uncle..."

"You're right, but in Shona, your mother's brother is *sekuru,* so is his son and all his male descendants."

"Well," I said, half seriously, "when you first mentioned him, I thought he might have been, you know,"

"I know wh...? You thought uncle Toby was my boyfriend?" She burst out laughing. The dimples that I had found so attractive when I first saw her seemed more pronounced at that moment. Her eyes seemed to sparkle and I found myself laughing with her without really knowing why.

"Were you jealous?" she asked when the laughter had died down.

"No! Well, may be a little, but I had no right to be jealous because you were not my girlfriend then."

"I'm your girlfriend now, am I?"

"Of course!" she could be so exasperating.

"Why, because we had sex?"

"Yes!" I said emphatically, then hesitated. We had not really said anything to each other about how we felt and it had all been rather spontaneous. Had she just done it because her body's need had been so great?

"Look, Sipho," she said after a while, "You are the first man that I have let in, emotionally and I know what rejection feels like. What happened here was probably the result of years of inactivity on my part, and, from what you say, on your part as well. So if that is all it was for you, please tell me now. I can deal better with an uncomfortable truth than with a lie."

"Rumbie," I was not quite sure what to say, "all I know is that I don't feel the kind of closeness that I feel with you, with anyone else. When I was away, I thought about you constantly and really looked forward to seeing you. My mother told me that every time I spoke your name, something in me changed and she was convinced that you were more than just a friend to me. Of course," I said looking seriously at her, "I did not expect to be attacked like that the moment I landed!"

"I did not attack you!" she protested feebly playfully throwing a pillow at me, "I suppose I did didn't I? I had not planned it that way but yes, I was so looking forward to seeing you again. I did not think that I would miss you that much and when you disappeared for a whole week into you village, I was so miserable that I thought my cousin Chipo was lying about you being at the village."

"Why would Chipo lie to you?"

"I don't know. She kept telling me what a good looking man you are and I thought that perhaps you two may have.. you know!"

"Chipo was very nice to me but, no, the thought never occurred to me. In fact, when she first came onto the bus with her immigration uniform and name tag, I thought about how ironic it would be to be arrested by someone with the Shona equivalent of my name!"

"Anyway," Rumbie said, getting up, "she thinks the world of you. And what does your mother expect me to do with the fabric? I've never sewn anything in my life!" She was holding the fabric against herself, "I suppose I could get a dress made. A dress from my mother in law!"

I needed to get back to my own place in Alexandria and I told Rumbie so.

"So soon?" She seemed to be protesting, "I was going to prepare a meal for us."

"I've been away for so long the place must be upside down! Anyway, both of us need to get ready for work tomorrow. Why don't you come over at the weekend and I'll cook you a meal?"

"Are you suggesting that I'll only see you at the weekend?"

"You'll see me at work every day.."

"Why don't I come with you now? I've never been to your place." It seemed the only natural thing to do.

CHAPTER NINE

I could not believe how much I had missed the place. The Van der Burger was much changed in the month that I had been away, but the smells were familiar. Early in the morning, the smells were of frying bacon and eggs, sausages and toast as Francois Myburg the Chef, prepared for the breakfast trade which would soon be upon us as the office workers – mostly young white office workers who lived alone and had neither the time nor the desire to make breakfast at home – came in for quick breakfasts before proceeding to the various office jobs they had in the many offices in the Sandton complex. Most of the faces were familiar although I did not know anything about them. A few of the customers appeared to recognise that they had not seen me for a while and I was duly rewarded with a nod here and a smile there in acknowledgement.

"SIFO!" A burley white man wearing a shirt that was a few sizes too small; or was it the stomach that was too big for any shirt, greeted me jovially. I had tried to explain to him that the 'ph' in my name was pronounced s 'p' and not 'F' as in English. He either did not understand or did not care.

"I thought the boss had fired you," he went on, unravelling his newspaper to read. He was one of the few customers that never seemed to be in a hurry first thing in the morning.

"No," I replied politely, "I had taken some leave to go and visit my home in Zimbabwe"

"You from Zimbabwe? I should have known. You guys work much better that our own blacks here in South Africa" It was probably meant as a compliment but I found it difficult to take it as such. White people always seemed to want to exaggerate the differences – real or imagined – between the indigenous peoples of Southern Africa; yet, in my view, we had much more in common.

"So, how are the Rhodesia ruins doing?" This was an old and tired joke, yet, after my visit, it was difficult not to see its poignancy.

"It's okay," I could not admit to a white person that things had gone badly wrong – as they had predicted – in my homeland. "I really enjoyed myself."

"How come you are back here then?"

"Well," he had caught me unprepared, "I have a job here and, well, I left with the intention of coming back."

"But why?" He was not letting it go. "Surely the job you do here is not very skilled and there must be cafes like this in Zimbabwe?"

The truth was I did not know and if there were or not but I had heard how difficult it was to get a job, any job in Zimbabwe.

"I just never thought about it. Look sir, I need to get back to the kitchen," I had to get away from his questions, so I hurried back to the kitchen to assist the chef with preparations. In the corridor, almost exactly at the point where I had punched her a month earlier, I bumped into Rumbie who quickly ducked in mock fear. "I should remember not to run into you in corridors," she gave me a quick peck on the lips and carried on towards Mr Vans office. For a few moments, I stood there, staring at the door into which she had disappeared. How could she be so casual about our relationship? I had hardly slept the night before just reliving the time I had had with her since my arrival back from Zimbabwe.

"I see you are doing the Shona?" I wished George would not put it like that. What I did with Rumbie was not 'doing'! It was making love! But then again, what did George know about love.

"She really missed you, you know. We never had a conversation in which she did not mention your name. In fact if you go into her office, you will see that she has been cancelling the days off on her calendar and even had a big red circle on the date that you were due to return. For a Shona, she is not bad looking." Why did he have to spoil it like that?

It had been an exciting reunion with George and the rest of the crew. They all seemed genuinely excited to see me and questions about my time in Zimbabwe rained. It was clear that for most of them, Zimbabwe was still home and there was the hope that things might be getting better. Unfortunately, I could not confirm what they all seemed to have been hoping for.

"Did you find yourself a nice Ndebele girl to marry?" Khumbulani had asked suddenly, almost as if he wanted to change the subject.

"He has no interest in Ndebele girls," George had responded for me, "he has his Shona!"

I smiled to myself as I carried on to the kitchen, recalling the excited chatter that had only been interrupted when Mr Van came in.

"Can you guys stop talking about bloody Zimbabwe and get back to work? Or do you want to go back there?" We had all scurried off to our various positions but I felt a deep disappointment. How could going back to your home country be such a threat. Yet it was!

"Sipho" Mr Van had called after me, "It's good to have you back. Please come into my office later. I have some news for you."

"Thank you, sir," I had said, wondering what sort of news he could possibly have for me.

It had been an exciting couple of days, I thought as I recalled the visit to my home in Alexandra Township the day before.

"Sipho, you have a girlfriend?" Sithembile, looking quite heavily pregnant had seen Rumbie and I come into the yard holding hands.

"Hello Thembie," I responded pleasantly, "Meet Rumbidzai..."

"You brought her from Zimbabwe?" She shook Rumbie's hand enthusiastically, "Welcome to South Africa Rumbidzai. I was getting worried about my brother..."

"I did not bring her..."

"I live here in Joburg." Rumbie and I spoke at the same time then burst out laughing.

"You live here? In Johannesburg?" Thembie sounded incredulous, "how come I have never seen you before?"

"Perhaps Sipho wanted to keep me his secret," Rumbie offered an explanation.

"Why would he do that?"

"I don't know, perhaps he has another girlfriend?" Was she jealous?

"No!" Thembie exclaimed, "he does not have a girlfriend, although he has many admirers in the neighbourhood. But we have all decided that he is not interested in girls!"

"And by 'we' you mean...?"

"Even my mother says that she worries about you. 'I don't know why you girls don't seem to see what a good man Sipho is', she always says to me as if she wants me to propose to you. I was so angry with her one day that I asked her why she does not marry you!.

'He's a bit too young for me' was her unexpected response. 'Otherwise I would have asked him without hesitation'."

"Then you would have a readymade family!" Rumbie had cut in. It had reminded me that my mother had said the same thing about the prospects of me marrying Rumbie.

"And have a delinquent like Thembie for a daughter?" I decided to carry on the light hearted banter, "No, thank you!"

Mr Mlambo had been so excited to see me that he, for the first time since I had known him, came round to my side of the fence.

"I see you're back," he had said as he vigorously shook my hand, "how was it back home?" I still found it difficult to see Mr Mlambo and myself as coming from the same home but he looked so genuinely happy to see me that I found myself warming to him. He had started to speak to Rumbie in Zulu, but then got even more excited when he realised that they spoke the same language. For a while, I had been ignored as they chatted away excitedly about what I could not imagine.

"We are both from Manicaland," Rumbie had said excitedly as she turned to me, 'but he is from Chimanimani, where they speak Chindau, and I'm from Rusape, where we speak Chimaungwe."

I was confused. Mr Mlambo had told me he was from somewhere else and the language they spoke sounded the same – and they seemed to understand each other perfectly..

"Mr Mlambo, I thought you said you were from..."

"Melsetter?" Mr Mlambo finished the sentence for me.

"That changed its name to Chimanimani; Melsetter was the colonial name," Rumbie had explained.

"And the language you speak is not Shona...?"

"No!" Mr Mlambo said emphatically. "It's ChiManyika."

He had me completely flummoxed!

"Well," Rumbie tried to explain to me, "The term 'Shona' refers to a group of languages that are fairly similar but with differences; rather like your Sindebele and IsiZulu. You can understand each other, but there are differences..."

"Or Setswana and Sesotho," Mr Mlambo added. "Do you understand?"

"Yes," I said. I did not. What about the other languages they had just said?

The rest of the afternoon had been pleasant – very pleasant. Rumbie was very complimentary about how clean and tidy my accommodation was, even though there was a thin layer of dust on everything as I had been away. I started to tidy up the room but it seemed that Rumbie had other ideas. At last after many years, my bed saw some action!

We had then tidied my rooms together and I had found myself imagining Rumbie as my wife. The thoughts were not unpleasant.

"Zimbabwe must have some pleasant memories for you," Mr Van had walked in on me without me noticing, "You've been walking around with that silly grin on your face all day."

"Yes sir," I could not tell him how bad my home country was; nor could I tell him the real reason for my 'silly grin', as he put it, "it was good to get home after so many years away."

"Well," he said, "you better get your head back here. You've got lots of work to do!"

"I know..."

"No, you don't," he interrupted me, "your cake convinced me of your idea about a bakery division for this establishment. I've been doing the numbers – well Rumbie did the numbers actually – and they make sense. So when the people next door moved," I had noticed a lot activity in the premises adjacent to us but had assumed that the Laundromat were renovating their premises, "I moved in and we are turning it into your cake and confectionery outlet, which I want you to run."

Just like that, a new chapter had started in my life. The next few weeks were hectic to say the least. I really had no idea what it took to run an organisation and I soon realised that the ability to bake was the least of the skills I needed. Fortunately, I had Rumbie to walk me through the various systems I had to put in place for accounting, loss control, procurement and so on. It meant of course that we were spending a lot of time together at work and outside work. She was a hard task master and could easily change from a passionate lover at home – we still lived in our two separate residences to a ruthless 'boss' at work. She was also a stickler for neatness and the bakery division soon got a reputation not only for its high quality cakes and other confectionaries, but for its cleanliness as well. I, of course was not only the head baker; I was also the washer upper, the cleaner, the accounts clerk and everything else that needed doing because, according to Rumbie, 'we could not afford to employ yet'.

Needless to say, we worked long hours seven days a week and often got home late at night and sometimes in the early hours of the morning. Mr Van seemed to have complete trust in Rumbie and although he checked over the books every week, he pretty much left us to our own devices except for the once a month meetings where he grilled us on the progress we were making. Sometimes it felt like I would have been better off staying in my old job! It therefore came as something of a shock when one Friday afternoon Rumbie suddenly said,

"I think we'll close up early tomorrow and take the rest of the weekend off."

"Why? I thought we agreed that Saturday afternoons is when we do the books for the week."

“Fuck the books,” she said, looking around to make sure that no one was within ear shot. I had never heard her use that kind of language before and I was caught completely by surprise.

“Don't look so shocked, Sipho. You deserve a break. I think we'll go and visit my uncle Tobias tomorrow evening. He is expecting us.”

I was relieved to finally have some time off; but I also felt nervous at the thought of meeting her uncle.

I need not have worried. Uncle Tobias lived in an apartment close to the University of Johannesburg Campus where he was working on his Doctorate.

“He has a passion for the history of the peoples of Southern Africa and the politics of the region,” Rumbie told me on the taxi, “I think you'll like him.”

“Hello Sipho,” uncle Tobias, dressed casually in jeans and a loose fitting sweater met us at the door and greeted me in the most fluent Sindebele, “Rumbie has told me so much about you. It's so nice to finally meet the man who's stolen my niece's heart. I was beginning to worry about her. Come in, come in...”

I was confused. When had Rumbie talked to her uncle about me? We'd only been dating for a few weeks and had, in that time, not had much time for anything other than the bakery.

“When you were back in Zimbabwe, she came to visit me often and talked about nothing else. I think she was worried you might have found an old flame...”

“Uncle!” Rumbie sounded like she was protesting. “I did not talk about Sipho,” she said in Shona, at least it sounded like that was what she was saying.

“I think she is in love with you,” uncle Toby, as Rumbie seemed to call her, said in English, with a wink, “and I can see why,” he added with a chuckle, “Sit,” he indicated a two sitter couch in his living room come office.

The apartment, though clattered, looked comfortable and well lived in. There were books everywhere and although I could not read all the titles, it seemed to me that they were predominantly historical and there were a couple of titles that I recognised like Nelson Mandela's "Long Walk to Freedom". It reminded me that South Africa was in the throes of their own freedom. I wondered what their 'freedom' would look like. By all accounts, Zimbabwe had been expected to do well with her own freedom fourteen years or so earlier. Yet the evidence of my recent visit was that the people of Zimbabwe, certainly the people of Matebeleland, were much worse off than they had been under Rhodesia's own 'Apartheid'.

"So, you've just come back from the homeland I hear. What did you think?" Uncle Tobias seemed more comfortable conversing in isiNdebele.

"Well," I was not sure what he expected me to say. In spite of his being fluent in my own language, I could not forget that he was Shona and the according to the people in my home area, they were doing much better as it was their leaders who were in power. "It was good to see my folks and all my childhood friends..."

"I presume it would be," Rumbie's uncle interrupted without sounding rude, "I was asking about the economic and political situation. What are the Zezurus doing to our country?"

"I did not see the rest of the country as I only spent time in Maramani and Beit Bridge."

"Rumbie, please make us a cup of tea," he was clearly very fond of his niece, "a friend of mine will be joining us for supper."

"You seem surprised that I speak such fluent IsiNdebele," he said turning back to me.

"I did not expect you to speak my language so fluently," I responded honestly.

"It seems Rumbie has not told you anything about me. Are you guys so busy that you have no time to talk about anything else?'

I was not sure what he was suggesting, so I did not say anything.

"Anyway," Uncle Toby went on, "I was born and raised in Bulawayo and although we always spoke Shona at home, I spoke isiNdebele everywhere else; at play, at school. In fact I'm a lot more comfortable speaking isiNdebele than speaking Shona! My parents were not exactly thrilled and I was always being reminded that I was not a *Mundevere."*

There was a knock on the door and Uncle Toby went to open it to let in his visitors who were, clearly expected.

"Steve! Sihle, come in, come in."

A tall, slim , very pretty – I thought – lady walked in followed by a tall bearded man who was not what I would have called good looking. I wondered what it was that she saw in him.

"Hi uncle Steve, auntie Sihle," Rumbie shouted cheerfully from the kitchen. "Shall I include you in the cup of tea?"

"Coffee for me, as usual," uncle Steve answered, "and I think your auntie brought some cake..."

"Yes, I did, but that's for later. I won't be able to eat supper if I have cake now."

"We would," Uncle Steve and uncle Toby spoke at the same time. They were clearly comfortable in each other's company and they were, all three of them, speaking in isiNdebele.

"I'm going to have to learn that language now," Rumbie was bringing in the teas and coffees, "Sipho, unfortunately, always speaks to me in English."

"So, you're the famous Sipho?" Uncle Steve said, turning to me. Had Rumbie told everyone?

"I can see why you're so excited, Rumbie, he's a good looking boy."

I felt awkward. No one had ever said that about me before – apart from MaMpofu and my mother – but I never really took them seriously.

"This is my friend, Steve Mpala," Uncle Toby introduced the new arrivals, "and his wife, Sihle. Steve and I have been friends for as long as I can remember."

"We met on our first day at school – iNduba primary School in Phelandaba in Bulawayo. He was being ignored by everyone because he hardly spoke isiNdebele; well he spoke a version of the language that had everyone in stitches. Most of the kids did not know any better, but there were a few that started to call him names – even some that turned out to be Shona who were fluent in isiNdebele – telling him to go back to *emaTshoneni* where he had come from. I thought he needed protection..."

"Some protector, he turned out to be. I did a much better job of protecting myself!" Uncle Toby sounded amused?

"Still," Mr Mpala retorted, "I got beaten up on your behalf; I took beatings that were meant for you!"

"You've been friends since your first day in school? How long is that?" I asked, surprised that people could have stayed in touch that long.

"More than thirty years," uncle Tobias answered, "we separated only when we went to High school. He went to Mpopoma High in Bulawayo and I went to Goromonzi near Sal.. Harare. But then we met up again at the University of Rhodesia..."

"...where everyone thought he was Ndebele," Uncle Steve completed the sentence for his friend. "It did not help that on moving to Bulawayo his family had decided to adopt their totem - Nyati - as their surname, which made their name sound Ndebele."

"And many of the boys I knew were from Bulawayo so naturally, I tended to spend most of my time with them."

"We had encountered some tribalism growing up in Bulawayo but it really did not affect us until we got to University, where the political awareness of the students meant that discussions on national issues came to the fore. The language one spoke became an issue at that point."

At this point, Auntie Sihle decided to go and join Rumbie in the kitchen. I found myself wondering what language they were going to communicate in. I need not have worried. The chatter and animated conversation coming from the kitchen soon told that they were comfortable in whatever language they were communicating!

"Remember our big brother Ernest Ncube?" Uncle Tobias was saying, well, he was more your big brother..."

"Yes, he had been long-time friends with my older brother, Phineas, who had asked him to look out for me when I got to University. He was in his final year of a Mechanical Engineering degree when we started at Uni.

'Watch out for these Shona girls', he would say to us, 'they are bad news'. It always made me feel uncomfortable because of course my best friend was Shona..."

"I didn't mind, really," uncle Toby said, "I always thought that people with those kinds of views were small minded. In any case it was comforting having someone that I could call a big brother in the strange world of University life."

The two of them then burst out laughing, which took me by surprise.

“Guess what? Big brother Ernest is still our big brother who now runs an engineering company in Harare making agricultural implements. He has three children and is married to a Shona woman that he met at University!” Uncle Steve was wiping the laughter tears from his eyes. “I reminded him of that the last time I saw him here in Johannesburg when he had come shopping with his family – he often stays with us when he comes down. He looked slightly embarrassed, but then recovered quite quickly.

‘Well,’ he said, ‘you know of course that our fore fathers used to raid the Shona and take away their women. I’m only continuing that tradition.’”

“In which case most of you are half Shona anyway,” uncle Toby said, “your fore fathers only took women of child bearing age...”

“...and gave them Ndebele children!” Uncle Steve responded. This was obviously a subject that was often debated between them. But it was all in good humour.

“I tried to reverse the trend of course.” It sounded to me like Uncle Toby was trying to make light of a situation he still found difficult. “I married a Ndebele girl that I had known for nearly as long as I’ve known you...”

“She did not deserve you, my friend,” uncle Steve patted his friend on the shoulder in a gesture that was meant to comfort him.

“I loved that girl,” he was looking into an unseen distance, “we got married against all opposition from most of her family – who had known me most of my life – and my mother. I believed that she was in love with me. Her family’s opposition was based not only on the fact that I was Shona, I had also fought on the wrong side in the war of liberation! She married me anyway.”

“These things happen...”

“How come they don’t happen to you and Sihle, Steve?” Uncle Toby looked as if he was close to tears. “I watch you and your wife and your relationship seems to grow stronger. Is it because you are both Ndebele?"

"Our marriage has had its fair share of challenges, Toby. You were just unfortunate to fall in love with someone who was clearly not as committed to the marriage as you were..."

"And now she's sleeping with that Nigerian professor. A Nigerian!"

"Oh Toby," Aunt Sihle and Rumbie had come into the room and were setting the table in the 'dining corner', "you're not still pining for Samantha are you? You know that that's not even her given name – Samantha. Her parents had named her Sakhile, and she decided that she did not like that name because it was too 'African', so she changed it to Samantha after some hit song by Cliff Richard made the charts!"

"I know all that but..."

"Toby," Sihle was unrelenting, "you are not getting any younger and you need to move on from that set back. You've overcome many setbacks in your life. Your experiences in the war were not exactly what you expected but you got over them - at least you've channelled your frustrations into studying why African leaders are the way they are, but you refuse to get over this? Was her ..."

She looked at Rumbie and I and it was clear to me that whatever she had meant to say was too delicate for our young ears.

"Anyway," she went on, "food is ready and I know someone who likes you very much at the University, but you won't even give her the time of day."

"And you've kept that from me? Toby, I thought I was your best friend and confidante." Uncle Steve appeared to pretend to be hurt.

"Uncle Toby," Rumbie spoke for the first time in a while, "I nearly rejected Sipho's proposal because I thought I just might have to marry you myself!"

"She's not really...." Toby tried to offer an explanation but it was clear that he did not have one.

"Not really what? Not really as pretty as Sakhile? I think she is prettier!" Aunt Sihle, it seemed to me, did not like uncle Toby's ex.

"I don't know what that woman did to my friend. Sometimes I think that there is truth in the stories that I hear that women give men certain portions to make sure that they don't look at other women. Tobias will not look at any other woman since Samantha..."

"Sakhile!" Aunt Sihle corrected,

'What proposal?' I was still thinking about Rumbie's statement about nearly rejecting my offer. 'She attacked me!' I knew of course that she was joking about marrying her uncle...

"She is white!" Uncle Toby said forcefully.

"Who is white?" It seemed that uncle Steve was as lost as I was.

"The girl," aunt Sihle explained, "the girl that likes Toby."

"Oh." That seemed to stop everyone in their tracks.

"So what if she is white? Does the colour of her skin disqualify her from loving or being loved?" Aunt Sihle was looking angry with all of us.

"Let's face it Sihle," uncle Steve said to his wife, "Whites are not exactly like us..."

"She's not just white; she's Afrikaans!" Uncle Toby sounded surer of himself now. Even I thought that he had said what should have been the game changer. Afrikaans people were notoriously racist – apart from the van der Merwe's who were, clearly an exception; but aunt Sihle was having none of it.

"Even before she met Steve, she was always respectful. She is studying the history of the indigenous peoples of Southern Africa and spends a lot of her time in the library where I work. When she found out that I was from Zimbabwe, she was genuinely interested in finding out about our culture and lifestyles. She did not judge us and even made me begin to realise that some of the values in our culture that are being eroded are what makes us who we are.

'The West,' she would say to me, 'would do well to look at African culture...'"

"They are normally quite condescending about that," Uncle Steve said.

"She was not! And when I introduced her to Toby, I detected some immediate chemistry, even from you, Toby."

"She's probably just curious," Uncle Steve was not giving up either.

"Curious about what?"

"You know how these white women believe that black men are, you know..."

"Is that all you can think about? I think that she genuinely likes Toby, but my brother here is busy obsessing about that Sakhile, who has moved on! I wanted to invite her here tonight but then thought that it would be inappropriate as we are meeting Rumbie's rather dishy young man for the first time."

"Do you think she would have come?"

"I know she would have come. She told me that she has told her parents about Toby..."

"What?" Uncle Toby looked almost alarmed.

"Not as her boyfriend. She says that she only told them that she is collaborating with this very handsome, very intelligent black Zimbabwean who has some very interesting input into her thesis."

"I wouldn't call what we do 'collaborating'..."

"She obviously thinks otherwise. Anyway, I exaggerated about the 'very handsome, very intelligent' bit. She's said that to me not to her parents. Let's eat." Aunt Sihle led us to the small round table meant for four but could fit five, which meant my elbow kept catching Rumbie's, which I did not mind at all.

"What is the girl's name by the way?" Uncle Steve asked during dinner. Up to that point, there had been silence as everyone seemed to concentrate on the meal, which was the best meal I had had in a long time and included millet *s'tshwala,* pumpkin leaves *(ibhobola),* chicken, and the actual pumpkin *(amathanga).*

"Aneka," Uncle Toby responded. "Aneka van Rooyen." He said that with so much feeling that uncle Steve looked up and said, looking at his wife rather fondly, "Thank you for bringing that up, Sihle, I think you've just opened my friend's eyes."

I woke up to an eerie silence the next morning, wondering for a while where I was. The bed I was in was smaller than my normal bed and I remembered that I was still at uncle Toby's. We had sat up late into the night talking and laughing. It had been the most pleasant evening that I could remember. The clear camaraderie between uncles Toby and Steve reminded me that I did not really have anyone that I was that close to. Rumbie was clearly very comfortable in their company and although the conversation changed from Sindebele to Shona to English, there was no awkwardness of any kind and everyone looked genuinely happy. I sat next to Rumbie most of the evening watching the goings on without really being part of the conversation; but also not feeling as though I was being left out. The subject of Aneka kept coming up and it was clear that although uncle Toby was not admitting it, he was very fond of her. In the end, it had been agreed that the Mpalas would host a *braai,* on the next afternoon – Sunday, to which she would be invited.

It had been well after midnight when the Mpalas left and we went to bed. I had been rather embarrassed when uncle Toby offered Rumbie and I the second bedroom, together! But Rumbie's uncle seemed perfectly comfortable with it. Nothing had happened of course because, well it was a small flat and I was afraid that uncle Toby might hear us! Rumbie did not make it easy for me to abstain either, snuggling so close to me in the small bed and making it clear that she had nothing on under her flimsy night dress. But I had years of celibacy and self-discipline behind me and I had resisted.

This morning, she was not in my bed and I wished that she were. In fact, I soon realised that there seemed to be no one in the house, hence the eerie silence. I took a look at my surroundings. It was a small room with just enough space for the bed and a small dressing table with a long mirror. In one corner stood a bookshelf that seemed too small for the number of books in it and a large number was piled on top of the shelf. I wondered idly if uncle Tobias got to read all the books – most of which were on the history of Eastern and Southern Africa. How many books did one have to read in order to complete a PHD? Lots, I decided. I was still debating whether to get up when I had a car arrive as Rumbie and her uncle arrived back from whatever escapade they had been on. Dressing quickly, I met them as they came in as I was making my way to the bathroom, toothbrush in mouth as I struggled to look presentable.

"There you are! You were so fast asleep I decided not to wake you," Rumbie said cheerfully as she carried the parcels from their shopping trip into the kitchen.

"He obviously had a busy night," Uncle Toby said winking at Rumbie, who disappeared into the kitchen looking as though she was embarrassed by her uncle's statement. If she was not, I was! What kind of relationship did she have with her uncle. I had expected him to disapprove – or at least frown at – my sleeping with his niece and he was making a joke of it!

Something was different with uncle Tobias this morning and for a while, I could not define it.

"Did you cut your hair?" I asked as I emerged from the bathroom having finished brushing my teeth.

"Yes. It was overdue..."

"What do you mean overdue?" Rumbie shouted from the kitchen, I've never known you to cut your hair – and shave..."

That was it! I thought. Uncle Toby looked as if he had been scrubbed; he was so clean. His hair was cut short and combed and his beard had been shaved, leaving a bit on the chin which was nicely trimmed with a thin line on either side of the mouth going up to a moustache that I had not noticed before – it obviously was always there but he had always looked so unkempt that it was difficult to distinguish the features on his face.

"*nakupenda Anekaaaaa!"* Rumbie was singing to the tune of an old Swahili classic, replacing *Malaika* with Aneka.

"It's not for Aneka!" Uncle Toby said emphatically.

"Of course not," Rumbie responded coming out of the kitchen. "After years of walking around looking like you have a dead cat in your mouth, you've just decided, on the day of your first date with Aneka..."

"It's not a date! Anyway, Aneka has known me for three years and she knows what I look like!"

"Okay," Rumbie said looking at me, "It's not for Aneka, but do you know what else he did this morning? He bought a pair of designer jeans and a very nice shirt. Normally he just goes to the flea market!"

“All my other clothes are dirty. You’ve not been here for weeks to help me with the laundry. In fact I’ve not seen you since Sipho came back!”

“It must be for you, Sipho,” Rumbie carried on, “He’s never allowed a small thing like dirty laundry stop him before. We call him the recycling king...”

Rumbie had to duck as her uncle threw one of the cushions playfully at her, “I’ll tell Sipho how I helped you shop for the clothes that you were going to wear when you went to meet him at park Station...”

“Uncle!” She looked flustered, “that is not true Sipho, I just needed his company...”

“Do you think he’ll like this? Does it show me at my best?” Uncle Toby was strutting around like a model, mimicking Rumbie’s voice.

“Come on Sipho,” Rumbie said to me as she turned to go back to the kitchen, “come and help me marinade the meat. I also need to make some salads for this afternoon.’

I followed her into the kitchen with Uncle Toby stage whispering to me, “I see she’s got you trained already!”

“Don’t mind my uncle. It’s his chauvinism that’s left him without a girlfriend all these years.” I could not tell if she was still joking.

“It’s because you spoilt me!” Uncle Toby appeared to be making peace. “None of the women were as good as you, my niece.”

CHAPTER TEN

There were the five of us sitting in a semi-circle in the Mpala's garden; Mr and Mrs Mpala; Uncle Toby, Rumbie and myself. Conversation had been lively and varied but I could sense that uncle Toby was getting restless. Aneka, who had been expected an hour earlier, had not shown up. White people are known for their time keeping and if she had been delayed, the expectation had been that she would have phoned – after all, she had a mobile phone and both uncles had one each. Uncle Toby had been reluctant to call her because he did not want to appear too anxious. But now his anxiety was plain for all to see.

"I told you she's not coming," he said suddenly.

"When?" Aunt Sihle asked.

"When what?"

"When did you say that she was not coming?"

"Well," uncle Tobias had looked and sounded frustrated, "You're the one who said she likes me, where is she?'

"I don't know, there must be a good reason, she's normally very reliable," aunt Sihle was on the defensive.

"The reason is that she's white," Uncle Steve stood to go and refill his beer, "can you imagine her coming to a gathering of *kaffirs?* Here, have a beer my friend." Up to this point uncle Toby had been sipping on a glass of wine because, as he put it, "I don't want to get too drunk before our special guest arrives."

"She's not like that," aunt Sihle sounded less sure of herself, "she'll be here, you'll see."

I saw uncle Toby hesitate as he looked at the beer that had been offered. He had got quite drunk the night before and I had seen how much he enjoyed his beer.

"No," he said at length, "I'll stick to the wine."

"You know of course that there's more alcohol in wine than in beer."

"Well, that might just be what I need right now," uncle Toby, looking as though he was feeling sorry for himself was replenishing his glass to the brim, so that when he picked his glass up, he spilt some of the red wine on his new shirt. He did not seem to notice.

"I'm so sorry I'm late folks," a tall, stunningly beautiful white woman came through the Mpala's gate looking rather flustered. I was surprised at how beautiful she looked, having grown up in a society where all white women were thought to be beautiful. I was thinking about how every time one of the girls in the village dressed up smartly, she was always described as 'looking like a Mrs' – Mrs being the generic term for white women. Also because I had never seen white women as anything more than the boss's wives and sisters, I had only always looked at them as, well beautiful. But Aneka was classically beautiful, like the white women on television adverts. She was tall and slim and although her clothes looked casual, they looked as though they were especially tailored for her. Her dark brown hair which came down to her shoulders looked fresh ad bouncy and as she threw her head back to move a lock of hair from her face, she revealed a long neck that was as flawless as her face. What was she doing with a black man? I asked myself. Perhaps uncle Steve was right about her curiosity. I was imagining what she looked like under those clothes...

"You'll swallow a fly," Rumbie whispered to me as she pushed my lower lip up to close my mouth.

"Welcome, welcome," aunt Sihle seemed to be the only one unaffected by the new arrival. She quickly offered Aneka a chair poured her a glass of wine without asking for her preference. These two clearly knew each other well.

Uncle Toby regarded his bottle of wine rather intently, a stupefied smile on his face. He seemed at a loss for words. Equally speechless was uncle Steve who suddenly needed a colder beer than the one in his hand.

"I told you she was coming," aunt Sihle sounded triumphant.

"Of course I was coming. I said I was didn't I?" The elegance with which she sat in the proffered chair had all the men watching her every move. "It was my mother."

"Your mother?" Uncle toby had found his voice.

"Well, she decided that she needed me to accompany her shopping this morning, and it was the longest shopping trip I've ever had with my mother. I think she was a bit worried about me coming to spend the afternoon with you guys."

"Surely she knows that you have black friends at the University." Uncle Steve sounded almost as if he was accusing her.

"I've never really told my parents that I have non-white friends. They are old school and, you know how it is. I've told them that I collaborate with Toby, but this was the first time I had told them that I was coming for a social gathering with" she hesitated, "you guys."

"Come on, Aneka. You are in your thirties, surely your parents..."

"They are particularly protective of me," Aneka interrupted aunt Sihle, "I was married before and it did not go very well. He was from a family I'd known all my life and they approved. But he was extremely abusive." Aneka was quiet for a few minutes as the memories seemed to make her very sad. I was stunned! I had never thought that white people could be abusive to their wives! They always seemed so in love; always walking hand in hand, kissing in public....

"I've not really dated anyone since, although my mother has tried hard to set me up," she seemed to have regained her composure, "but always with macho beer swirling, meat eating white guys with little or no regard for women." She laughed nervously, "You do understand that she would be a bit worried that the first social invitation I've accepted in a while is from non-whites."

"No, we don't understand. We are University graduates and are as civilised as any white man!" Uncle Steve was not going to let her get away with that one.

"I know," she said with equal conviction, "but we live in a society where we have been socialised in a certain way. My parents are by no means racist, but they have never seen a situation where their daughter would befriend black people who are not their workers!"

"That sounds racist to me..."

"Guys, guys," auntie Sihle intervened, "we are here to have a good time not to fix the racial problems of the Republic of South Africa. After all, we will soon have a majority government in this country and everything will be great. Toby, put some meat on the braai, I'm starving."

"They do need fixing though, Si," Aneka was not giving it up either, "and I would not hold my breath regarding the new majority government that we are expecting, if what has happened to the rest of Africa is anything to go by."

"We thought the same in Zimbabwe," Uncle Toby was mixing the meat into the marinade before putting it on the braai stand. "We were more educated and we had seen what had happened to the rest of Africa and learnt our lessons. Look where we are now."

"The truth is, humanity does not learn from the mistakes of others. We need to make our own mistakes; otherwise our children would not be arguing with us as we argued with our parents and as their children will argue with them. It's the cycle of life; it's what keeps life interesting."

"I think South Africa will be different, you'll see," auntie Sihle sounded convinced.

"Not unless South Africans begin to look at life from the perspective of the African, not from the perspective of the coloniser!"

"Here we go again," uncle Toby said under his breath.

"Toby doesn't like me to talk about this subject," Aneka, looking rather fondly at Uncle Tobias, I thought, said to the rest of us. "He believes that I am not qualified to talk about how Africans should feel…"

"Are you? How would you know having lived all your life as a privileged Afrikaner?"

"I know that I have never gone through what you guys went through but I have spent the last few years studying about the history and culture of the indigenous people of Southern Africa and…."

"That qualifies you to tell us how to feel. Typical!" Uncle Toby looked and sounded angry with Aneka, yet there was something about his manner that said that he was not really angry, but perhaps needed to make an impression.

"*Wena,* you'll burn the meat trying to impress Aneka here about your philosophical prowess!" Uncle Steve may have seen what I had seen, or perhaps felt the need to diffuse the situation, I could not decide which.

"That's right, Steve. Toby seems to think that only black people can understand their history fully, but I think that an outsider, without the emotional baggage of having suffered the traumas of colonialism, may have a more balanced perspective."

"Can I show you where the bathroom is, Aneka?" Aunt Sihle clearly wanted to change the subject. Aneka looked like she wanted to carry on the subject but seemed to change her mind.

"Sure," she said, getting up and following aunt Sihle into the house.

"Rumbie, please get another bottle of wine from the house," aunt Sihle said over her shoulders as she linked arms with Aneka to lead her into the house, Those two were, clearly, very close.

"I wouldn't mind having a piece of that," uncle Steve said as soon as the women were out of earshot. "She is dynamite!"

"She is very pretty," I said.

"Young man," uncle Steve addressed me, "the flowers in my garden are 'very pretty'. That is a work of art. She even has a backside like our women!"

"Not bad," uncle Toby said, looking a bit embarrassed by uncle Steve's praise of his friend.

"Then how come you've not, you know...?"

"It's difficult. White women are not like our women. You cannot be sure that her fondness is not a condescending fondness for a lesser being. They are very fond of their dogs you know."

"I see what you mean," uncle Steve was looking thoughtful.

"I mean," uncle Tobias continued, "How do you even start the conversation? 'Aneka, I love you?' that sounds stupid even to myself."

"What sounds stupid," Aneka, looking even more radiant – she must have freshened up or something – was coming out of the house carrying a tray with some cutlery and glasses on it.

"Nothing," uncles Steve and Toby spoke simultaneously.

Aneka looks suspiciously at both of them in turn but must have decided not to pursue the subject. She put the tray on the table beside the braai stand and went to stand next to uncle Toby.

"You're very good at this, aren't you?" she said, putting her arm lightly on his shoulder.

"Hmmm," he seemed unsure how to respond.

"For an African," she said looking directly into his face.

"What do you m..." He had turned sharply to her, seemingly annoyed by her comment but as soon as their eyes met, he could not continue. For a brief moment, it looked as though they might kiss, but then uncle Toby looked away, and the moment passed.

The rest of the afternoon was extremely pleasant. The meal, a mixture of western and traditional dishes went down well and we all seemed to over indulge. I had not had so much roast meat for as long as I could remember – well, the last roast meat I had had back in Zimbabwe was not marinated and it was an old ox, so I could not compare it with this. It seemed to me that everyone was being careful about what they said and how they said it, but full stomachs and the alcohol that was flowing freely by now seemed to loosen tongues.

"I'm really looking forward to an apartheid free South Africa," aunt Sihle said as she sat down after serving the desert of ice cream and chocolate.

"With the freeing of Nelson Mandela and the pending elections, I think that we have already begun to see the benefits of the end of apartheid," Uncle Steve agreed.

"I can't believe that we are finally going to see the end of white privilege, sorry Aneka, but it's been a very unfair system." Uncle Toby glared at uncle Steve for saying that.

"Why are you apologising to me?" Aneka protested feebly, "I'm not responsible for apartheid."

"But I don't hear you protest too much about your privileges," uncle Steve insisted.

"Would you protest, if you were in my shoes? Look, Steve, not many people will complain too much if the unfairness does not affect them, but it does not mean that they agree with the prevailing system. Look what happened in your own country recently. How many Shona people protested at Gukurahundi? Does that mean that all Shona's agreed with the atrocities committed against the people of Matabeleland?"

"Most Shona people did not know what was happening..."

"I do not believe that!" Aneka interrupted uncle Toby with feeling. "I believe that when people are not affected, they don't want to know. Most white South Africans knew what was happening but it was better, or convenient to bury their heads in the sand and pretend that it was not happening!"

"Those of us affected by Gukurahundi," uncle Steve said quietly, "will never forget what it was like."

To which aunt Sihle burst out in uncontrollable laughter.

"It is not funny, Sihle!" Uncle Steve chided his wife seriously. But it was as if she could not help herself.

Try as she might, she could not stop laughing. She took out a tissue to wipe the laughter tears from her eyes but the more she tried to stop laughing, the harder she laughed. On his part, uncle Toby was trying to keep a straight face with little success.

"It is not funny!" Uncle Steve repeated.

"It is funny, actually," uncle Toby, it seemed, could not contain himself either and he had started giggling at his friend's obvious discomfort. Aunt Sihle was besides herself and the rest of us had started laughing without really knowing why. Uncle Steve first glared at his friend and his wife in turn, but also joined in the laughter.

"Well," he said trying to regain some composure, "it is funny now. Then it was not so funny!"

"It was!" Aunt Sihle rolled in her chair as another fit of uncontrolled laughter swept over her.

"What happened?" Aneka was as curious as I was to know what it was that was evoking such mixed emotions.

"Well," uncle Steve started reluctantly, "I was coming from church one Sunday afternoon. We had gone to worship in Magwegwe that morning because that was where Sihle's parents lived and the idea was to visit them after church. Sihle had gone ahead of me and I had stayed behind because there was a men's meeting to plan a men's retreat. Although I was a visitor to this congregation, the retreat sounded quite interesting and we – Sihle and I – had decided that it was worth me finding out if I could join it." He hesitated and looked at his wife, whose face was still looking like she could burst out laughing again

"On our way to Sihle's parents, I was with three other guys from the church, we took a shortcut that meant we would pass the sewer ponds at Old Magwegwe – they were still functional then; I believe they have since been decommissioned," Again he looked at his wife. "There were soldiers that appeared to be guarding the ponds although I could not understand why. They called and beckoned us towards them. Innocently we went over, not quite sure what they wanted.

'*Muri ma dissident?'* The apparent leader asked. We laughed nervously at his absurd question. How could we possibly be dissidents? We were in suits on our way from church, for heaven's sake! But he was having none of it. They had information, he told us in Shona – which thanks to my friendship with Toby, I understand reasonably well, unlike my other friends – that guns have been hidden in the sewer ponds and he wanted us to go in and look for them. We laughed, of course because the suggestion was just so ludicrous.

'*Murikutoseka?* I said go into the ponds and find those guns! If you laugh at me again....', he indicated his weapon in a gesture that was unmistakable. When I explained to the others what was expected of us, they all looked down at their clothes – as I did – to indicate to him that we were not suitably clad for the task he was expecting us to carry out. He seemed to think that this was funny and the soldiers all burst out laughing.

'Don't worry,' one of them said, 'you will get other suits from your supporters.'" Uncle Steve, who looked close to tears, picked up his beer as if to drink but, apparently, could not.

"I can still smell that bloody sewer!" he said.

"What did you do?" Aneka asked.

"What do you do when men brandishing AK 47's tell you to get into a sewer pond and search for guns? You get into the sewer pond and search for guns, even in your Sunday best suit!" He was looking as resigned to his fate as he must have felt that afternoon.

"So we went in, feeling with our feet as we tried to keep or faces as far away from the sewer as possible.

'Bend down and use your hands!' he shouted.

Anyway, we had to go to my in laws after that." That seemed to be the end of the story as far as uncle Steve was concerned. He was not, I realised, going to tell us the details of his experience inside the pond, but I was sure that we were all imagining what it must have been like.

"My mother," aunt Sihle started, still clearly struggling to supress her laughter, "was the first to see her favourite *mkhwenyana* approaching my parents' house. She could, of course not comprehend why her son in law looked like he was wet in the October heat and why he was having trouble walking. And Steve's face..." she could not continue as laughter overtook her again.

"I'm so sorry my darling," she said at length, "but it is the only time I've seen you looking like a lost little boy." This time her tears were not laughter tears. "A lost little boy being followed by all the little boys in the neighbourhood – and all the flies too!"

"My mum in law had to hose me down – much to the amusement of the hordes of children," uncle Steve appeared to have regained some of his humour.

"And you had to borrow my father's suit – two sizes too big for you – which got some strange looks on the bus back to our flat in town."

"I hadn't even finished paying for that suit and I had to give it away! I could not get rid of the smell!"

"What about me? I had to share the same bed for days while you had that smell. In fact, I'm not sure it ever completely went away. I think that in the end I just got used to it!"

For the next few minutes, we all took turns at making fun of uncle Steve and his amazing coat of shit!

"I don't understand why you guys seem to think that that is so funny. That is abuse of the highest order!" Aneka looked outraged.

"They could have been killed," uncle Toby said simply.

"You're not serious!" Aneka was incredulous.

"Mankind is supposed to be God's crowning glory; made in his image. But it is amazing what we are capable of when we are in positions of power and are assured that our actions will not lead to any negative consequences. A soldier with a gun will use it to kill particularly if the 'enemy' is different."

"How is a Ndebele different from a Shona?" Aneka was looking confused.

"They speak different languages."

"Yes, but, without them opening their mouths, could you tell that this one is Shona, this one is Ndebele and this one is Nigerian, even?"

"Nigerians are different, I mean they speak funny..."

"Sihle," Aneka looked pityingly at her friend, "I said 'without opening their mouths'."

"So, it's okay to discriminate on the basis of looking different?"

"No! Toby," Aneka was looking and sounding frustrated, "you just said that armed men will kill if the enemy is different, so, I'm trying to show you that, in the case of Gukurahundi at least, the differences were only superficial," she shrugged her shoulders, "then again, when you think about it, all human differences are superficial."

"Yet, for well over three hundred years, black people in this country were disenfranchised on the basis of the 'superficial' differences?" uncle Steve was pleased to have moved from the subject of his encounter with the soldiers.

"That was also wrong, of course, but humanity is strange in that we are the only species, as far as I know, who will find all kinds of differences to separate us. Tall people versus short people; light skinned people versus dark skinned people. Even beautiful people – depending of course on one's definition of beauty – versus ugly people."

"Would you put yourself among the beautiful...?"

"Toby please be serious for a minute. There is something that is so... so, fucked up about our world, yet we are supposed to be the most intelligent of the species."

"Isn't that why so many whites are leaving South Africa? They see the end of their privileged status and will not wait around to see that eroded."

"I think that many of them are worried by what they have seen happen in the rest of Africa and are leaving before the same happens to South Africa."

"In other words," uncle Tobias cut in, "they do not believe that an African can run this country successfully?"

"Do you blame them? They have seen the rest of independent Africa..."

"They will not even give us the benefit of the doubt!"

"I think that perhaps we have started this conversation from the wrong angle" Aneka said, placatingly, "We need to understand the history of how we got to where we are before we even begin to apportion blame."

"We were colonised, disenfranchised and had our land taken away, that's how we got to where we are!" Uncle Toby was looking irritated, "what else do we need to understand?"

"I think that," Aneka sounded like she was choosing her words carefully, "Unless we understand the European's mind-set and motivation at the time of colonisation, we will not understand what informed their behaviour. And unless we understands the indigenous people's belief systems and culture, we will not understand their response to colonisation, and their apparent acquiescence to being dominated."

"Meaning?" Aunt Sihle was looking confused.

"Look, Africa had always been a bit of an enigma to Europeans. Apart from a few adventurers who ventured into the interior, what was known about the 'dark continent' was mainly along the coast where they had built staging posts for their voyages elsewhere..."

"Like India," Uncle Steve said.

"Yes, India was one of their main destinations. But remember also they had Ports from which they collected slaves that they took to such lands as the West Indies, the United States and South America. By and large it was Arab Traders and in some cases, other Africans that brought the slaves to the coast." She paused, as if to let what she had just said sink in.

"Then Europe had an attack of conscience and the lucrative trade in slaves was abolished. There was need to fill the gap left by the abolition, and adventurers like Henry Stanley and David Livingstone, among others, were bringing back stories of untold riches to be found in the interior of Africa. Remember of course that the people who lived in Africa had been traded commodities and were therefore considered somewhat less than human, so as far as the Europeans were concerned, this vast land was uninhabited and was anybody's for the taking!"

"Which is why David Livingstone has gone down in history as the 'discoverer' of the Victoria Falls, even though there were people living there!" Uncle Steve sounded disgusted. All of us were mesmerised at the story that was being told to us by the daughter of a coloniser, yet she seemed to know more about African history than we did.

"Yes. But there were many other things found in Africa that suggested an organised and civilised group of people that Africans were not given credit for. The most famous of course being the pyramids of Egypt. But, did you know that Timbuktu was a great seat of learning and has one of the world's oldest libraries?"

"Come on. That is far-fetched!" Again, uncle Steve was the quickest to react.

"It is true," uncle Tobias said getting up to refill Aneka's glass. "These people will not even acknowledge that Great Zimbabwe was built by blacks. They have tried to prove that someone else did. In fact there have even been suggestions that it might be aliens from outer space who built Great Zimbabwe!"

"Of course acknowledging that Africans were responsible for such structures means that they would have to acknowledge that Africans may have had some intelligence and knowledge superior to their own. I mean, they are hard pushed to explain how the pyramids were built, given that the ancient Egyptians did not have the scientific knowledge (they believe) that we have today and did not have the technology!"

"I'm told that even Moses from the Bible, had a black African wife," aunt Sihle added.

"That's another thing, religion," was there nothing that this woman did not know about African history? "Most African religions believe in an all-powerful God, the creator, who is represented by certain spirits who are either ancestors or other spirits that mediate between the people and God. Is that so different from the Christian God? Take the Dogon tribe of South East Mali." She rummaged through her handbag and brought out a wad of papers that she flipped through. "I was reading about them only yesterday. Although they did not come into contact with Europeans until the late nineteenth century because they live in a well secluded place in the mountains, they have an all-powerful, all knowing God called AMMA, whose son NOMO is the water spirit. There are two other spirits, LEBE, the agricultural spirit and YURUGU, the representative of fallen man before AMMA. Does that not sound somewhat similar to the Christian God? Yet African religion has been denigrated as heathen and worthless!"

"We have an all knowing creator in Shona religion, *Musikavanhu (*the creator of humankind). But I find it difficult to take him seriously. People talk about going under some tree and after some ritual, food would appear! How ridiculous is that?" Uncle Toby seemed pleased with himself.

"And you find that hard to believe?"

"Of course it's hard to believe…."

"Yet you believe that the children of Israel received Manna from heaven?"

There was some nervous laughter as most of us in the room were professed if not necessarily practicing Christians, but I was keen for Aneka to continue her story.

"Look," Aneka said at length, "I'm not denigrating Christianity. I am a practicing Christian myself. All I'm saying is that Africa needs to tell her own stories in her own way. Africans must not allow themselves to be defined by the views of others."

She was quiet for a few minutes. I had the impression she might have felt that she had gone too far.

"Well," she went on after a while, "religion is a whole other subject area. But I need to get back to the story of colonisation. The surge in interest for things African meant that there were bound to be clashes between the many countries that were trying to get a foothold into this untapped, unmanned source of wealth. This was a time, remember, when most of Europe was ruled by Royalty and the royals tended to marry into each other's' families, so there was need for some order in the 'scramble' so that they did not tread on each other's toes. So a conference to discuss Africa's 'Partition' was organised in Berlin by then German Chancellor Bismarck, to which everyone with interest in Africa was invited."

"Everyone except the Africans, who happened to be the ones living in Africa at the time."

"Yes Toby," Aneka agreed, "but remember Africans were still considered..."

"Less than human." Uncle Steve completed the sentence.

"So," Aneka carried on, "In 1884 and 1885 these powers – Germany, France, Great Britain, The Netherlands, Belgium, Portugal and Spain – sat down around a conference table in Berlin, and parcelled out Africa. The United States had been invited but did not attend because they had no desire to build an empire, they said." She was looking quite angry now, although I was not sure that it was not the wine taking effect. "They drew lines on a map," she said emphatically, "and with those lines drawn in faraway Berlin, Africa's narrative was changed!"

Apparently subconsciously, she put her hand into uncle Toby's hand and their fingers intertwined. I noticed then how white her skin was against the darker skin of Rumbie's uncle. On his part, uncle Toby did not resist although the grin on his face told its own story.

"What fuckin' pisses me off," the wine was definitely taking over, I thought, "is that today's African leaders have bought into that narrative."

"What narrative is that?" I got the impression that uncle Toby was not necessarily interested in the answer.

"The lines that were drawn by those men in Berlin are what defines Africa today. Lines that did not take into account linguistic or tribal groupings, existing kingdoms and empires. Lines that turned neighbours into foreigners and made relatives need passports to go and visit relatives."

"Are you suggesting that borders are removed? Surely that is not practical," uncle Steve sounded a bit tipsy.

"I personally don't think it would be such a bad idea, but, as you say, it may not be practical. But, look Steve, when I go to the border with Zimbabwe for example, I see that the people on either side of the border speak the same language yet, when they come across to our side, they are treated as foreigners. How is a Zimbabwean *Venda* a Mukwerekwere, and a South African Venda is not? This is replicated all over Africa!"

"Actually," Rumbie seemed to remember something, " I think I did hear that our people may have come from Tanzania, but I wasn't really paying attention so I don't have any details."

"That would not surprise me," Aneka said. "There was, generally, free movement and there were no restrictive passports. Because of the free movement, you will notice that the languages of this region are very similar, if not the same. Sesotho, spoken in Lesotho, and Setswana, spoken in much of South Africa and Botswana are virtually the same language – and you'll get traces of the same language in Zambia – among the Lozi – and parts of Zimbabwe. Then you have IsiZulu in Natal, IsiSwati, spoken in Swaziland, isiXhosa spoken in the Cape and isiNdebele, spoken in Western Zimbabwe – again, virtually the same language. Yet these groupings are sometimes thousands of kilometres apart, and because of the lines drawn in Berlin, are in different countries! Does that make sense to you?

"Yes, I mean No!" Uncle Toby was still holding on to Aneka's hand, "In fact, you can go as far North as Kenya and Uganda and you will hear certain words that are common to our languages. But we have been divided by the lines that Aneka keeps talking about. But if it is not practical to abolish borders, what is the solution?"

"I don't know," Aneka said honestly, "But have you taken a close look at the map of Africa? Some of the lines don't make sense even to the casual observer. Look at the border between Zambia and the Democratic Republic of Congo for example. Southern DRC appears to have a long finger that pokes into the middle of Zambia! How much sense does that make, at least to the Africans living there?"

I stood up and went to look at a map of Africa that I had noticed on uncle Steve's dining room wall. Sure enough, there was the 'finger' as described by Aneka. It was not the first time I was seeing this, but I had never questioned it before, accepting that Zambia was shaped that way without asking why it was shaped that way. For the first time, I wondered about the people living on either side of the 'finger' Would they have to go round it's tip to get to the other side, or did they need passports to pass through DRC territory? Then I also noticed that Malawi was strangely located; seemingly swallowed by Mozambique. Were the people in that area different from each other, or was it colonialism that made them Malawian and Mozambican? When I came back to my seat, I asked Aneka why the borders were so senseless.

"They made sense to the colonisers, of course, not to the indigenous peoples. Remember that Northern Zambia is what's commonly known as the copper belt. Copper was one of the most sought after minerals and the Belgians – or more accurately, the Belgian King Leopold, who owned the country in his personal capacity at the time – wanted some of the copper!"

"He owned a country?" I was astounded.

"One of Africa's largest and most mineral rich countries was, at one time, owned by one man!"

"How come they have not changed the borders after independence?"

"Because their colonisers defined them as two separate countries, one English speaking, and the other French speaking. Who wants to give up some of their copper?"

"But why don't they sit around a table, like the Europeans did and come up with more sensible borders?" I asked.

"I'm not a politician," Aneka said, looking at her watch, "but why is there reluctance to form some sort of unity? They've been talking about African unity for decades but nothing happens; because those that were colonised by the British – the Anglophones – take pride in their being British; the Francophone countries take pride in being French; the Portuguese and so on..."

"We really take more pride in the language of our colonisers than in our own languages!" I had never really thought about it that way. Speaking good English had always been considered an important part of one's education and always stood one in good stead.

"Can you imagine," Aneka went on, "how economically powerful Africa would be if they pooled their resources – natural and human - and formed some sort of Federal State, not necessarily covering the whole continent, but, you know Southern African Federation, Central African Federation, East African Federation and so on. Those would not only be more economically viable; they would be more attractive to foreign investors."

"How so?"

"Look, Steve, if you had millions to invest, would you invest in India, with a population of one billion people or would you invest in Botswana, with just over one million people. But if you pool the countries of Southern Africa together, depending on who you include, you now have a population of one hundred million or more to cater for and that begins to make sense."

"I wonder why no one has thought of it," I said.

"Oh they have thought of it alright. But I think politicians – all politicians are by nature, selfish. They think about themselves first."

"Who, for example," uncle Toby said, shifting position so that his arm was virtually over Aneka's shoulder, "would be President of Southern Africa? I cannot see South Africans accepting a Mukwerekwere for President..."

"Or Shonas accepting a Mundevere, or a *Mubwidi..."* it was becoming some sort of game.

"Exactly my point," Aneka said excitedly, "you guys are defining yourselves by the definition of your colonisers! They are happy because it keeps Africa economically weak and dependant on them, and when you start wars against each other, they supply the weapons, making their economies even stronger while Africa continues to bleed."

"Then, why do we not tell our own history. The history of Africa before the colonialists came?" I asked innocently.

"Because," uncle Toby answered, "we never wrote anything down; because they convinced us that our history before they came was worthless; because, young man, history is always told from the point of view of the victor."

"You don't have to go very far to look at that last statement," uncle Steve said, with feeling, "our own fairly recent history is being told in a one sided manner. We only hear of Mbuya Nehanda and Sekuru Kaguvi, yet even in school, we learnt that the Ndebeles rebelled first, yet no Ndebele heroes of the time are mentioned."

"If you do your research," Uncle Toby countered, "you will find that the Ndebele heroes are mentioned. It is only because the politicians speak loudest about these things that the impression is given that the first Chimurenga was only about Mbuya Nehanda and Sekuru Kaguvi. There are many heroes – Shona and Ndebele – that hardly get a mention when politicians speak."

"Gosh! Look at the time," Aneka said, standing up in something of a panic, "I have to go."

"Where are you going to go at this time of night?" Aunt Sihle said looking at her friend rather disapprovingly. "Phone your mother and tell her you are staying the night. You can go in the morning."

"Yes, stay," I thought Uncle Toby was looking rather hopeful.

"Yes, let me call my mother," Aneka stood up and went into the house to make the call.

"And you, Toby," Aunt Sihle was looking at uncle Toby sternly, "will go to your house."

"But Sihle..."

“No buts. Her parents let her come because she was coming to me. I don’t want to be responsible for, you know, whatever you have in mind.”

“But Sihle, you know that Toby has...”

“STEVEN!”

I saw Uncle Steve literally wilt under his wife’s severe stare.

“Well,” Aneka said, coming out of the house, “that went better than I thought. My mum was a bit concerned but I assured her that I’d be okay, I’ll join them for church in the morning.” She went across to uncle Toby, gave him a peck on the cheek and put her hand on his shoulder.

“That was very pleasant,” she said. “We must do this more often. it’s always good to be in intelligent company.”

With that, the evening ended and we headed back to uncle Toby’s apartment after a rather lingering handshake between Rumbie’s uncle and Aneka.

“Is that all she sees me as,” Uncle Toby said after some time as we walked back, “intelligent company?”

“She clearly likes you, uncle Toby” Rumbie reassured him. “I’m going to have an Afrikaner as an auntie,” she said skipping away from her uncle who was chasing her, all in fun, I thought.

CHAPTER ELEVEN

On the twenty fourth of December, 1994, I sat on the same rock that I had sat on earlier in the year when I was observing the preparations for my welcome home party after ten years away. The village was a hive of activity again on a larger and more intense scale. The following day, Christmas day was going to be the big celebration of my marriage to Rumbie and she was finally going to be officially welcomed into my home and family. We had got married a few months earlier in a civil ceremony in Johannesburg but it had always been our plan to have a celebration 'back home'. There had been some pressure from family to have two celebrations – one in Rusape, at Rumbie's parents home and the other one here at Maramani. This had led to probably the biggest argument between Rumbie and I as she was in agreement with this idea. Thankfully, I had been able to convince her that as we were footing most of the bill, particularly after I had paid a significant amount of my savings for her *amalobolo/roora,* it would not be in our best interest to spend so much on the wedding celebration.

"After all, we are already married with both our families' blessings," I has said.

"But Sipho, there are people in my home area, after my..." she had hesitated, "after I got pregnant, that wrote me off and said that I was a whore who would not amount to much."

While I understood her need to 'stick her finger up' at those people, the financial imperatives that faced us were too great to spend on a second celebration just to spite people who no longer really mattered in our lives. In any case, many of them had gone on to mother children from different men; what did it matter what they thought?

"You want to spend so much money just for your ego...?" I did not get to complete the question.

"Do you know what it's like to have people look at you as if you were a piece of nothing? Girls laughing loudly behind your back every time you pass them; and boys – every boy in the village – believing that you were anybody's for the taking?"

I had never seen Rumbie so angry. I had always assumed that after she had confided in me, and I had assured her that I accepted her, with her daughter, she had got over her anger. There had been nothing in our relationship, up to that point that had suggested that that period of her life still bothered her. I of course had had my own struggles with the idea that some man had had the temerity to violate her against her wishes – if indeed that was true – and that were it not for that man, I would have met a virgin – if her story about not being with another man since was true. Was she genuine in wanting to cleanse her reputation or did she just want to show off to her friends; to say to them 'look, after having my fun as a teenager, I've found this Ndebele fool to marry me!' I had found myself getting angry with my wife.

"Look," I had said angrily "I was not there when you slept with your teacher and I don't car..."

"I did not sleep with that teacher," she had shouted back angrily, "I was raped! So what is this then? You feel sorry for me? There are many virgins out there if you wanted to marry one. You could have left me alone with my life. I was okay..." She had stormed out of our bedroom and slammed the door behind her leaving me staring angrily at the door. I had wanted to tell her that there were not as many virgins out there as she seemed to imagine but the more I had thought about it, the more I had realised what a mistake that would have been.

I smiled to myself as I remembered how I had thought through what had just happened and realised that I had to apologise to her. It was her daughter Kupakwashe , who came to my rescue.

I had finally met Kupa, as everyone called her for short, after the traditional marriage ritual that, in my view was just her family asking for as much money as they could extract out of me. It virtually wiped me out of all my savings. I had waited anxiously outside Rumbie's childhood homestead in the Chiduku Area of Rusape District, while my *Munyai* – or negotiator – Mr Demo, a local who had been recommended to us by Rumbie's uncle, Mr Nyati who was the husband to Rumbie's father's sister, went in with Uncle Peter. There was nothing much for me to do except pace the ground and try to stay calm. Every so often, the negotiator would come out with uncle Peter to appraise me of the progress and how well things were going.

"I think we may be a little short," Uncle Peter had said during one of their excursions.

"What?" I had retorted, surprised that what I had put together, expecting that there may be some change for a bit of a celebration with Rumbie, was going to be short. "Does that mean I cannot marry Rumbie?"

"No," he had said reassuringly, "you are generally not expected to pay everything today, but I think you will have gone quite a long way by the time we finish."

Indeed, it turned out that most of the requirements were met on that day and the only things left were a few live cattle and some clothing for Rumbie's parents. With those formalities completed, I was brought in to meet the family. Rumbie had shown me pictures of her mother, but they did not do her justice. I could immediately see where my wife, as I was already thinking of her as, got her looks from. Her father was a tall, slim gentle man who seemed to have dressed his best for the occasion. Apart from the greeting, which seemed to be a series of hand claps that went on endlessly, he did not seem to have much to say and it was his younger brother who did most of the talking. I did not understand most of it myself but Uncle Peter tried his best to help me follow the conversation, which seemed to suggest that the family was very happy that their daughter had found herself a life partner who had shown his commitment to her by coming to do the right thing.

I was not particularly interested in the speeches which seemed to go on for an inordinately long time. I was looking at Rumbie who was dressed in a simple floral dress with the traditional head scarf covering her hair. She looked very pretty and I could not take my eyes off her. There were other people in the room, a very large round hut in which everything had taken place. They were introduced to me but I really did not remember many of them.

Finally, a pretty, smartly dressed little girl that I had seen without particularly noticing, was brought in and I came face to face with Rumbie's daughter for the first time. Up to now, I am still not sure what I felt then. How could a rape produce something so pretty and bubbly? She had her mother's large eyes that seemed to smile all the time and they looked directly at me with the innocence of childhood. She seemed to be examining me, almost as if she wanted me to say something to her. I could not think of anything to say because I suddenly felt a twinge of jealousy as I thought of the man who had fathered this flower. What kind of man would abandon such a blessing? She came to shake my hand with a courtesy, her eyes still looking directly into mine and a smile on her lips that reminded me of her mother. I was immediately drawn to the child although a part of me was still telling me that I could not love the child of my enemy!

Anyway, by the time we got back to Johannesburg – I had insisted that we take her with us in spite of Rumbie's mother's protestations that we needed time to know each other before introducing her fully into our lives – she had taken to calling me *baba* which felt awkward at first but I was slowly getting used to it.

"What a lovely little girl," Aneka had said as soon as she saw her. She and uncle Toby had become 'an item'; and she had virtually moved in with him. Needless to say, his flat was looking a lot more organised. "Sifo," she still could not get the way my name was spelt and still pronounced it the way that Europeans would pronounce the 'ph', "you are so lucky!" it did not help that sifo, in my language, means a disease!

I did not understand how she could see a child that was not biologically mine as being some sort of 'luck' for me.

"Look at her," Aneka was grinning broadly, "Imagine if she had your looks. Sifo!"

I think she was joking!

Anyway, on the day we had the argument about whether to have one or two wedding celebrations, Kupa had come knocked on the bedroom door and bounced in without waiting for an answer. She did this all the time and her mother and I had often joked that one day she was going to walk in on us during one of our most intimate times!

"Baba," she said jumping on to the bed happily, "I got ten out of ten in the English test again today. Look, the teacher even gave me a star," she said excitedly, her big brown eyes looking expectantly at me for the usual reward. But my mind had still been preoccupied with the earlier argument.

"Did you see your mother when you came in?" I had asked.

"What is it today?" She had responded, looking crestfallen, "first my mother says nothing at all to me and now all you do is ask me about HER!" It was one of our secret codes when Rumbie was not particularly happy with either one of us that we would emphasise the SHE and HER when we spoke to each other.

"Well I think that SHE may be right this time," I had said thoughtfully.

"Right about what?"

"About us having two wedding celebrations..."

"Are you getting married twice then?" she had asked innocently.

"No, we are already married remember? This will just be a celebration."

"Then why not make it one BIG celebration?" She had extended her arms to indicate the size of celebration she was talking about.

So now I sat on the rock watching the preparations for the BIG celebration. Again, I was being barred from participating in the preparations because it was for my big day as everyone kept reminding me. Rumbie and I had finally agreed that we would have the one celebration to which both families could contribute. They had contributed mainly in kind with whatever they could spare from their produce. Uncle Peter, representing my father, had given one of his older cows to be slaughtered for the occasion, and, once again, I could smell the roasted meat as the slaughterers enjoyed their mantshontsho. Everybody was walking around with purpose although for some of them, like my friend Promise, the purpose was not immediately apparent. I had not seen Rumbie, or Kupakwashe for the last few days. They were in faraway Chiduku, although I knew by then they should have been on their way for the celebration on the next day. I missed them both terribly.

The other big event of 1994 had been the first universal franchise elections in South Africa which had ushered in majority rule and Nelson Mandela had been installed as the first black President of South Africa. The excitement in the country was sky high and business was good although there were now more black customers coming into the Hamburger and its subsidiary The Hambaker. Mr Van had offered Rumbie and I minority shareholding in the business and we were both excited at the prospect of one day owning the business as Mr Van kept hinting.

"It's your country now" he would say, "and the communists in the ANC don't want us whiteys."

I, of course had begun to look at white people with a different mind-set after the many discussions with Aneka about how the Europeans had usurped our country and our land. Mr Van, I believed, was only righting past wrongs.

"Here you are, Sipho. I've been looking for you. Here, have some meat." Promise approached me with a plate of roast meat. It was good, tender meat for such an old cow.

"It's from the adder," he explained. "Only men eat this."

"And only men eat the bull's testicles?"

"Of course," Promise said with conviction, "We cannot have women eating that! They'll start to think that they are men!"

I found myself wondering what Rumbie would have made of that.

In fact I found myself wondering about the differences that were supposed to be between the people of Matabeleland and the people of Mashonaland. Was it all part of the narrative that had been fed to us by the colonisers? I remembered that in school we were always taught that the Matebele were 'war like' and that the Shona were their victims. While there may have been some truth in some of these assertions, as MaMpofu had confirmed for me over the years, was it not true that during that period and earlier, there had been wars and battles fought between the different Shona groupings? Yet those hardly got any mention in history. Was it not a fact of life that all people, all over the world have at one time or another, fought battles and wars that would probably not make sense to us today? In any case, did not the whites themselves resort to war in order to subdue the local people? Yet they were never described as 'war like'. It seemed to me that there had been a concerted effort to exaggerate the so called language differences in order to divide and rule us. In the 1890's there had been, after the initial Matebele rebellion, efforts to co-ordinate the response to the colonialists when a Spiritual leader in the Matopo Hills, Mlimo, I think his name was, whose influence seemed to go across tribal lines tried to co-ordinate the response to the colonisers.

Unfortunately, communication was poor and the uprising was easily defeated. Also during the war of liberation – the so called 'Second *Chimurenga*' – the Patriotic Front had been formed to bring together the different armies, broadly representing the two main tribal groupings in the country. Why was that not carried forward into independence?

"Politicians," Uncle Tobias had once said to me, "are essentially selfish. They will do whatever it takes to get their way. The Patriotic Front was a good idea and made good sense. But once the prize was in sight – the prize being the rulership of Zimbabwe – tribal politics came to the fore because, well, you do the sums."

I remembered another heated discussion between uncles Tobias and Steve, and Aneka.

"All politicians," Aneka had said, "are to a greater or lesser extent, Machiavellian!"

"You cannot be serious!" Uncle Steve had responded vehemently, "Machiavelli was a fool. He thought that people should seek power for the sake of seeking power..."

"Is that not what African politicians do?" Aneka had interrupted.

"Now, now children, play nicely," uncle Tobias had obviously felt the need to diffuse the argument. "Let us think this through. What was Mr Machiavelli's main theory?"

"That the only reason to go into politics is to get power and to keep it, at whatever cost."

"Now, tell me of a politician that does not subscribe to that," Aneka had sounded triumphant.

"Surely there are politicians whose sole aim is to help the people..."

"Name one," Aneka interrupted uncle Steve again.

"Nelson Mandela," Uncle Tobias had said.

"Well," Aneka conceded somewhat reluctantly, "maybe, but he is still new. Let's see what happens in a few years."

That had seemed to put paid to the argument until uncle Tobias stood up, went across the room and found a book he was looking for on the bookshelf. Sitting back down, he paged through the book until he found what he was looking for then read out loud;

"'A man who wishes to make profession of goodness in everything must necessarily come to grief among so many who are not good. Therefore it is necessary for a Prince who wishes to maintain himself, to learn how not to be good, and to use this knowledge and not use it according to the necessity of the case'. Niccolo Machiavelli." Uncle Tobias closed the book looking satisfied.

"What is he saying?" Uncle Steve asked.

"He is saying that in politics, you cannot afford to be good. That you cannot succeed by being good." Aneka said.

"Is he not the guy who also says that in politics, it is good to be feared?" Uncle Steve asked.

"'Since love and fear can hardly exist together, if we must choose between them, it is far safer to be feared than loved'. Does that not sound like our African Politicians?" uncle Tobias had read from his book again.

"What I am saying," Aneka was looking quite passionate, "is that, all politicians everywhere in some way subscribe to Machiavelli. In the so called democracies of the West, they will tell the people what they want to hear in order to get elected, then forget about them until the next election."

"Never attempt to win by force what can be won by deception..."

"Oh quit quoting from that bloody book Toby," Aneka was looking fondly at her boyfriend. "We get the picture. But what I am saying is that although Machiavelli has been derided in some quarters, he spoke the truth about politics and politicians."

"So, what is she like?" Promise brought me back to the present.

"Who?"

"The Shona," he made a pumping action with his arm, "You know."

It was not the level of conversation I was used to. I had become fascinated with history as I spent a lot of time with Uncle Toby and Aneka, but Rumbie had also got me to enrol in a business administration Diploma in order to 'equip me for the business challenges ahead' as she put it. She was frustrated that I seemed to read more history than My Business Admin books and would always remind me of what was important.

"What has history ever given anyone?" she would ask, "you certainly don't need it to run a company."

My explanations that I was just interested in knowing where we came from and how we got to where we were did not impress her at all.

"You know, Sipho," she would say, sitting on my lap and rubbing my hair, "there are things that we all want to do because they are 'nice' and they make us feel good. Then there are things that we have to do because those are what put food on the table. When we have enough food on the table, we can then do the 'like to do' things."

Between work and college, there was not enough time for those, so I 'stole' moments to read what I liked rather than what I had to; sometimes putting the history text inside the Principles of Accounts book so that she would not see what I was reading. Needless to say, I had been caught on a few occasions and it had led to some chastisement from her. Promise's conversation topic was not one I engaged in very often.

"Is that all you can think about, Promise?" I said gently to him. "There are more important things..."

"More important than sex?" He interrupted, "name one."

"Well," I hesitated, "Where do we come from, for example?"

"Our parents had sex and we were born," he responded rather smugly.

"I don't mean that!" I said, thinking how frustrating it was to have a conversation with someone with such a closed mind.

"What do you mean, because even in the Bible, God told Adam to go and multiply. I personally think that God said, 'Go and have sex'. Just that the bible is written in polite language."

I had to laugh. "Promise, what do you know about the Bible?" I asked him.

"I go to church," He did? "sometimes."

"So you know that God created Adam and Eve..."

"Who were white according to the pictures I have seen."

"We don't know that for sure." This conversation was getting tedious.

"So," he was not giving it up, "If God made white people, where do we, the black people come from? And the Chinese? And the Indians?"

"I thought you just said we all came from the sexual exploits of our parents," I tried to be flippant.

"No, no Sipho, you started this discussion. You said that it is important for us to know where we came from, so tell me, where did black people come from because, according to the pictures I've seen, they were not created by God – and if you look at how we live, God does not seem to care for us that much."

"We were all created by God, in His image," I said without too much conviction, " and he loves us all."

"So we all look like God?"

"In a way yes..."

"I look like God, You look like God, Shonas look like God, Kalangas look like God and white people look like God. Is that what you are saying?"

In spite of what seemed like Aneka's very strong views, she was a practicing Christian and had, in fact got Rumbie and I going to church regularly. I wondered then how she would have answered Promise's question.

'We'll never understand everything about God,' she'd probably have said, 'we just have to take it on faith.' But how could I explain faith to Promise when I hardly understood it myself?

"God is not like us," I said at length, "all we need to know and accept is that He loves us and we are made in His image."

He seemed to think about that for long while then decided not to pursue the subject.

"So, what is she like?" he returned to his original question.

"Promise, that is my wife you are talking about," this was irritating. "Would you talk about Bridget in that way."

"I suppose not," he said after a pause, "just that she is Shona and..."

"And nothing. All women are the same!"

He was quiet for a few moments then asked me what I thought was the most ridiculous question.

"You know that time when you came to visit, did you sleep with Bridget?"

"Promise, what do you take me for? I would never do that!" I was almost shouting.

"Well," he looked almost embarrassed, "I heard you slept with a few of the girls and, well," he hesitated, "I just wondered."

He must have agonised over that for some time, I thought. He was unemployed and in spite of his appearing not to care, it must have hurt him that he could not provide for his wife; he must have thought that she was vulnerable to approaches from any man with money or the means to provide. That was what our country had reduced us to. There was very little prospect of employment and many men lived in fear of losing their wives. I thought of my mother and what she had had to do. Would married women resort to the same profession if their lives got difficult? Had Bridget given Promise reason to believe that she could offer her charms to any man with money?

"Would you come to South Africa to look for work?" A thought was forming in my mind.

"Of course I would," he said enthusiastically, "but I don't have a passport and I believe life is not so easy down there." Was he looking for excuses?

"It didn't stop me," I said with a chuckle.

"I am not crossing over the Limpopo like you did! And look what happened to your friends..."

"I'm not suggesting anything of the sort," I reassured him. "Anyway, do you know that we could have been part of South Africa?"

"Oh? How so?"

"The whites of this country decided against it." I said, thinking about Aneka and her assertion that our narrative had been determined by our colonisers. This was just another example of it.

"Did you know that," I went on, "this country was first colonised by a private company?"

"*Haibo!*" He exclaimed, looking incredulous, "Now you're making up stories."

"Cecil John Rhodes, After whom the country was named, owned the British South Africa Company (BSAC) which colonised Southern and Northern Rhodesia (now Zambia). All with the blessing of the British Crown, of course, and although there was a Legislative Council in place, they still reported direct to London."

"Is that when they declared UDI?"

"No. UDI was much later. But in the early 1920's, some of the politicians of the time – all white of course – wanted to become a self-governing Colony, while others wanted to join the Union of South Africa, as it was known then..."

"Why?"

"Why what?"

"Why were they called the Union of South Africa?"

"It's a long story. The colonisation of South Africa was quite complicated, because first the Dutch came and set up the Cape – in the 16 hundreds, then later on the British came and I'm not sure how it happened, but they took over and the Dutch started moving North. The two white groups did not seem to get on and it culminated in the Anglo Boer War at the turn of the century. Anyway, some of what are now Provinces of South Africa were actually States – like the Orange Free State and the Transvaal, for example. Presumably because the white community realised that they were in the minority and their common interests were bigger than their differences, The Union of South Africa was formed, joining the various states into one Union."

"You mean like the Ndebele's and the Shonas realising that they have more in common than their differences?" He was cleverer than he let on.

"Yes but the histories are somewhat different. The black people of this country did not agree to be one nation; the boundaries were set by the whites and we were presented with a *fait accompli...*"

"A what?"

"A position already set for us. We had no input into how we wanted to coexist. It was presented to us and we've accepted it – although I'm not sure that everyone accepts that position."

Promise did not say anything for a while so I carried on with the story.

"Anyway, the decision on whether to join South Africa or stay independent was put to the all-white electorate, and, in 1922, they voted to stay independent of South Africa..."

"Why did they do that? We would be part of South Africa today..."

"Not necessarily," I corrected my friend. "Have you heard of the Federation of Rhodesia and Nyasaland?"

"Not really," Promise admitted, "although my mother always says, when she wants to express that something is really old, that it is from 'the days of Federation'."

"This was a Federal state that included Zimbabwe – then called Southern Rhodesia, Zambia – then called Northern Rhodesia, and Malawi – then called Nyasaland. Essentially, that meant that the three were one country. However, because they had originally been defined – in Berlin – as three different countries, when the Nationalist movements arose in the 1950's, they fought for independence not only from white rule, but also from each other. So it is just possible, that even if the whites had voted to be part of South Africa in 1922, we may have fought for independence as the originally defined state – defined, not by us, but by the colonisers in Berlin!"

"I prefer to think that if they had voted to be part of South Africa, we would still be part of South Africa! And, we would be calling the Shona's, Makwerekwere!"

"The Shona's would also have been part of South Africa," I said, "but they probably would not have been as dominant as they are in Zimbabwe."

"Why did those whites choose not to join South Africa? That was the most stupid decision they ever made." Promise was looking quite disgusted.

"I don't know," I said honestly. "They probably felt that they had enough to make a success of this country; but some may have felt that it was easier to get to the top in Rhodesia, a much smaller economy with a smaller population, than it would be in the much larger economy of South Africa. Politicians can be selfish, you know."

"Promise! I've been looking for you all over the place. There is still so much to be done and you keep skiving off!" Uncle Peter stood over us with his hands on his hips. He was clearly not very happy with Promise.

"I had to come and keep our star for tomorrow company. I thought he looked quite lonely."

"No, Promise," Uncle Peter was determined, "you ran away as soon as you heard that we needed to start moving the benches from the school. Anything to avoid physical labour! I wonder how you even can look after that pretty girl you call your wife."

"I don't just call her my wife. She is my wife! And as you've probably noticed, she is pregnant. That is my baby inside her!"

I found myself worrying about Promise and Bridget's baby. What would become of that child with a father like Promise? Rumbie and I had decided to wait for a few years until we were established, yet the likes of Promise made babies without any thought of how they would provide for them. Were we being too careful? Or was Rumbie just making sure that her daughter was well catered for before we had another child? It was one of the many moments of doubt that I had been having since the decision was made. I remembered my conversation with MaMpofu several months earlier. It struck me then that I was not even sure that I was capable of making babies! Would Rumbie.... Could Rumbie cheat on me if she thought that I could not have babies?

"As soon as we are married..." I said out loud without meaning to.

"What will happen as soon as you are married?" Uncle Peter asked curiously.

"Nothing. I mean, we decided not to have a baby until after the wedding. Rumbie wanted to look her best on her wedding day."

"You mean she's not pregnant?" Promise sounded as though he thought that I was the most stupid man he knew, "How can you be sure that she.... well you know that. But how can you be sure that when the baby comes, it will be yours. I mean, she has tasted another guy..."

"PROMISE!" Uncle Peter advanced menacingly at my friend, "Sipho here has grown up a lot since he left home as a sixteen year old. I trust his judgement, and I have met Rumbie. They are devoted to each other and I know that their marriage will be a happy one because they love each other and Sipho can provide for his family." I had a feeling that the last remark was a rebuke to Promise but he did not seem to notice it.

"But what if Sipho can't, you know, make her pregnant...?"

"Don't worry, he will," Uncle Peter said with conviction.

"I will," I repeated without the same conviction.

CHAPTER TWELVE

It rained for most of the night on the eve of Christmas, 1994, the eve of my wedding. The rainy season thus far had been very erratic and the deluge that came was, I'm sure, welcome for most people. But did it have to be on the night before my wedding? It bucketed down with thunder and lightning, making it difficult for me to sleep; although I'd been feeling so nervous that I'm not sure I would have slept anyway! As I tossed and turned in the old single bed whose springs had long lost their 'spring' and which sagged in the middle so badly that I felt like I was sleeping in a bath tub, many thoughts came to my mind. How was my relationship with Rumbie going to change after tomorrow? Was it going to change? How were our families going to relate? How would Rumbie fit into my family and its structures? I decided that it was just as well that we were going back to Johannesburg and would be away from the politics of families. We would, of course be expected to visit both families regularly, which meant that we would have to save up for the frequent trips back home for Christmas and other holidays. We were going to have another two children – hopefully both boys as we already had a daughter. A boy and a girl would be acceptable too of course. Come to think of it, so would two girls!

I sat up with a cold sweat. What if Rumbie didn't get pregnant? We had decided that she be on the pill until after the wedding so there was no chance that she would have got pregnant. Although we did slip up on one or two occasions when we forgot to use protection before she was on the pill; and she still had not got pregnant! I had not exactly sown any wild oats so I could not be sure! Would she cheat? The very thought caused me to lie down and cover my head!

I must have drifted off to sleep because I woke up to the sound of birds. They sounded particularly chirpy this morning although it took me a while to remember where I was and what day it was. It sounded as though the home was already a hive of activity and I could hear my mother and MaMpofu giving instructions for the yard to be swept, the meat to be turned and water to be put on the fire for the groom's bath. I looked at my watch and realised that it was just after seven in the morning. I had slept a lot longer than I had intended; yet I did not immediately get up. I lay in my bed for a while listening to the sounds of the morning. They reminded me of my childhood Christmases which were very exciting times for me as Christmas generally meant new clothes, new toys that I would lose quite quickly and lots of nice food – tea with lots of bread and jam in the morning, rice and meat for lunch and of course lots of sweets and cakes in between. My father would be home, which made Christmas a very special time.

I remembered the one Christmas when he had bought me the first and only bicycle I ever owned. It had been hidden in the bush somewhere to be revealed as a surprise on Christmas morning. And what a surprise it had been! We had all laughed as my father comically rode into the yard on a bicycle that was obviously too small for his tall frame I had had no idea that this was meant for me and I laughed and pointed as my father did a circuit round the homestead before stopping in front of me, getting off and handing the contraption to me.

"Now, you can ride to school," he had said with his deep booming voice and the wide smile that I always remembered fondly. My mother, in her new Christmas frock, stood in the background looking at her husband, my father with a pride and joy that I don't remember seeing again – at least not until that day in Beit Bridge when she saw me for the first time in ten years. Those happy times were long gone but at least for this one day, there was the sound of laughter round this home. I even heard Khulu laughing, a very rare sound these days.

"And where is that boy?" I heard MaMpofu ask.

"He's still sleeping," my mum responded, "let him rest, he's got lots of work to do over the next few nights. I need a grandchild as soon as possible!"

It was time to get up and let them know I was awake and could hear them!

In spite of the earliness of the hour, it was already stiflingly hot and I found myself sweating profusely. The air though seemed fresh, just as I remembered if being after such a storm in my childhood. There was a lot of activity as the entourage from Rumbie's family was expected quite early, having spent the previous night in Beit Bridge – Rumbie and her brides maids in a hotel in rooms that I had paid for. I was not sure where the rest of them would have slept although I imagined that they probably would have slept in their cars or whatever transport was bringing them to the wedding. I was surprised at how many people were already here; it seemed as though the whole village had woken up and come to our home. Or had they spent the whole night? Every face I encountered had a pleasant smile and although I did not know all of them, I felt obliged to greet them pleasantly and pretend to know them. After all, today, I was the star of the show, until Rumbie arrived of course.

"Another one taken by a Shona," I heard someone say. It was Sifiso, my first sexual encounter. "I don't know what these Shona girls have."

"I believe they are trained on how to, you know, please a man..."

"She can't have had a lot of training," Sifiso interrupted Bridget, "he didn't seem to know what to do..."

"What do you mean? Don't tell me you..."

"Well," Sifiso was sounding quite smug, "he was lonely and, well, I didn't know about the Shona and I thought ..."

I cleared my throat to make them aware of my presence.

"Sipho! How long have you been standing there?" Sifiso at least sounded embarrassed.

"Long enough" I said wanting her to know that I had heard a significant part of their conversation.

"You must be very excited," Bridget wanted to change the subject.

"We've been living together for a while so ..." I hesitated. It was exciting that the whole family was here and we were all going to meet Rumbie's family and begin to know them. "But yes, I am excited. You guys will get to meet my wife and please be nice to her."

"We will, of course," Bridget said although I had the feeling that Sifiso wanted to say something else!

I moved on. Everywhere I went, there were beaming faces, most of whom I did not recognise, but they all greeted me with enthusiasm and wished me well. Even Khulu was a bit more lucid this morning.

"Whose wedding is it?" He asked me as I walked past. I had had no intention to speak to him because I thought that he would have been in his usual uncommunicative mood.

"Mine, Khulu," I said stopping to talk respectfully to him.

"So who bought all the food that the women are cooking?"

"Members of the family, khulu. We all chipped in.."

"How come I'm not getting anything to eat. I'm hungry!"

"They are still preparing the food, then everyone can eat when the bride comes."

"Why? I am hungry now!"

"Okay, Khulu," I said, "Let me see what I can organise. I thought you might have wanted to wait until the wedding starts..."

"Whose wedding?"

I went off to look for MaMpofu who I knew would be able to rustle something up quickly for Khulu. She went off to prepare something for him complaining about why he didn't just wait like the rest of them. Of course I knew that she did not mean it.

Promise looked like he had bathed that morning and although his clothes needed renewing, they were clean and nicely pressed. No doubt Bridget's housekeeping, I thought.

"I hope your Shona relatives don't keep us waiting too long. I'm hungry and thirsty." I knew the kind of thirst he was talking about. There was home brewed traditional beer aplenty as well as some western style lagers, of course. I had had to compromise here because my new found Christian beliefs did not allow the consumption of alcohol, but I had been overruled by the family.

"What kind of wedding will it be with no beer?" Uncle Peter was incredulous.

"And how do we explain to our neighbours that they will not be allowed to drink?" MaMpofu was looking down at me with a severe stare that seemed to ask if I had gone quite mad. In the end, it was agreed that the alcohol would be kept out of sight and people would be asked to be discreet about it. It was a decision made to satisfy my sensitivities. Who has heard of drunk people being discreet about anything?

"Why do you keep calling them my Shona relatives, Promise?" I asked my friend. "After all. With a *Sibongo* like Sibanda, you could be Shona yourself. Many Shona's with the totem *Shumba* when they come to Matabeleland..."

"I am not a Shona!" Promise almost looked angry. "My great, great, I think great again grandfather came from South Africa!"

"And you know this because...?"

"Because his name was not Sibanda. He was Sebata, from the Sotho tribe in South Africa. He only came here because his wife had been taken by the King and the King wanted him dead. So he ran away!"

I burst out laughing. This was one of the most ridiculous stories that I had heard from someone trying to prove that they were not Shona.

"Who told you this?" I asked after a while, having noticed that Promise was not laughing with me.

"My father. I asked him the other day when you told me that it was important for us to know where we come from. He was surprised, of course, and thought that I was drunk as usual."

"You're serious...?"

"Of course I even asked my father whether he had tried to find our South African relatives but he said that it was too long ago and he wouldn't know where to start."

"Perhaps we should make it our project," I said seriously. "'Find the Sebatas'!"

"Then maybe I can come to look for work in South Africa among my relatives."

He too, it seemed to me, had given up on any prospects of him finding work in Zimbabwe. I had had an interesting conversation with Mr Moyo a few days earlier when he told me that he was a veteran of the war of liberation.

"But Mr Moyo," I had said with disbelief, "I have never heard that mentioned by anyone!"

"No one in this area knows," he said simply, "I deliberately kept quiet about it."

“But why, Mr Moyo, You are a genuine war hero, if what you are telling me is true of course.”

“Why would I lie about something like that? There were too many disappointments after the war and I preferred to be unknown.”

“Political disappointments?”

“No! Well, those came later.” He was quiet for a few minutes as though he was deciding whether to tell me about his disappointments or not. He seemed to debate in his mind for a while then opened up as one who wanted to unburden himself.

“There was this girl,” he said in a monotone, “who had promised to wait for me when I went to war. We were going to get married and have many children,” his smile was not at me, but was with his innermost thoughts. “She was what kept me going during the war. I could not die and disappoint her by not coming back to fulfil our promise. I did everything – including hiding away from the heat of battle if things were not looking good for us – just to make sure that when the war was over, she would welcome me home”

“What was her name?” he had not said anything for a few minutes and I felt the need to prompt him to go on. He seemed to ‘come back’ from his thoughts.

“Roselyn,” His smile broadened at the mention of her name, “I thought that it was the most beautiful name I had ever heard.” He seemed to retire into his thoughts again.

“So, what happened to Roselyn?” I asked, wanting to find out about the disappointment that made him not want to be known as a war hero.

“She married our Form Two English teacher!” He looked at me with eyes that pleaded for an answer to the question, ‘how could she betray me like that?’

“Did you speak to her?”

"Only as to the wife of my former teacher. She did not seem to have had the commitment that I had and I understand she started dating him only a few months after I left."

"She must have assumed that you were not coming back..."

"Obviously! She probably prayed that I be killed in the war!" He was getting worked up.

"Mr Moyo, sometimes these things are not meant to be. Your level of commitment was not..."

"This was meant to be, Sipho. I carried her picture everywhere I went! I even showed it to some of the women I slept with in the bush..."

"So, you were not exactly.. without fault yourself?"

"Sipho, When you are in a war situation, you don't know how long you have to live. Every day could be your last. So you live for today. If a girl is available, whether willingly or because she is afraid of the gun you carry, you sleep with her because she could be your last. Those girls meant nothing at all."

Mr Moyo seemed so convinced of his own 'rightness' in this that I hesitated to tell him what I was thinking. In the end though, I felt that I had to tell him.

"Mr Moyo," I said tentatively, "Do you not see that, just as you saw your liaisons in the bush justified by your uncertainty about your life, she too had uncertainties..."

"What uncertainties? All she had to do was wait!"

"And if you had not come back?"

"I promised her that I was going to come back and I did!"

"I know you did. But let us just say that you had not come back. She would have missed the chance to marry a man that she probably came to love and would have been a widow without ever being married."

"What about me?" He was almost in tears.

"What about you, Mr Moyo? You are alive, healthy, physically unscathed by the war and you are a good looking man. Did you ever marry?"

He seemed to sober up a bit and for the first time in a while, his smile was directed at me.

"For such a young man, you are very perceptive," he said. "Well, I could not stay in that area. Everyone knew of my relationship with Roselyn and they kept telling me how sorry they were that it had not worked out. I had to go somewhere where no one knew me or Roselyn. So I moved from Kamativi, you know, the old tin mine, to here, where no one knew me. I had just got my demobilisation pay from the army so I bought the shop and was going to spend the rest of my life sleeping with any woman that would have me!"

"What happened to that dream?"

"AIDS." Mr Moyo said simply, "and the realities of a failing economy. Of course as you get older and the girls get younger, you become a lecherous old man and having a wife becomes important. But when you are the wrong side of forty, finding a wife is not so easy either!"

"So, you are telling me that because things did not work out with Roselyn – mind you she could have waited for you and then both of you found out that the years apart had changed something in your relationship and it was not working anyway – but because this imagined perfect relationship did not work for you, you spend your days mopping about someone who has moved on? Do you not think you should be moving on yourself?"

"I'm too old..."

"Too old for what exactly, Mr Moyo? You have twenty, thirty, even forty years ahead of you. Unless you do something different, that shop will soon close and then what?"

"What can I do Sipho? Having gone out to fight for this country, I expected better; but it's as if those of us who fought on the side of ZIPRA made no contribution to the struggle. Our leaders were vilified, our commanders were imprisoned and the history of the struggle is told only from one side. We are depicted as traitors, yet we shed blood for this country too; we sacrificed our lives, our education, our loves to see this country liberated from the yoke of colonialism and where are we today. Right back where we started; worse off than when we started!"

"When you went to fight," I was treading on thin ice, "you were going to overthrow the colonial government right? Did you ever think about what you were going to replace it with?"

"With a black government of course!"

"Of course," I agreed, "But what sort of black government? The colonialists were very clever. They destroyed our own forms of government and introduced us to theirs, while they excluded us from participating. What that did, was that the new black government that came in only knew how to rule as the colonialists did!"

"Are you saying that we had a better form of government before the whites came?"

"I don't know" I said honestly. "All I know is we do not seem to understand who we are any more. All our values, our clothes, our language even..."

"So now you think we should go back to wearing *amabhetshu?"*

"No, Mr Moyo. I am saying that we have thrown away everything that identifies us as a people; look, the Indians were colonised but did not lose their identity, neither did the Chinese nor the Arabs. They have adopted what they need from the West but have kept the essential characteristics of their societies. Only Africa has adopted the colonial system wholesale. Perhaps this is the reason why Africa continues to lag behind the rest!"

Mr Moyo seemed to ponder this for a long time while I watched him still trying to make up my mind about the truthfulness of his assertion that he was a hero of the war of liberation. It struck me then that if what he was saying was true, then as a country, we had failed our heroes. How many other Mr Moyo's were living like this with no hope and regretting their role in freeing this country?

"You know, when Gukurahundi happened, I could not afford to be identified as a former freedom fighter.They would have killed me for sure, so I just went deeper into the persona that I had created for myself; a simple rural peasant with a shop but no knowledge of anything beyond my little shop. Of course some of my problems started then because they would come and take things from the shop that they never paid for. And if they wanted to drink until all hours, I had to stay up and entertain them, all the time worrying that the so called dissidents would come and find me drinking with their enemies..."

"Did they ever come, I mean, the dissidents?" I asked.

"Thankfully, no. They seemed quite adept at hiding themselves and the accounts of their activities that I came to know about were from the soldiers."

"Is it likely that there were no dissidents at all?"

"I think that there were enough people who were disappointed by the way we were being treated and I believe that some of them may have tried to start an insurrection. I do not believe that they were that many though. But that is only my opinion, I don't know for sure."

I noticed that Mr Moyo's demeanour had changed. He looked very sad and was quiet for a long time as though he was not sure whether to express his thoughts. Finally, he stirred, obviously having made his mind up.

“Do you remember Gift? The young man I got to accompany you to your home when you first came back?”

“Gift, yes I remember him. What happened to him?”

“He has found one of his ‘real’ relatives and gone to live with them.”

“Wasn’t he your grandson?”

“No.” Mr Moyo shrugged his shoulders and sighed. “I had adopted him.” Again, Mr Moyo sighed. He was quiet for a few minutes then went on, “he was from Tsholotsho and he, and a few other young children had lost their parents when the soldiers burnt their parents alive in a hut.”

“How terrible!” I said, not sure what else to say. “Why would anyone do that?”

“There was a former freedom fighter in their village who, fearing for his life – and the lives of other villagers – if the soldiers found him at home, was having to live out in the bush with some of the villagers taking food out to him. For some reason, one of the youngsters, inadvertently or to ingratiate himself with the soldiers, told the soldiers about this man who had food taken to him in the bush. Of course the whole village had to be punished and so they shut them in a hut which they set alight and then waited outside with their guns to shoot anyone that tried to escape!”

Mr Moyo was quiet for a few minutes and I had the sense that he was trying very hard not to cry. After some time looking into the distance, he carried on.

“The whole village was wiped out, except the children who then went from village to village trying to get help but no one wanted them. Somehow, their misfortune was seen as infectious!

Ironically, the parents of the youngster who had reported to the soldiers were also killed."

I was stunned. How could people be so cruel?

"Anyway, when I heard of their plight from people who had come from Tsholotsho, I decided to take one of them in. It turned out that he had an older sister who had turned to prostitution to survive. Some international organisation – I think it's Save the Children – took her in, sent her to school and she is now rehabilitated and working for the organisation. She came looking for her brother and how could I deny her?"

It was one of the saddest stories that I had heard about the period and while it had a happy ending for the young man, I was not so sure that it was a happy ending for Mr Moyo.

"Gift was too young at the time so he did not remember much but many of the children were traumatised by their experience. Can you imagine what it does to a child to have its parents taken away like that? The bodies apparently lay there for days until neighbouring villagers felt brave enough to go and bury them. They were afraid of course and in their hurry to get away as quickly as possible, they dug only shallow graves which the dogs could easily get into. Stories of dogs being seen carrying human limbs were common and many of the dogs were killed – even those that had not visited the shallow graves – for fear that they might get used to the taste of human flesh!"

Mr Moyo's eyes were moist as he held back the tears. Yet it felt as if he could not stop himself telling the story. It was a sort of unburdening for him.

"In the other villages, girls as young as thirteen and fourteen had become the soldiers concubines..."

"At thirteen and fourteen? Surely they were too young to..."

"They were raped to start with! But they soon got used to that way of life. Then of course they were told that every week they had to go and report to the soldiers about dissident movements – even if it was only to tell the soldiers that no dissidents had been seen in the area. Their fear was if they did not go, their villages may be attacked and their parents killed, so they went faithfully every week to satisfy the soldiers' lusts. Many of them became prostitutes even after the soldiers had gone."

Mr Moyo sat back, an indication that his story was finished. I was not sure what to say. I felt numb at the thoughts of how cruel human beings could be to fellow human beings. Was this the soldiers' mandate from their leaders or did they just abuse the unbridled power that they obviously held over the villagers? I wondered.

"Of course now there is the Unity Accord that brought an end to the problem of inter party and inter-tribal animosities?" I ventured, wanting to diffuse the tension that had built up.

Mr Moyo laughed in a manner that suggested that he did not think much of the so called Unity Accord.

"You know what we say about that in these parts? That the new name for ZANU reflects the amalgamation of the two parties into a new united Party." He was still laughing. "The 'ZA' came from ZAPU and the 'NU' came of course from ZANU?" he had stopped laughing, I noticed. "ZAPU," he went on "completely lost its identity and was simply swallowed by ZANU."

"Is that such a bad thing?" I asked.

"I don't know. You tell me." He had an opinion, I was sure, but he was not going to share it with me.

It had seemed to me that there was a lot more to the Gukurahundi story than I could ever understand. But today, there was no thoughts of such things. It was the day of my wedding and the village was ready for the biggest party that they had seen in a long time. Mr Moyo had also arrived, looking, as usual, quite distinguished in the new suit that I had brought him from South Africa. It was nothing fancy but it was certainly a lot better that the one I had seen him wearing earlier on in the year and he seemed determined to stay apart from everyone else, so he sat regally in a chair in the shed of the grain store in which I had had my first sexual encounter

"There you are, Sipho," he said as soon as he spotted me, "How come you are not yet dressed for the occasion?"

"Good morning Mr Moyo," I responded cheerfully, "last time I checked, they had not yet left Beit Bridge. I don't want to get my suit dirty before the bride arrives!"

We made small talk for a while and he clearly felt comfortable around me as the only person who knew his real history. He had made me swear that I would not tell anyone.

"Aren't you envious?" I asked him after a while.

"Envious of what?"

"Of me getting married. Doesn't it remind you of Roselyn and what might have been?"

"NO," he said with conviction, "after our discussion the other day, I realised how foolish I had been, and how I had been blinded to other possibilities,"

"Other possibilities...?"

"Well, that I may have been so consumed with Roselyn that I did not see other people that may have brought me happiness."

"You mean there is a possibility?"

"Maybe," My Moyo was being very coy.

"Who?" I asked excitedly. I was so happy for him.

"All in good time, young man" he said, "all in good time."

I had to scramble as the sound of approaching vehicles was heard with the customary honking of hooters to signify that the bride was on her way. I had kept myself busy all morning but suddenly, the excitement of the moment caught up with me. I had been living with Rumbie for a few months and had not expected that I would be so excited at 'wedding' her in front of my family and her family.

I went outside fully expecting the cars to be inside the homestead, but there seemed to be a problem. The cars had stopped some way from the entrance into the home and there seemed to be no movement. Uncle Peter went to investigate thinking that there might be a problem with their vehicle. He came back shaking his head.

"I had forgotten how these people operate," he said, slumping into a nearby chair.

"What do you mean?" I asked, my anxiety making my voice sound strange, even to me.

"We must pay before the cars enter our space..."

"I already paid them lots of money!" I was feeling agitated, "What do they want more money for?"

"Well," uncle Peter said patiently, "It's all part of the fun of a wedding. When the cars do come into our space, they will want more money for the bride to alight, then more money for her to come into the house and whatever else they can think of. They may even ask for money in order for the bride to reveal her face!"

"And you call that fun? I've already spent a lot of money on this wedding..."

"Don't worry young man," uncle Peter said calmly, "I have you covered. It's only for this one day and lets let them have their fun."

"This is what happens when you marry foreigners!" Promise was looking a bit tipsy.

"They are not foreigners!" I shouted at him, "they are Zimbabweans."

"Ngama Shona," Promise insisted, "They have strange traditions."

With the monies paid, the entourage drove into our homestead singing loudly and excitedly and although I could not understand everything they sang, it did not sound complimentary at all. To my utter disgust, uncle Tobias was leading the singing , with Aneka in tow. She was clapping her hands in time with the rhythm of the song and was looking a little too happy for my liking. As uncle Peter had predicted, there were a few more payments before Rumbie finally emerged from the car. My side of the family, who had been trying to outsing Rumbie's family went silent. So stunning was Rumbie in her cream, body hugging wedding dress that I was glad uncle Peter had agreed to pay them.

"She is Shona?" I heard Promise whisper to someone. "I didn't realise they have such beautiful women."

"Her mother is probably Ndebele," a female voice I did not recognise said.

I smiled to myself as I recognised the kind of bigotry that people seemed to display without even thinking about it. I wondered whether this kind of ignorance was a result of being somewhat marooned in this neibourhood and never having been anywhere outside of Maramani. It was the kind of sentiment that saw many foreigners in South Africa feeling more and more unsafe of late. Yet, as I had been reading and discussing with the likes of uncle Tobias and Aneka, there was so much mixing even historically that there was hardly anyone who could claim to be pure anything. Then again, it depended on one's definition of 'purity'. Even in the so called coloured community, where people were clearly of mixed ethnicity, there were said to be 'pure' coloureds, I had found out!

Anyway, as I looked at Rumbie, my Rumbie as she smiled while women from my village were throwing rice and other small projectiles towards her, it did not matter what tribe or where she came from. She was the most important person in my life and she was beautiful. My mother and MaMpofu were leading what appeared to be a contest to outsing each other between my family and Rumbie's. It all seemed in good fun and everyone was in good spirits. The faces of the people from both sides seemed genuinely happy and in spite of the difference in language, communication, it seemed to me, was taking place. Aneka, who I had found out spoke quite fluent Zulu – with an Afrikaans accent – was having the time of her life arguing with people from my side of the family, in a common(ish) language. Looking at all the smiling faces reminded me of what she had once said to us about the fact that one could not tell, simply by looking at faces, what ethnic group one came from. We were going to be okay, I told myself.

Finally, after what seemed like ages of singing, counter singing; dancing and counter dancing, I was united with Rumbie with a simple ceremony of Uncle Peter and uncle Tobias each leading their protégé to the centre of the human circle that had formed and helping us hold hands, we were married! Uncle Peter of course explained that we were already legally married and that this was just to fulfil the families' wishes for a celebration.

And what a celebration it was! There was enough food for all the guests – invited and uninvited – because in these communities, people do not get invited to weddings or funerals. It is an obligation that many feel they have to fulfil because they may also need guests at their weddings. But of course there is always the extra incentive of free food particularly in these very difficult times. It struck me then that probably made sense in days when people did not travel far and only the local communities were involved. Here, there were people from as far away as Harare, Bulawayo, Rusape, Mutare and even South Africa. Still, there was enough food and I saw some people go back several times for more. For a time, Rumbie and I, who by now were seated in a make shift grass shed specially constructed and decorated for the occasion, were forgotten as everyone seemed to concentrate on the food. And for a while, Rumbie and I sat holding hands without speaking but comfortable to be sitting next to each other after so many days apart. It had been the longest we had not seen or spoken to each other for many months. Rumbie was the first to speak.

"I did not realise how much I would miss you," she said, looking at me with that smile that always melted my heart and tightening her grip on my hand. "I am so happy this has finally happened."

"I missed you too my love," I said earnestly, "it has been miserable not being able to at least talk to you. The battery on my mobile phone died a day after I arrived here and there has been nowhere to charge it."

"I did wonder whether you'd forgotten about me, you know, found an old flame..."

"Rumbie! How can you even think..." I started to protest.

"I'm joking Sipho!" We both burst out laughing, at which point the women from my village burst into an impromptu song about the forwardness of a *malokazana* who can laugh at her own wedding. It sounded as if it was being made up as they went along and I had to listen before translating to my wife.

Wamhle lomfazi
Noma engowezizweni
Kodwa usile lomfazi
Uhlek' emtshadweni wakhe

Loosely translating to

This woman is so beautiful
Even though she is a foreigner
But this woman is forward
She laughs at her own wedding!

It was all of course in jest although her family tried to counter with their own song which Rumbie said was talking about how I had had to go to faraway lands to find a good woman because the ones in my own land were too short, or too tall; too fat or too skinny, depending on who was leading in the singing.

It all stopped when the food came and it was some feast! There was rice, *is'tshwala, um'nqutshu* and of course meat; lots of meat which included beef – from uncle Peter's cow, goat that had been bought from the neighbourhood and chicken also from the neighbourhood. The bridal table of course had other additions like salads, wine and some fizzy drinks. The rest of the party were more concerned with the alcoholic beverages which had been hidden away from the main festivities but which slowly seemed to find their way into the main wedding 'arena'. The talking got louder as the music being played from a large high volume speaker, got louder; the dancing became more raucous as inhibitions were removed by the alcohol and even those that were not drinking joined in as the party came into full swing. My mother was dancing, I noticed with Mr Moyo, which made me somewhat uncomfortable. Was she 'picking him up' I wondered.

Occasionally, a group of older women – who all looked like they were way past the age of sixty, but who called themselves 'The School Leavers' – would be given opportunities to present their renditions of traditional singing and dancing to traditional drums. For obvious reasons, their dancing was not as energetic as one would have expected, but everyone seemed to enjoy their performances and others, even from Rumbie's side of the family, joined in, trying to emulate their dances. Of course some of them were also partaking of the traditional alcoholic beverages and the presentations became quite disjointed and comical, but no one seemed to mind.

As the party started to wind down once the food had been consumed and he alcohol induced singing and dancing had run its course, I noticed that Mr Moyo was still lingering around my mother and their dancing was embarrassingly intimate. I was going to have to talk to her. Not at my wedding surely! They even disappeared for a while in the early evening, and reappeared looking like love struck teenagers, coming to where Rumbie and I were sitting while holding hands to congratulate us. How could she do this to me?

"Is that your step father?" Rumbie asked after they had left.

"NO!" I said, almost shouting. "He's just a good friend and neighbour..."

She burst out laughing "A good friend and neighbour hey? I think that they are a bit more than..."

"No. That's Mr Moyo. He runs the shop at..."

"The one you bought the suit for?"

"Yes. I thought he deserved it and I've just found out that he is a liberation war hero!"

"Is he now," Rumbie seemed to be enjoying my discomfort, "I think that he and your mother look suited to each other."

I wanted to tell Rumbie that Mr Moyo knew what my mother did and that there was no way he could take her seriously. But this was my wedding day. I did not want to think about my mother's profession and what she had had to do. It was frustrating enough that she had scoffed at the suggestion of coming to stay with Rumbie and I in Johannesburg making the lame excuse that couples have enough problems of their own without bringing mothers into their lives. It had suggested to me that she probably enjoyed what she did and now she was getting her 'teeth' into Mr Moyo, still reeling from the loss of Roselyn more than a decade ago.!

"I think Mr Moyo is just drunk," I said lamely.

"He looks sober to me," Rumbie insisted, "and he is looking smitten."

'That's what my mother does,' I thought to myself, 'get men to fall in love with her for a while until...' I could not get myself to think beyond that.

"I'm smitten," I said, looking at Rumbie and trying to change the subject.

"He reminds me of you when you first came to my flat."

"Who?"

"Mr Moyo, of course! Same sheepish look of not being sure whether to say how he feels..."

"Rumbie, I really don't want to talk about my mother right now..."

"I think she is in love."

"Yeah, right," I said sceptically.

"Sipho, I'm a woman. I can see a woman in love."

"Rumbie, I'm a man. I know how women like my mother do to, you know..."

"You do? From experience, I suppose." She could be so frustrating!

"Anyway, let me introduce you to Zenzo," I was relieved to see Zenzo, with his now trademark limp walking towards us, grinning from ear to ear as though he did not have a care in the world. He probably did not, having had as much to eat as he would for the next few weeks.

"Ah!" Rumbie seemed to take her mind off my mother and Mr Moyo, "the man who brought you to me. Hello, Zenzo," she said standing up and hugging Zenzo like an old friend, "Sipho has told me so much about you."

I was surprised. The contrast between Rumbie in her smart wedding dress and Zenzo in his ragged clothes that needed replacement could not have been more stark. Yet Rumbie seemed not to notice and she hugged my erstwhile friend with what looked like real warmth. Even the few people who were still dancing, including my mother and Mr Moyo, stopped to look at what must have seemed a strange spectacle. Zenzo regarded me over Rumbie's shoulder with a smile that contorted his whole face, almost as if he was in pain. Rumbie stood back, but continued to hold Samson's hands.

"Thank you, Zenzo," she said, "for bringing my husband to me."

"Yes," Zenzo was looking confused, "he is my very good friend, you know." He then turned to me and said, "She is a good woman, even though she is a Shona."

Now why did he have to go and say that? But Rumbie seemed to take it in her stride.

"You're a good man Zenzo, for a Ndebele!" Rumbie responded without flinching.

Did I deserve this woman?

"We have to do something to help Zenzo," she said that evening as we were getting ready for bed.

"Like what?" I asked guiltily. I had not really thought of doing anything for the people that I had spent a few weeks in the bush all those years ago. I had given Zenzo a few of my older clothes -which he did not wear to the wedding because he was keeping them for 'a special occasion' as he put it. I had been mildly irritated that he did not consider my wedding special enough to wear more decent clothing than he had on!

"I don't mean that," Rumbie was looking very serious. "Is there nothing that can be done with his leg? Surely there must be some operation that can be done to improve his mobility?"

"I don't know," I replied honestly, "I can find out, but it must be quite expensive for..."

"You, Mr Dube, can afford it I'm sure."

"You mean 'we' can afford it?"

"Yes. We can afford it. And the man needs a woman in his life."

"I'll look into it when we get back to Johannesburg. As for the woman in his life, he tells me that since his encounter with the soldiers, he is incapable of, you know, having sex."

"Poor guy. But relationships are not always about sex, surely? He needs companionship, someone to talk to, someone to help him wash his clothes and to grow old with..."

"Would you have married me if I couldn't make love to you?"

"I don't know Mr Dube," there was a naughty glint in her eye "there are other ways to satisfy a woman, and I think you have a good enough imagination to..."

"Thankfully, I don't have to find 'other ways'," I said thinking about the 'other ways' that we had never tried and not finding them appealing at all.

"So, if something were to happen to you in that area," she pointed at my crotch, "should I divorce you?"

"I'd hope not, but how many women do you know that would live with a man without sex. She'd probably only cheat on him!"

"I think that you guys overate the importance of sex in a marriage. Companionship, friendship and growing old together – rather like your mother and Mr Moyo..."

"Leave my mother out of this," I said tersely.

"Why. You don't think your mother needs a man in her life?"

"She has many men..."

"You don't understand, do you? She did what she had to do to survive. But that was just sex; there was no emotional connection with any of those men," this conversation was becoming more and more uncomfortable for me, "every pot has its lid," she went on, conjuring up obscene images in my mind of Mr Moyo being my mother's 'lid'.

"Can we not talk about this? We don't know for sure that anything is going on there..."

"Are you blind? Come on, be happy for your mother. She'll be good for Mr Moyo's business, you'll see. And because Mr Moyo knows about her history but seems to still like her, it will be a good union!"

She was being too logical about this, but then again, it was not her mother who was a prostitute. Anyway, I was not sure what I felt about the possibility of my mother and Mr Moyo becoming an item. I thought that Mr Moyo might have been getting the short end of the stick. Would my mother stop her 'professional' activities? Could she?

"And what makes you think that she'll be good for his business?"

"She's a woman, and she's had some experience dealing with different people. Mr Moyo has not been too motivated about anything but I think that having someone else to think about in his life will give him the necessary impetus to want his business to be a success!"

"I love you Mrs Dube," I needed to change the subject and besides, it had been many days since I had made love to my wife and I hoped that, as we had agreed, she had taken herself off the pill. We had to do it on the floor, of course because the single bed with the springs was not comfortable for two people to share and the springs would have made embarrassing noises that may have given away what activity we were involved in for a good part of the night.

I woke up the next morning to find Rumbie no longer besides me, and, after the initial disappointment at not being able to partake in what we, between us, called 'morning glory', I realised that as a new daughter in law, there were certain chores that she was expected to take part in that morning. It struck me then just how cruel our culture could be. A newly married couple had to interrupt their 'married people activities' because the family expected to be served! Anyway, we were only going to be here for another day or so then we had to go back to our home, our lives and our business. I sat up as I realised that after ten and a bit years away, this place no longer felt like home. South Africa did. Yet because of the border imposed along the natural barrier of the Limpopo River, I was still considered a foreigner in the country that I had known and lived in all my adult life. For a few minutes, I thought about this and the study of the map of Africa that I had been doing. Many of the borders did not make sense. Our Northern and Southern borders, for example, ran along the Zambezi and the Limpopo rivers respectively, but how were the Eastern and Western borders decided on, and why were they not straight lines? Why were some borders straight lines and others not?

"I suppose," Mr Moyo had said during one of our conversations, "it depended on what the colonisers wanted in a specific part of Africa."

"Like the Belgians wanting copper," I interrupted.

"Yes, but it was not always about wealth. I am told that the border between Kenya and Tanganyika would have been a straight line were it not for Mount Kilimanjaro."

"Tanganyika?"

"You know it as Tanzania, of course. But Tanzania is the name given to the Federation of Tanganyika, the main land, and the island of Zanzibar. They took the first three letters Tan and Zan to create Tanzania,"

"I did not know that," I said honestly.

"Anyway, Kenya was a British Colony and Tanganyika was a German colony..."

"So what happened?"

"Well, the Germans lost the war and part of their 'punishment' I suppose, was that they lost their African colonies; the main ones being Tanganyika and South West Africa – now known as Namibia. Tanganyika was taken over by the British and South West Africa was put under the administration of South Africa."

"So," I was astonished by this revelation, "they fought their wars in Europe and decisions were made about Africa that did not take into consideration African views?'

"I don't think they ever considered that we had any views on the subject. After all, we had been running around in loin cloths and killing each other – according to them – and we were doing nothing with the vast wealth that the continent has!"

I had thought about this for a few minutes and could relate what Mr Moyo was saying to Aneka's assertion that big chunk of African History was determined outside Africa and that this continued to this day!

"So what about Mount Kilimanjaro?" I still did not understand what he had meant about the border not being a straight line because of Mount Kilimanjaro.

"If you look at the map, you will notice that had the line from the Indian Ocean going North West towards Lake Victoria, been a straight line, Africa's tallest mountain would have been in Kenya..."

"So?"

"I cannot vouch for the accuracy of this information, but I'm told that the Germans asked the British to change the trajectory of the border because they had Mount Kenya, itself a significant land mark, so they could 'spare' Kilimanjaro for the Germans!"

I smiled to myself ruefully as I thought of the arrogance of the Europeans. But thoughts of Mr Moyo reminded me of the previous night and what might have happened with my mother. In spite of Rumbie's confidence about their relationship, I still worried that my mother might not have the same idea as Mr

Moyo, who was vulnerable because of his obsession with his imagination of what might have been with Roselyn.

I got up quickly, dressed and went outside. The first thing I saw was my wife carrying a bucket of water on her head. I was surprised at how easily she was walking without holding onto the bucket, and yet none of the water was spilling. She seemed deep in conversation with Bridget, Promise's wife and they clearly understood each other because there was a lot of laughter as they walked. What language, I wondered, were they speaking in?

"There you are, my boy," I wished mother would stop calling me that!

"I'm a grown man, mother..."

"But I'll always be your mother, and you'll always be my boy!" She retorted to my protest. "Anyway, your wife is a hit."

"A hit?"

"She is a happy child and she has done everything that is expected of a malokazana, cheerfully too. You know how we are in these parts. Everyone was up early to see what this Shona malokazana from Joburg would do. Whether she'd be able to do all the chores expected of her. And she has and more, with such ease. It's as if she's done it all her life!"

"Well, she has, mother. She did not always live in Johannesburg you know. In her home village, she grew up doing all the chores that all girl children in Zimbabwe are expected to do..."

"I know, but there are people who, after being away from Zimbabwe for a few years can tell you that they can no longer do those things. You wife seems to be very comfortable doing them."

"What is he still doing here?" I had seen Mr Moyo walking towards us.

"Who?" My mother turned to look in the direction I was looking. "Oh Mr Moyo, well, he never left. We spent the night together..."

"MOTHER!"

"...talking. He is such a gentleman and we talked until daybreak without realising how long we'd been talking."

"Talking about what?"

"About your father and his disappearance; about me and my 'work'," she made inverted comas in the air with her fingers, "about the war of liberation, about Roselyn, about you and Rumbie. We even gossiped about some of our neighbours..."

"Good morning Mr Moyo," he was within earshot and I wanted to warn my mother,

"Good morning son," had he ever called me that before? "And good morning dear," he said cheerfully to my mother giving her a peck on the cheek, an action that embarrassed me no end.

"Well, I better get going," I said trying to walk away.

"WAIT!" There was an urgency in Mr Moyo's voice that made me stop. I turned round to find Mr Moyo looking sheepishly at the ground almost as if he had been caught stealing, "You may as well be the first to know, I have asked you mother to," he hesitated, looking at my mother as though he wanted her approval, "marry me."

"And?" What else could I say?

"A girl has to think about these things," there was a naughty glint in my mother's eyes, "after all, there are all these men to choose from..." why did she have to go and say that? She seemed to realise her mistake and looked embarrassed.

"I'm so sorry Sipho," she could not look me in the eye, "That came out wrong. I was trying to make a joke..."

"You're over eighteen, mother," I said turning to walk away.

"I said yes," she said, sounding as though she was pleading. I turned around to see my mother in tears, "he is a good man and I said yes to him. I am going to be Mrs Moyo."

"And I promise you, Sipho," Mr Moyo was looking less unsure of himself, "I'll try my best to make your mother happy after all that she has gone through. And if I can make her half as happy as Rumbie seems to be, the rest of my days will be worthwhile." There was an honesty in his voice that said that he meant every word! I was ecstatic. I could talk about my mother without worrying about letting something slip that might give away her profession – assuming of course that she was giving it up.

"Are you sure about this, mother?"

"Yes," she said straightening her back as if she was going to salute. She dug a hole in the ground with her foot and spat into it, using her foot once again to cover it with soil. It was her way of saying that she was turning over a new leaf; spitting out her old ways and burying them.

"My life has gone full circle," she said. "My son has come back to me; I have a good malokazana and now I have a good man for a husband. God has been very kind to me."

Rumbie, I thought had been right after all. Again.

I hardly saw Rumbie for the rest of the day. She seemed to take her being a malokazana very seriously and she was immersed in the goings on of the village. Bridget had become her constant companion and every time I saw her, they were together and seemed to be laughing all the time. Several times during the day, I saw Mr Moyo who seemed to be watching my mother constantly. It seemed to me that my mother had replaced Roselyn in his mind and he was not going to let her go.

Sometime during the afternoon, I had to say farewell to uncle Tobias and Aneka who were on their way to Bulawayo before proceeding to Johannesburg. Aneka had apparently been very impressed with the wedding and the people of Zimbabwe.

"For a people that have suffered so much," she said as they were getting ready to leave, "these people are extremely cheerful And I sensed no animosity towards Rumbie's family."

"Why would there be animosity? We've given them one of the most beautiful girls in our whole tribe!" Uncle Toby was joking, I think, "they should have given us another cow in appreciation!"

"But the wedding was so beautiful in its simplicity. I think we should have one like it!" Aneka looked at uncle Toby questioningly.

"Well," said uncle Toby, clearing his throat, "I haven't exactly asked for your hand..."

"What are you waiting for?" Aneka and I spoke at the same time.

"Well," uncle Toby seemed at a loss, "there is the little matter of racial differences. I'm not so sure that your parents will accept me as a son in law."

"So what? It's my life and I'm going to live it with you. What does it matter what they think?"

"Did you see how our family came to support Rumbie? That is what will be expected; that your family will come to support you. It will look strange if it is just you and I with no one from your side of the family."

"What are you saying Toby? That your family will not accept me if I'm not accompanied by members of my family. They seemed to accept me as part of the entourage that came to support Rumbie?"

Uncle Toby was looking uncomfortable and seemed unsure what to say.

"Did someone say something? Have they told you that I'm not acceptable?" Aneka's face had turned a bright red.

"Not exactly..."

"What EXACTLY was said?"

"It's my mother you see..."

"Your mother? She's the sweetest most loving mother I've ever met. In fact she's the one that's made me feel most welcome!"

"Has she now?" Uncle Toby sounded surprised "She has always said to me that she will accept any daughter in law from any tribe except whites and coloureds, because she does not like the idea of her grandchildren calling her a kaffir!"

"Why would our children call their grandmother a kaffir?"

"Coloureds in this country have, in fact been known to not acknowledge their black relatives and yes, they do sometimes call them kaffirs," I felt I had to rescue Rumbie's uncle.

"That's just ignorance!" Aneka spoke with passionate anger. "But, come to think of it, they are as much victims of the segregationist policies of past governments as the rest of you. The rest of us, in fact!"

"Now, that is just silly, Aneka. How are you a victim? How are coloureds victims? They had better lives than the rest of us!" Uncle Toby was not looking happy.

"It is not easy to explain, but by segregating people, you create artificial boundaries. Look, ethnicity has always created boundaries, look at the different tribes in this region; although their languages are similar, because, as far as I'm concerned, they came from the same root, they are still boundaries that have even led to major conflicts. During the days of slavery in America, slaves of mixed blood – what we call coloureds in this part of the world – would get the easier jobs inside the house partly because they were the slave owner's biological children and partly because they were considered to have more 'refined' features that were easier on the Caucasian eye! In Australia, there was a deliberate policy to encourage white men to make Aborigine women pregnant so that their children would look more refined; so that today, there are more mixed race Aborigines than full blooded ones. It is what I have always said that the narrative of the black man has always been decided on by the white man. In Southern Africa, they created a 'new' race of Coloureds which is inferior to them but superior to the blacks. In so doing, they not only created a buffer between themselves and the 'African', they divided the two groups so that they cannot unite against them!"

"Are you suggesting that the white man told them to call us kaffirs?" Uncle Toby sounded sceptical.

"No, Toby. They did not tell them to say that. But by making them feel superior, it was inevitable that they would want to demean those below them."

"Well," Uncle Toby was sounding less hostile, "they have succeeded because my mother now does not want grandchildren that will call her names."

"Young people will always call older people names," I got the impression that Aneka was trying to defuse the tension that had built between them.

"Not those kinds of names" retorted uncle Toby.

"Are you saying then, Toby, that because of your mother you will not consider a more permanent arrangement. What is this then? 'Date a white woman and dump her'?"

"it's not like that..."

"Tell me what it is like!"

"It's important to me that my mother approves the woman I want to..."

"I thought you said she did not approve of Samantha or Sakhile or whatever she calls herself?"

"She did not..."

"But you went ahead and married her regardless. Was that because she is black?"

"You guys have a good trip," I said walking away. I could see that uncle Toby was stumped, but that it would be easier for him to climb down if there was no audience.

"So you are abandoning me now Sifo?" Aneka was not looking happy.

"You know I'd never do that, Aneka. But I think that you guys have things to talk about and I believe it would be easier if it was just the two of you."

They drove away waving cheerlessly at us although most of the people there were not aware of the simmering tensions.

"You seemed very close to Bridget," I said later that evening to Rumbie, "what language did you speak to each other?"

"Language doesn't matter. The important thing was that we were communicating," Rumbie looked and sounded tired, but she also looked very happy. "I've been in South Africa for a few years and my colleagues all speak isiNdebele, so I've picked up one or two things. She has a little knowledge of Shona, so, we spoke." She looked serious for a minute.

"You know that Bridget is a very clever girl, but she's in a very difficult position."

"What do you mean 'difficult'?" I was puzzled.

"Well, before the apparent joviality that you saw, she balled her eyes out at me, crying about the difficult position she finds herself in." I did not respond, so Rumbie went on.

"Her first pregnancy was a mistake and she paid for that mistake by getting 'married'," she made inverted comas with her fingers, "to a man she did not love. She accepted that and grew to respect, if not love Promise. But she was determined to improve herself and one of the decisions she made was not to have a second child until their situation had improved significantly..."

"Then how come she's pregnant again, their situation is hardly..."

"That is why she is so upset!" Rumbie drew close to me and held my hand, "'Society', or more accurately, the village, put such pressure on her by starting a rumour that perhaps the first child was not Promise's because 'how come she is not getting pregnant again'? perhaps promise is barren and she must have named him because he was the easier target. It is a well-known 'fact' that all the eligible young men in the village, teachers, agricultural extension worker, and even salesmen who came to the township were after what was considered the prettiest girl around. She must have slept with one or a few of the other suitors and Promise was the unwitting victim of her uncertainty of who the responsible man was!"

"But she told me that she had only had one sexual encounter with Promise before..."

"They don't believe her of course. I was raped and yet to this day, there are people in my village who still say I must have asked for it!"

I could see that she was getting quite emotional. But I could also understand how she would empathise with Bridget. On the other hand, I was not there when this happened and I could not vouch for Bridget's claimed purity at the time of her 'encounter' with Promise.

"Do you believe her?" I asked.

"Sipho! Do you believe me?"

"Of course I do..."

"What if I lied to you? What if I went to that teacher's house fully aware of his intentions? What if I had done it with him many times and only cried rape because I got pregnant...?"

I was stunned! Was she confessing? Did she now feel confident that she had successfully ensnared me into marrying her and wanted the truth to now be known? I was livid.

"You lied to me!" I said taking my hand away from hers.

"No! Sipho, all I am saying is as much as you believe me and have always understood how..."

"I was believing your lies! What an idiot."

We had the most heated argument since our relationship started made all the more dramatic because we were having to whisper for fear of being heard! I was furious. How could I have been so taken in by this Shona? After about an hour of me accusing her of all sorts of things, going as far as to suggest that she had probably slept with Mr Van in order to get the job at The Hamburger, She seemed to calm down and in a childlike voice, she asked, "Do you want a divorce, then?"

That stopped me in my tracks. I looked at my wife's teary face as she looked up at me with what looked like real sadness and I realised how much I loved her.
"Of course not," I started.

"Because," she went on in the same calm voice, "if you believe all those things that you are accusing me of, then there is no point to this sham that we are calling a marriage. We don't have to announce it now. We can go on pretending and finalise things when we get back to Joburg."

"I'm so sorry, Rumbie," I said, sitting down besides her, "I just started to imagine all those things you were saying as happening to you and..."

"So, you've never really believed me? I fell in love with you because you were such a gentle man and you made me believe again. After years of not trusting men, you got me trusting again. Yet at the back of your mind, there must have been some doubt..."

"No. Rumbie, there has never been any doubt in my mind."

"Then why did you react like that? It must be something that you've always thought about." She was worryingly calm. What an idiot I was being!

"Rumbie," I tried again, "you are the first woman that I ever loved and you've never given me any reason to doubt you. It may have been the excitement of the day and the thought that some of the things you said about yourself may have been true, I don't really know what it was but the thought that you may have been complicit to the incident with your teacher just infuriated me. It would mean that you were probably in love with him and..."

"Of course I was in love with him! That is why he violently took away my virginity and ignored me afterwards; why he disappeared from the scene as soon as he heard that I was pregnant. That is why I kept myself busy with my studies, not wanting to think about what was to become of me. I even considered becoming a nun!" the sarcasm in her voice was unmistakable, and I found myself on the defensive.

"Rumbie," I said, trying to sound calmer than I really felt, "please let's not do this. It has been a good day and I don't want it spoilt with a stupid argument..."

"So, now I'm being stupid?"

"No, Rumbie," I started then realised that she was just too angry to try and reason with, so I held my peace. That did not stop her talking but I decided I was not going to answer her, which seemed to infuriate her even more! I'm not sure at what point her tirade stopped because I must have dozed off. The next thing I remember was waking up to her caress in the most sensitive part of my anatomy and although I was still annoyed with her, the relevant 'limb' was responding and we made long and passionate love without speaking. Afterwards, we turned our backs on each other and I finally fell asleep. Sated but confused.

CHAPTER THIRTEEN

That was twenty five years ago this Christmas. As 2019 comes to a close, I find myself reflecting on what has been a wonderful twenty five years of marriage – with some challenges here and there but nothing to rival the argument of our wedding night. Our children – we were blessed with unidentical twin boys (Bongani and Tendayi) some five years after our marriage; Rumbie having admitted that she had not taken herself off the pill as a result of the wedding night argument – have done well. Kupa finished law school and is now employed by a leading law firm while the boys are currently at University here in South Africa; Bongani pursuing studies in Information Technology while Tendayi appears more inclined to the Arts and is therefore pursuing a degree in Humanities. Their ambitions are as diverse with the former wanting to go overseas and specialise in computers while his brother wants to stay on at University and become a lecturer and researcher in the Social history of Southern Africa.

"It was only one night, but for a couple of years after that, I had begun to doubt if our marriage was as good as it seemed," she had explained. "Of course when I did try to get pregnant, it took a while..."

" ...by which time, there were already whispers about my own fertility," I had interrupted her, "and, I have to admit that when you did get pregnant, I wondered – only until the boys were born of course – if I was the father!"

"You dog!" She had said throwing a pillow playfully at me, "You mean, that for the nine months of my pregnancy, you were doubting me? Imagining me with someone else?"

"Well, yes and no. It was all MaMpofu's fault. She had said some things to me during an earlier conversation – about how some women, on recognising their husbands shortcomings, would find other ways to have babies, knowing that in our society it is always the woman's fault."

"I'm hurt," she had said sitting on the bed and looking quite upset. I had started to worry until she looked up at me and said, "It had been suggested to me and I have to admit the idea was not totally without merit..."

"You wanted to sleep with another man?" I had roared at her.

"No Sipho. It was that very thought that repulsed me. I could not see myself being with anyone else but you and I had decided that if we were not to have children of our own, well, there was Kupa who you always loved."

"What are you smiling about?" Rumbie, still looking rather handsome in spite of her advanced years, was carrying some laundry and interrupted my thoughts as she walked past.

"Oh, just thinking about how blessed we are and what a good marriage we have had."

She put down her basket and came to sit on my lap.

"You are a wonderful husband Mr Dube. I only wish you would give up on your dream of ever going back to Zimbabwe."

This was an area of mild disagreement between us. Thirty five years ago, I had come to South Africa to escape the violence that was bedevilling my home in Zimbabwe. It had never occurred to me that I would still be in South Africa with very little prospect of ever going back to Zimbabwe. Three weeks ago, we buried my old neighbour, Mr Mlambo whose longevity in South Africa had once surprised me. I had been surprised at how many of Mr Mlambo's contemporaries there were and that none of them wanted to go back. But the most surprising thing over the years has been the number of Zimbabweans – and other

Africans – that had made the trek south by whatever means. It was as if, once independent, Africa had found out that independence was not what they wanted! It is now estimated that there are about three million Zimbabweans living in South Africa and many more in other parts of the world, mainly in Western Europe but I had heard of Zimbabweans in Viet Nam and South America.

"My mother..."

"Your mother," Rumbie interrupted forcefully, "is married to a wonderful man called Jokoniya Moyo!"

We always called Mr Moyo by his full name between us, "and she's having a wonderful life. What makes you think she needs you?"

She was right of course, as she had always been about Mr Moyo and my mother. They had had a traditional marriage ceremony the year following our own Christmas ceremony. I was too embarrassed to attend the wedding and I made some excuse for my inability to attend what turned out to be the beginning of a happier life for my mother. Rumbie had accused me of being unfair to my mother and said that it was my own guilt at not being there for her in her darkest days that made me not want to allow her happiness with someone else! I disagreed with her at the time but saw her point later although I had never admitted it to her. She also had been right about her being good for Mr Moyo's business because she quickly took over the financial management and became a cross border trader, regularly travelling to South Africa to bring in the many goods that were in short supply in Zimbabwe and reselling for good profits. This meant that, in the early years of their marriage, we saw her quite often and occasionally she would bring Mr Moyo along with her.

My conversations with Mr Moyo had been quite awkward to begin with as I was not sure what to call him. My mother had no such inhibitions and always brightly called him 'my father'.

"I'll be bringing your father along with me this time," she would say over the phone. "You'll need to show him around Joburg."

"I will," I'd respond wondering whether I was being disloyal to my long lost father.

"History is always written by the victors," he had said to me one evening after a long silence during which we had appeared to be concentrating on one of the South African 'Soapies' on television.

I had heard that somewhere but was not sure where – probably during one of our conversations with Aneka – but as I was not sure where this was going, I decided to say nothing.

"Do you know that if one listened to Zimbabwe's history of the struggle as told by ZANU, one would believe that only ZANU, and only the Shonas fought for that country." This was a conversation that I always found difficult to participate in.

"Yet," Mr Moyo went on, "the first uprisings against white colonial settlers was in Matabeleland!" He had cleared his throat as he seemed to warm to his subject. It had not occurred to me at the time but I later realised that he felt safer talking about these things outside Zimbabwe because, as he later explained, "In Zimbabwe, the CIO are everywhere. You never know who is listening."

"You know, son," he had gone on, "It does not matter how bad our history is, the truth is that we cannot 'unlive' it. But if we only want to tell those bits of our history that puts us in a good light, we will not learn from the mistakes of the past and we're likely to repeat them, or have them repeated by others down the line."

"What do you mean Mr Moyo," I was genuinely puzzled.

"If you listen to our Politicians in Zimbabwe today," he went on looking quite serious, "You'd be excused for thinking that the history of our liberation was perfect; that no mistakes were made. As a result, they will not admit any mistakes they may be making now."

"What mistakes were made?"

"First of all, we allowed ourselves to be divided by the settlers, who came in and highlighted our differences and minimised what we have in common," Mr Moyo looked at me, his face animated, "did you know that after the first of what they call the Matebele Rebellion which culminated in the battle of Mbembesi, where the superior fire power of the British annihilated the greater numbers of the Ndebele, there was an effort to coordinate the next rebellion through a spiritual leader based at Matopo Hills, whose influence seemed to go beyond the Ndebele? Unfortunately, the communication was poor and the attacks were uncoordinated leading to another defeat."

"That was more than one hundred years ago, Mr Moyo,"

"Yes. But the rift has continued to dog our politics so that many of our Political Parties are based on tribal, not ideological considerations."

As I said nothing, Mr Moyo went on.

"ZAPU and ZIPRA were predominantly Ndebele, while ZANU and ZANLA were predominantly Shona. Were they fighting for the same things? Why did they have to split their resources to fight a common enemy? In fact when we met each other in the field, we would more often than not turn on each other!" He had looked at the television but I had the feeling he did not see it. He would have commented at the appearance of a gay couple that seemed to be fashionable on television these days.

"The other thing," Mr Moyo went on, "is that we had no plan. Rather, the only plan we had was 'remove the white man', but there was no thought about what we were going to replace him with! Which is why we have ended up with white men in black skins, whose responsibility is only to themselves and to their kith and kin and hangers on. The rest of us can go to hell as far as they are concerned!"

I wondered whether the bottle of whisky that I had bought for him was taking effect.

"They have allowed our health care system to rot because they and their cronies can go to other countries for treatment; they have killed our education system because their children go elsewhere for schooling! There is no sense of responsibility for the nation. They don't care that our roads are bad, that our railway system has collapsed. They continue to build mansions but no roads to get to them, and to buy the most expensive cars to drive on those roads!" He stood up and unsteadily went over to pour himself another glass, the first time he had ever done so, normally waiting for me to pour for him.

"And we Zimbabweans don't know our responsibility."

"What responsibility is that, Mr Moyo?"

He stopped and looked at me. "Why do you insist on calling me Mr Moyo? It sounds so formal. I am your father you know. Well as good as, anyway."

"Okay Mr... I mean father," it sounded so weird.

"Argh you're just like the rest of them. They know what they don't want but they don't know what they want."

"Who?"

"Who are we talking about. The bloody Zimbabweans!" He sat down and promptly fell asleep, his rather large shot of whisky sitting on the table in front of him.

I later repeated my conversation with Mr Moyo to Rumbie.

"He's right," Rumbie had said calmly.

"About what?" I asked confused.

"About everything he said. That history is written by the victor; that we've allowed ourselves to be treated as if we don't matter by those whom we have given power over us and that we have reneged on our responsibilities to not only hold our rulers to account but also to take charge of our own responsibilities to build the Zimbabwe we want."

"It's somewhat difficult to take charge of anything when you're being oppressed and your views being suppressed by an authoritarian leadership who won't allow anyone to disagree with them, surely?" I protested feebly.

"No one said it would be easy. But if the truth be told, the unfortunate thing about the nature of power is that it is never given up easily. It generally has to be taken away from those who have it!" She stood up and looked at me directly, looking quite serious, "you are the history enthusiast" she said, "look at all the changes in power throughout history. Oliver Cromwell had to fight to remove, or at least reduce the power of the monarchy; the Americans had to go to war to get rid of the British colonialists. I mean, we had to go to war to remove the white settlers..."

"Are you suggesting that Zimbabweans should go to war?" I interrupted.

"Not necessarily. But I think that they should be showing more resistance to what is happening in their country. As it is, they seem to acquiesce to everything their government throws at them!"

I noted that Rumbie was talking as though she was not Zimbabwean herself. I wanted to point that out, then paused. Was I Zimbabwean still? Were our children? They certainly did not display any particular loyalty to Zimbabwe nor did they display any to South Africa either. Was this what globalisation meant. It occurred to me that we were probably the last of a dying generation; a generation that tied itself to a particular geographical space. I remembered the many conversations with Aneka over the years where she had always argued that this was a phenomenon that came with colonialism. That Africans had always moved freely around this vast continent, with no borders and no passports. Were we getting back to that, unintentionally?

But I was also thinking about Rumbie's comments. I had recently visited Zimbabwe, looking at the possibility of expanding our business to that country, primarily, I suppose because I still considered it home. What I had found was extremely disappointing, to say the least. The people appear to be totally defeated and seem to have lost all hope of ever getting their country right again. So they spend their days in fuel queues making jokes about their President and leadership and complaining about how the rich are getting richer and the poor poorer. Yet none of them seem able to offer any solutions. There is not enough cash in the formal banking sector, yet the black market is awash with both foreign currency and the Zimbabwe Dollar. Everyone complains about corruption, yet, it seemed to me, that everyone participates in it. For example, I met a parent who had just had to fork out one hundred American Dollars (which are more than a junior doctor's monthly salary) to ensure that their child could get into what is called Early Childhood Development – or ECD – which is pre-primary school! Even when people have broken the law, they are more likely to discuss 'what can be done to make the case go away' with the arresting officer than they are to call a lawyer! By all accounts, business in virtually every sector of the economy is conducted on a 'what's in it for me' basis.

I had found Uncle Peter, whose employer had closed up shop and moved elsewhere, making shoes from his home. He had a big order for safety shoes from a large organisation. I was most impressed until I found out that he had had to pay the buyer of the organisation he was supplying – a large nickel mining company, a substantial amount of his profits – which of course meant that his shoes were more expensive than if the buyer had gone to a retail outlet to buy. When I asked him how he could justify that, he simply shrugged his shoulders and told me that that is how business is done in Zimbabwe! I had, of course heard that similar things were happening in the relatively newly emancipated South Africa, but it was not so rampant, surely?

"Do you know," Uncle Peter had said to me, "that even getting into such institutions as nursing school and teacher training college is about who you know or who you pay?"

"Surely that is not right!" I had exclaimed in disgust, "it means that it's not always the best candidates that get in."

"Yes," he responded with another shrug, "but how do you define 'best'?"

"Level of education and examination results are a good measure usually." I had responded smugly.

"Which is probably why virtually every year, papers are 'leaked' to some students in advance, and I'm not so sure that the marking is always fair."

"But how can that be uncle Peter. Surely someone needs to account for that!"

"Yes, well," Uncle Peter had the demeanour of one resigned to his fate, "a few are caught and publicised in the newspaper's, but I've never heard of anyone serving time for leaking exam papers and anyway, how do you prove that you've been marked unfairly because markers are trusted to be fair and there is no way of checking.

"Would you complain if you passed when you did not expect to? And if you did not do as well as expected, how do we know that you did not panic during the exam?"

Uncle Peter had looked at me for a long while and then suddenly stood up and said, "let's go for a walk."

Not far from his home in Glen View was a hive of activity with all sorts of things being made on the street. Decent looking furniture, shoes, clothing were being manufactured before our very eyes. There was even a car panel beating shop and a timber merchant among the many businesses that seemed to be doing a roaring business.

"Many of these will end up in the big department stores in the City," Uncle Peter explained. "Can you tell, by looking at the furniture, that it was made on the street in Glen View?"

"But how many people do they employ and do they pay taxes to the government? Do they pay rates to the City?"

"Why should anyone pay anything to them? They'll only abuse the money by paying themselves hefty salaries, holding expensive but useless meetings in hotels and going on expensive foreign trips."

"But Uncle Peter," I persisted, "is it not important that monies are paid to a central authority so that amenities and infrastructure can be improved..."

Uncle Peter burst out laughing.

"Look at the state of our streets. Every month, they charge us and we pay them for 'refuse collection'. Does it look like refuse is being collected? And look at the state of the roads. We have no running water, no electricity for much of the day..."

"We're also getting power cuts in South Africa..."

"For eighteen hours a day, if you are lucky?"

"No, but perhaps these are the teething problems of a newly independent count..."

"For how long can a country be considered newly independent? It is nearly forty years for us. Are we still newly independent? Anyway," uncle Peter seemed less animated, "The point I wanted to make with this tour is this; all these people you see working on the street have nothing but basic education. Yet by doing what they do, they are able to fend for their children, even sending them to University, after which they come home to sit and watch television and play games on their phones and computers because there are no jobs to be had and they are too educated to join in the family business!"

"But surely they could use their newly acquired education to improve the family businesses and formalise them..."

"Unfortunately, most of us have been socialised to be educated so that we can go and get a job and working in the family business is not a job – and most family members don't get paid salaries; only allowances, if they are lucky. That is why so many, like you, have left the country to go and get menial jobs in countries like the United Kingdom and others. Many, as you know, have gone to South Africa, Botswana and Namibia and increasingly, they are going to Mozambique and Zambia, countries whose economies are on the rise because the whites have come back!"

I found myself getting seriously depressed as I thought about these things. By all accounts, Zimbabwe had been a thriving economy at independence; the country has a wealth of natural resources and claims one of the most literate populations on the continent. Why had we not been able to take the country forward rather than regress it as we seemed to have.

"The colonialists were very clever," Aneka had said during one of our many conversations on the subject. She and uncle Toby had got married against both their parents' wishes but they seemed very happy – apart from some cultural challenges early on in their marriage, and we were regular visitors to each other's homes. "They introduced an education system based on their own, which was class based and taught learners how to be employees." Judging by my experiences in Zimbabwe, she was probably right! "They denigrated everything African," Aneka had gone on, "as primitive and inferior to such an extent that the African himself believed it! So now, to most Africans – certainly in Southern Africa – the indigenous languages are dying in favour of the languages of the erstwhile oppressor, indigenous culture and values, some of which are, in my opinion, far superior to our own, have been consigned to the dustbin of history and the African has lost his identity. The result is that the leaders who have taken over at independence, have taken over a culture and identity they hardly understand, because they were never part of it during colonial rule, yet are expected to deliver as the whites did. Do you know that it took Western Society centuries to develop their political culture and political institutions – and they are still far from perfect – yet the African, having had his whole political system destroyed with all its institutions, is expected to just take on the new system and run with it.."

"What institutions did we have?" Uncle Tobias had interrupted.

"I don't know. But there were empires and Kingdoms in Africa whose history we do not know; whose demise is only explained to us in terms that convince us that such Kingdoms were inferior and doomed to failure!"

"But surely, they fast tracked us into modern society without us having to go through the pain..."

"What pain?" Aneka looked almost angry. "Which is the fastest growing economy in the world today? China." She answered herself. "In fact I'd be very surprised if they were not the world's biggest economy right now, but of course all the measuring is done by the West. Did China lose its culture and identity? No. They have continued to plot their own trajectory in spite of denigration from the West. They continue to speak their own languages which they have been able to adapt to modern science; they use their own hand writing and they have a political system which is far from perfect, but it is delivering for them!"

"So, our leaders are right in looking to China for.."

"NO!" Aneka said emphatically, "We are not to look to anyone but ourselves."

"We?" I had asked, "Surely you are not suggesting that you are one of us?"

"Why not? I married into a patriarchal community where I take on the husband's culture. But that's not the point."

"What is the point exactly?" Uncle Steve had asked.

"The point is," Aneka was shaking with indignation, "that Africa, with its wealth of resources and population, would do better to look inwards, at better communication between the countries. Instead of competing for foreign direct investment, they should be looking to invest in themselves. Look, there are enough wealthy people in Africa to start the process. The problem is that even those that have got their wealth from stealing from the public purses of Africa, do not invest in Africa; because of the belief that the more developed institutions of the developed world are more trustworthy. What Africa needs is men of vision. Men who will look at Africa fifty years, even one hundred years from now and see where they want Africa to be..."

"Well, Zimbabwe is talking about vision 2030..."

"What can be done in ten years? In any case it is not just about talking up a vision; it is about putting in the plans and the hard work to ensure that the vision is realised."

"I had interesting conversations with some employees of the City of Harare, which is also talking up the vision of being a world class City by 2025," I said remembering. "When I asked them what steps they were taking to realise that vision, they had no idea. Just that they had been told that this was the intention. In any case, I understand that Harare was a world class city in 1980."

"It was you know," said Uncle Toby, "most of the new arrivals particularly in the diplomatic community were very surprised how much 'like home' it was! But our leaders like to make such noises. Before the year 2000, we had all sorts of platitudes about 'Health for all by the year 2000', 'Education for all by the year 2000'. What happened to those?"

"They just disappeared and no one has asked the powers that be why they were never fulfilled. I reckon the same will happen with the current 'visions'. By 2030, we will be so engrossed in other self-inflicted problems that no one will even remember that such promises were ever made." I was feeling quite depressed about my home country's prospects.

"Does anyone know what OPEC stands for?" Aneka asked.

“Organisation of Petroleum Exporting Countries!” We all answered at the same time.

“You see, once these countries realised that the oil in their countries was not infinite; that it was all they had, they decided to take control of their resource and ensure that they got a fair price for it. Some of those countries have become quite wealthy by investing their wealth back into their economies. The reason why the Middle East will never know peace as long as they have oil is that the dominant countries of the world want control of that oil. Africa is a different scenario altogether. We have been convinced that the so called hard currencies of the world are worth giving up our wealth for. So, they are free to come and take our resources, in exchange for cash – which by the way in not wealth; it only represents wealth. Before we know it, our resources will have been depleted and, as our greedy leaders bank their cash outside Africa anyway, we will not even have that!”

What could we say? She was making so much sense although it still sounded too ‘conspiracy theory’ like to me.

“The only African leader one of a very few at least – who saw this, was Robert Mugabe...”

“Now you are talking crazy woman...”said uncle Toby.

“What?” said I.

“What did you smoke?” Uncle Steve cut in, all of us speaking at the same time.

“Hear me out. I did not say that he was necessarily a good leader. Only that he could see what was going on. Unfortunately, he was a bit of a narcissist, and narcissists typically have an arrogance that does not respect other opinions. So if you don’t see things his way, it’s because you are too stupid to understand....”

"And therefore you should be killed for your stupidity? Like he did to the Ndebele's, and later on to anyone in opposition to him?"

"And never having apologised for Gukurahundi, he went on to call it 'a moment of madness'." Uncle Steve had always had issue with that statement from the former President.

"That was wrong, of course," Aneka relented, "but whether you are a Christian who believes that the world as we know it is six thousand years old, or an evolutionist who believes that it is billions of years old, three to four years do constitute a moment; and the world has had its share of such moments of madness – or shame. Hitler's attempted elimination of the Jews was one such moment; as is the situation in various countries around the world where ethnic cleansing has been attempted. Domestically, the current sporadic waves of xenophobia are another example."

"You seem to be doing your best to defend Robert Mugabe and his policies," I said somewhat testily.

"No, I'm not. I just think that his methods may have been questionable, but his motives were probably misunderstood but had good intensions. And I'm not talking about his domestic policies either. His speeches at such fora as the United Nations, the African Union and so on..."

"Where the rest of Africa cheered him on without joining him...." Uncle Toby started.

"...as a result of which their own countries benefitted from Zimbabwe's isolation and economic malaise!" I finished the sentence.

"As I have always said, the borders that were created in Berlin for the benefit of the colonisers continue to work for them even today. Africa continues to view itself in terms of those borders, so that each entity created by those borders sees itself as different from the rest and will selfishly defend its own 'national Interests!"

I was reminded of a conversation I had had with a Mozambican who told me that most of eastern Zimbabwe should be in Mozambique; the basis of his argument being that the Portuguese got there before the British. It struck me then that what he was saying was, "our colonisers got there before your colonisers, so that part of the land belongs to us!"

"Promise and Bridget are here," Rumbie interrupted my thoughts. We were expecting a few of our Zimbabwean friends for a Christmas lunch and Promise and Bridget, who we had helped to come into South Africa, had become part of our close knit circle of friends who included uncles Tobias and Steve and their wives, Aneka – who for some reason we never called 'auntie' – and aunt Sihle. Zenzo and Sifiso were also expected. We had arranged for Zenzo to come to South Africa to have his leg looked at by, ironically, an orthopaedic surgeon who had emigrated from Zimbabwe. He still walked with a limp but with much improved mobility. He had returned to South Africa a few years after his surgery with Sifiso in tow, the surgery having miraculously cured his 'engine' as well! They lived in Alexandra Township and were expected later as they were still using public transport. Promise and Bridget, who ran a Hamburger branch in Soweto had just bought themselves car which he was proudly showing off to Rumbie.

"I don't know how to thank you guys," he was saying to my wife, "imagine where we would have been now had we stayed in Maramani!"

"You've done all the hard work yourselves..."

"What hard work?" I interrupted Rumbie, "let him grovel because without us he would have been a drunken bum with no prospects whatsoever. And Bridget would be barefoot and pregnant with probably another five or six children!"

"Sipho, my man," Promise was as cheerful as ever, "I know for a fact that it was Rumbie who organised everything for us. You wanted us to stay back in Zim so that you could come and look down your pompous nose at us. I really think that Rumbie could have got herself a better husband than you!"

We hugged heartily. Promise had become one of my closest friends in South Africa.

"Any of the offspring joining us?" I asked my wife.

"Kupakwashe said she may make an appearance later. I spoke to the boys but they were a bit iffy. I think that Tendayi has a new girlfriend and Bongani said he will come if he can finish the paper that he is working on..."

"He's working on Christmas day?" Promise sounded incredulous.

"Well, he says he doesn't believe in Christmas," I said, "Its apparently part of the mental colonisation that the whites foisted on us! What about your two?" I asked Promise.

"Promise junior took his little sister to some secret destination. I think he too has a girlfriend that we don't know about." It was Bridget who answered, looking fondly at her husband.

"Come in, come in," I invited the new arrivals into our rather large house – unnecessarily so now that the children had all left. We left Rumbie in the Kitchen with Bridget while we continued to the back garden where chairs were already set up in a semi-circle on the lawn with a prepared but unlit braai stand on a concrete pedestal away from where we would be sitting.

"You guys normally go home at Christmas. What happened this year?" I asked Promise as we took our seats.

"Children's school fees, mainly but hey, Zim is so depressing you know."

"You can say that again. I'm really not sure if our country will ever come right," I said, thinking about my experiences during my recent business trip to the country we still called home but was too depressing for us to visit at Christmas. The last twenty years or so had been particularly bad for the country we all said we still loved and hoped one day to go back to. There had been the Economic Structural Adjustment Program (ESAP) that had been attempted in a bid to get more support from the Western Financial institutions that seem to control the economy of the world. It had been an unmitigated disaster for most ordinary Zimbabweans, Then as we ushered in a new century and a new millennium, the Government of Zimbabwe finally decided to tackle the land question where, again because it was done, in most people's opinions, for political rather than reasons of correcting past injustices, it failed again and only managed to raise the ire of the West and its financial institutions. It had always been a mystery to me why our leaders seemed unable to read the mood of the world; to understand that, as a poor country with plenty of resources but little capital and know-how to exploit them, they needed to have the wisdom to keep the support of those who could help them until they economic legs grew stronger. Instead, the country's agriculture, once the envy of Africa, had suffered what seemed like irreparable damage and the economy, highly reliant on agriculture, had collapsed. With little or no job prospects, most young Zimbabweans, reputably highly educated and of all races, left the country in search of better lives for themselves and their families left behind because they were able to support them from afar. This had become one of Zimbabwe's main sources of foreign currency although most of it was being traded on the black market

Up to November 2017, one man had been blamed for the hiatus in Zimbabwe. It was Zimbabwe's founding leader, Robert Gabriel Mugabe who was seen as the main stumbling block. He refused to change course even when it was clear that whatever he was doing was not working; he continuously insulted countries that were in a position to help his country out of the mess it was in and when he lost elections – as was widely believed in 2008 and 2013, he just refused to go and engineered the results to make sure that he stayed in power. There were, of course, some who said that it was the army in whose interests it was that Mr Mugabe stayed in power, who ensured – with widespread violence some of which mimicked the violence of Gukurahundi – that ensured that he did not lose those elections to the opposition Movement for Democratic Change (MDC).

In 2017, the army was finally fed up, apparently, of Mr Mugabe's rule and the growing influence of his much younger wife, so he was thus removed without much violence and his erstwhile ally and deputy, Mr Munangagwa, had taken over the reins. The country had exploded in joyous celebration as they saw the dawn of a new era. Alas, two years down the line, it was looking more and more like a false dawn. For most Zimbabweans, the so called 'new era' was a worse refection of the old era whose demise they had so celebrated. The economy was in more rapid free fall and the many who had left the country 'until things got better' were losing any hope of that ever happening; and those inside the country were looking for opportunities to get out!

"Cry the beloved country," I said with a sigh, quoting the title of the old South African Novel by Alan Payton.

"Come on, Sipho, it's Christmas! Forget about Zimbabwe for today." Aneka and Uncle Toby had arrived unnoticed and had walked in on my musings.

"Who says I'm thinking about Zimbabwe," I protested.

"What other beloved country can you speak so mournfully about?" Uncle Toby sounded like he'd had a few drinks, "and anyway, how come there's no meat on the braai? I'm starved!"

We got busy roasting the meat with Promise serving drinks all round. In a short time, all who had been expected for the party had arrived except my mother and Mr Moyo who had been delayed at the border but, thanks to mobile phone technology, we knew that their bus was approaching Johannesburg and I was going to have to pick them up when they arrived. All the women, except Aneka, were in the kitchen while we sat around making small talk. Zenzo was, at his own insistence, manning the braai and the smell of the meat was getting to us.

"Where's the 'pap'?" Uncle Steve asked loudly enough for those in the kitchen to hear, "The meat is burning!"

By the time my mother and Mr Moyo arrived – Rumbie having offered to pick them up from the station – we had all eaten and those who were partaking of alcoholic drinks, everyone except myself, were having a merry Christmas indeed. Rumbie had also been drinking some wine but, as usual, limited herself to a few glasses.

“Welcome people of M'nangagwa,” Promise said hugging my mother and shaking Mr Moyo's hand. “How is your President?”

“Oh? He's 'our' President now? Who is yours? Ramaphosa?”

“Why did you decide to travel on Christmas eve?” I asked, concerned because they looked so tired.

“Well,” my mother answered, “normally it is not a problem because most people are travelling North to Zimbabwe with very few coming this way. This time it seemed as if there were as many coming South as going North.”

“You must be tired,” Rumbie said, “Shall I run the bath for you? I've had your luggage put in the guest wing as usual.”

“No! I'm OK.” Mr Moyo was eying the array of drinks on the table, “Let me have some of that meat before I get stuck into some Christmas,” he said licking his lips.

“Moyo!” My mother looked sternly at her husband, “We last bathed before we left home yesterday morning!”

“So? Do I have to bath every day?”

“You've been sweating in that bus for nearly two days...”

“Okay, okay. I'll bath before we go to bed. Alright mother?”

My mother looked at her husband and for a moment looked like she was going to insist, but then seemed to change her mind.

"I don't know if it is to do with his age, but your father does not like to bathe these days," she said looking at me.

"Do I look dirty to you?" he asked looking at me.

"Of course not, dad. I think you..."

"Did you hear that?" Mr Moyo interrupted me, "he called me dad without hesitation. I told you he will come right!" he addressed my mother triumphantly.

"He's had twenty five years to get used to the idea and I think he can relate to you more now. He too did not like to bath as a youngster!"

The laughter that followed seemed to break the ice and we had a pleasant afternoon of drinking and eating too much food particularly meat.

In spite of all our best efforts, the conversation did turn to Zimbabwe and its current situation. By this time, we had been joined by Bongani who arrived dressed in jeans that looked like they had been recycled several times and a sweater that appeared to have been taken straight off the wash line. He ate so much food that his mother commented on his appetite.

"Your cooking, mother, beats beans on toast any day!" he responded.

"Any cooking beats beans on toast" I said.

"Yes, but the allowance you give me does not cover canteen meals..."

"As well as alcohol," his mother interrupted.

"Of course," Bongani seemed unfazed by the mild disapproval from his mother, "It is impossible to attend boring lectures all day and be sober at night!"

"You used to be such a sober young man, and you loved going to church."

"Yes, mother. But then I realised that the religion that was used to subjugate and oppress me, cannot be the same religion that will be responsible for my ultimate redemption. How is that possible?"

"So, alcohol will redeem you?" Rumbie sounded indignant and disappointed.

"There is no redemption that will come from some supernatural being! That is the problem with Africa. We have been sold this religion that says we can suffer here while we wait for God to come and take us to heaven and we have stopped thinking for ourselves. The rest of the world is innovating and amassing wealth at our expense and we are in church singing praises to God and waiting for him to come and take us out of our misery?"

"Fortunately for you young man," Rumbie said, clearing up the table, "our God is very forgiving..."

"That's another thing!" Bongani interrupted his mother, "they tell us about forgiveness, yet they are the most unforgiving people on the planet!"

"What do you mean?" I asked my son.

"Can you imagine a white Nelson Mandela? After all they did to him, he came out having spent most of his adult life in prison and what does he do? He extends the hand of reconciliation. In fact, if you look at the history of Africa and the atrocities that have been committed against us, Is it not surprising that whites – who are generally in the minority in Africa – live happily alongside their former slaves and servants?"

"That is the forgiveness that God expects of us," Rumbie said. "'Forgive us our sins AS WE FORGIVE...'"

"My point, mother, is that we do forgive, and that must be something in our psyche; something that must have been instilled in us by whatever belief system we had in the past. Christianity, after all, is what teaches 'an eye for an eye' and our colonisers seem to believe in that more than they believe in forgiveness! Even our own Robert Mugabe tried to forgive and forget and they took advantage, as they always do, of our essential goodness."

"Now you are talking foolishness," Mr Moyo joined in, "Mugabe was more cruel even than the whites..."

"... and we are not just talking Matabeleland here. Look what happened after the referendum in 2000, when, for the first time since independence, an opposition party was able to mobilise against ZANU PF's flawed supposed new constitution. He unleashed so much violence not only against his own people but also against those white farmers that had decided to stay!"

"In subsequent elections in 2003, 2008and 2013, we saw levels of violence that were unprecedented in Zimbabwe..."

"Unprecedented, grandpa Moyo? How were the so called rebellions of the 1890's put down, and throughout the decades of colonial rule, how many people were imprisoned, killed or just disappeared for asking for what we now call basic human rights...?"

"At least then we knew we were up against a government led by people who did not like us," I proffered an explanation. "The same killings and disappearances are still happening today, when the government in place is supposed to understand..."

"But they don't, dad!" Bongani was virtually shouting. "Our independence leaders came from a situation where they had no say and no rights whatsoever; where the white government stifled and crushed any form of opposition. So when they took over, that is what they understood to be the way to rule. Why should people who lived without a voice under a white government suddenly have a voice under the new one?"

"But they went to war to free us from oppression," Promise said, then seemed not to have anything more to say.

"Did they?" It sounded like a rhetorical question from Bongani. "Look they may have had good intensions to start with, but let's face it, the whites lived a significantly more opulent lifestyle than their black counterparts, because, as we saw it, they were the rulers. So why should the new rulers expect any less?"

"Young man," Mr Moyo said in a voice that, it appeared to me, was meant to convey to Bongani that he could not know any better than those that were involved in the struggle, "I went to war, to fight colonialism and oppression. I did not fight so that we replace an oppressive white government with a repressive black one. I went to fight so that we could all live in a society in which we would all be equal..."

"I'm sure you did grandpa, but did your leaders have the same vision? I think that one of the great tragedies of Zimbabwe, if not all of Africa, is that those that are governed seem to know what they don't want, but have no idea what they want."

"Of course we know what we want," Mr Moyo, who by this time had had a few helpings of whiskey looked and sounded quite aggressive. "I did not go to war without knowing what I was fighting for!"

"Don't take this personally grandpa. I am talking about us as a nation. What I am trying to convey is this: In 1980, we celebrated the coming of independence, right?"

"Yes!"

"Did you know at the time, what sort of government you wanted, or did you just take it for granted that the new government would be better? In other words, you all knew that the white government was what you did not want, but did you know what type of government you wanted to replace it?"

"Bongani is right." Aneka spoke for the first time in a while. "Even as late as two years ago when Mugabe was finally removed from power, Zimbabweans went onto the street to celebrate the removal of what they did not want, but was any thought put to what they wanted to replace Mugabe with"

"Thank you, Aneka," Bongani said looking triumphant, "someone at the same intellectual level as me at last!" I think he meant it as a joke but it was not taken as such by the rest of us.

"What?" I said.

"Young man that is insulting," said Mr Moyo.

"Is it because she's white?" Promise weighed in.

"I think you misunderstand the youngster," Aneka came to his rescue, "he meant it as a joke."

Everyone seemed to calm down and Rumbie quickly called the other ladies to help her with the desert.

"More food?" Uncle Toby was holding hands with Aneka and seemed quite relaxed, "I don't think I can eat any more!"

"I can," said Bongani. I looked at my son and wondered where all the food went. He still looked thin and haggard.

The dessert, which was very sweet and very rich, was eaten in silence. Even uncle Toby had a second helping.

"Thank you my darling," I said to Rumbie, "what was that?"

"Sipho, you know that is trifle with some..."

"Of course I know what it is. I was asking for the benefit of Zenzo here. You've been very quiet, Zenzo?"

"I am enjoying this nice food. Sifiso must come for some cooking lessons. I'm tired of *is'tshwala* and *m'bhida* every day."

If looks could kill, Zenzo would be history with the look he got from Sifiso.

'There is a theory," Aneka said, "called 'The trauma of colonisation'..."

"Darling do you have to? Please let us digest the dessert in peace!" Uncle Toby looked half asleep.

"Is anyone going to have that steak that's left on the braai?"

"YOU HAVE IT!" we all said in unison to Bongani.

"Thank you!" The young man said as he enthusiastically went to get the rather large steak that was looking quite dry as it had spent so much time near the fire. "Now, Aneka, please tell me about this theory of yours."

"I don't know," Aneka hesitated, "there are those among us who'd rather go to sleep..."

"Oh come on Aneka, you know you want to. Never mind the old man!"

"Toby is not old! Are you my darling."

"You tell me," Uncle Toby had a naughty glint in his eye I was sure that Aneka's face turned bright red!

"Well," Aneka said at length, "I've only come across it in my readings and don't really know much about it but it basically talks about how, by disrupting ways of life and cultures, whole societies can be traumatised. European colonisers had this arrogant stance that they had a duty to 'civilise' the 'uncivilised' non-Christian world. Prompted perhaps by their strong belief that they had the mandate from Jesus Christ to "Go ye therefore", they went out with the idea that anyone outside this religion was a heathen and therefore uncivilised, although, in the case of India, there is evidence that the subcontinent had many centuries of a different kind of civilisation and religious culture – which is why Christianity never took hold even after two hundred years of colonisation." She paused and looked around to see if anyone was listening. We all were, including uncle Tobias.

"But," she went on, "because the British had used the religious differences among the people of India – which by the way included Pakistan and Bangladesh – they created such hatred between the religions that many people died ..."

"Wait a minute," Aunt Sihle interrupted, "What do you mean India included Pakistan and Bangladesh?"

"They were all one country called India. But the bloodletting that took place when independence was imminent led to the country being split along religious lines, creating first India as we know it today then east and West Pakistan with East Pakistan later changing to Bangladesh. Some of the fissures that became apparent then are still sources of conflict today with border disputes and so on. In fact India, and China, funnily enough, tend to see the period of colonisation as humiliation because their own civilisations were disrupted..."

"China?" Rumbie asked. "Who colonised China?"

"They were not exactly colonised but for many years they were dominated by the Japanese – on and off ..."

"That is surprising, considering the relative sizes of the two countries." I had not really read anything of the history of the Far East.

"Not so surprising if you look at the size of Britain and the empire she built. Must be to do with the ambition of island nations. Anyway, when the Europeans came to Africa, particularly Southern Africa, their idea was to settle – as they had done so successfully in Australia and New Zealand and even the Americas. But settling meant getting rid of the indigenous people somehow. They had successfully 'got rid' of the Aborigines and the Maoris in the Pacific countries to such an extent that the indigenous people of those countries are now an insignificant minority. The same with the American 'Indians' and the indigenous peoples of South America whose civilisations are still being 'discovered' even today!" Aneka was clearly warming to her subject and she stood up and poured herself a glass of wine despite uncle Toby's protest that he could have done that.

"Darling, my glass has been empty for a while," she responded as she came back to her seat.

"In Southern Africa, well, take Zimbabwe for example, once they had subdued the indigenous people, they dispossessed them of their land and moved them into 'Reserves' later renamed to 'Tribal trust Lands'. In South Africa they tried to create whole 'sub countries' in the form of the much hated 'Bantustans'. They then built a modern economy that benefitted them. By encouraging the immigration of Europeans, they had hoped to increase the white population to the extent that they would outnumber the indigenous population. Unfortunately, two things worked against them. There was an explosion in the growth of the indigenous population – which can be attributed to modern medicines being introduced – but the immigration of whites was not as much as had been hoped because parts of the country were thought to be not fit for European habitation!"

As no one said anything, Aneka went on.

"The effect of all this was that the indigenous people felt like they were not part of the country. None of what was happening belonged to them. So that even though at independence, they took their country back, there is no conviction that it belongs to them! The mines, the farms, the companies the banks, all do not belong to the indigenous peoples."

Again Aneka paused as though she wanted the point to sink in.

"That is why," she went on, "even the leaders of the countries of Africa do not bank their wealth – ill-gotten or otherwise – in their own countries. They prefer to bank it in those countries (the former colonisers) in whose institutions they trust. And the rest of us, well, we are also looking to leave and go to the same former colonisers. Imagine what would happen if all the Zimbabweans in the diaspora came back. Surely that would change the political landscape as more people who have tasted life in 'normal' societies came back. Currently, most Zimbabweans in Zimbabwe are still so traumatised by the legacy of colonialism that they do not believe that they can change the direction of the country."

"You know what I heard during my recent visit?" I said. "You know that some white farmers have been given back their farms in Zimbabwe? I heard many people say that the 'real' owners of the farms had come back..."

"Exactly!" Aneka said, looking quite excited. "Colonisation has so traumatised them that they do not believe that they are capable of doing anything! The same is happening in South Africa. How is it that xenophobia targets other 'foreign' Africans but protects the real foreigners to this continent? Because the blacks of this country are not convinced that the vast wealth of this country belongs to them!"

"But, Aneka, our leaders steal from .."

"Because they do not believe that it is theirs. Why would you steal from yourself? Look," She was getting quite worked up, "if we were all convinced that this is our home, that the countries of Africa that we live in belong to us, we would all work towards improving our lot and not run away to those countries that have already got it made. Do you know what the irony of it all is? Given the opportunity, the Europeans want to come back to Africa!"

"And the Chinese are coming in in large numbers," Mr Moyo said.

"But we want to leave. Africans are dying in the Mediterranean, fleeing from their continent. Going in search of 'better' lives..."

"I'm going Canada!" Our daughter Kupakwashe waltzed in, looking rather glamorous, if a little tipsy. "What a start to the new year!"

"My favourite niece!" Uncle Toby stood and hugged Kupa.

"What do you mean 'going to Canada'?" Rumbie looked somewhat concerned.

"Well, mother, I've been applying to Canadian Universities to further my law studies and I've been accepted by The University of Manitoba to read for a Master of Laws degree!"

"I thought you were doing so well with your current employers?" I said.

"Of course. But one has to explore new horizons. Besides, SA is becoming strange and I want to leave before the rush..."

"What do you mean by strange? South Africa is still one of the best economies in Africa..."

"That doesn't take much doing," Bongani interrupted me with a chuckle.

"Yes, my brother," Kupa went across and gave Bongani a peck on the cheek, "They used to talk in similar terms about Zimbabwe and look where that country is now. And the corruption that is said to have brought down Zimbabwe is escalating in this country. So, as I say, I'm leaving before it's too late. You should consider that too Bongani. This country is going nowhere fast!"

"I'll turn off the lights," said Bongani, "besides, if we all leave, who is going to correct the mess that these old people are creating?"

"What mess is that?" Tendayi walked in with a tall – almost as tall as Tendayi – slim, dark, stunningly pretty girl on his arm. "Merry Christmas everybody!" My son had the air of one who knew what effect his companion was having on everyone who saw her, "meet my friend Margaret Obonyo. She's from Uganda."

"Hello Margaret," Rumbie and Aneka said almost in unison.

"Welcome. I'm afraid there is not much food left, although I had saved some for Tendayi just in case."

"Please don't worry yourself Mrs Dube, I couldn't eat any more today. We've been visiting friends and have had so much to eat." He voice was as beautiful as she was.

"I'll eat," said Tendayi, "It's not Christmas until you've tasted my mother's Christmas faire," he addressed the last comment to Margaret, who looked at him with a face that seemed to say 'I don't believe this!'

As my wife went off to prepare Tenday's food, my mind was in turmoil.

'Uganda!' I was thinking, 'Why couldn't he get himself a nice Ndebele, well, Zimbabwean, even Southern African girl? Uganda is so far. First Kupa is talking about Canada, and now this.'

"You are from Uganda? And you are so beautiful?" Zenzo sounded as incredulous as he looked.

"There are beautiful girls everywhere you know," Mr Moyo came in to rescue a potentially embarrassing moment, "That is the problem with you people who've never travelled..."

"Moyo," said Zenzo with a sceptical smirk, "where have you travelled?"

"I've been to Uganda you know..."

"Oh! Where in Uganda did you go?" Margaret sounded relieved.

"We did not exactly go into Uganda," Mr Moyo sounded almost embarrassed, "We just stopped over at Kampala airport during our flight to and from Eastern Europe during the war of liberation..."

"Now you are going to tell us you were in the war?"

"I was in the war of liberation," Mr Moyo said emphatically.

"He was, you know," I said to confirm Mr Moyo's story as he had confided it to me.

"So, you are responsible for the mess that is Zimbabwe?" Bongani meant it as a joke I'm sure but Mr Moyo took it to heart.

"No!" He shouted, "it is the selfishness of our leaders that is responsible! They are not interested in the welfare of anyone but themselves!"

"We are all responsible," Uncle Toby said quietly, "we have all reneged on our responsibilities to building a better, more prosperous nation."

"How do you contribute when they will not listen?" Uncle Steve chipped in, "they will go to any lengths to silence descent; people have disappeared without trace and, people have died mysteriously, there is wholesale intimidation, particularly at election time and to add to all that, the integrity of the election process is compromised! How does one contribute?"

"At independence," said Mr Moyo, "I had first-hand experience of what it is like to have power over other people."

"You did?" We all spoke at the same time.

"Yes," he said, "being a hero of the war gave you certain 'privileges' beyond everyone else. Everywhere we went, we were wined and dined, women threw themselves at us and even guys who would not have had the guts to approach beautiful women found themselves overwhelmed by them. If that was happening to us mere foot soldiers, can you imagine what was happening to the guys at the top?"

"They were deified. Treated like Gods and I think they began to believe that they were gods!" Uncle Toby was looking into the distance, as if he was dragging back some memories that he'd rather have kept hidden. "You know what they Say?" He went on, "'Power corrupts; and absolute power corrupts absolutely!'"

"Zimbabweans were so grateful to their liberators that they were willing to forgive them such minor indiscretions like open infidelity, nepotism and what seemed like minor cases of corruption. We did not question them or hold them to account. After all, they had been willing to make the ultimate sacrifice; to die so that we could be free!" Mr Moyo was swaying a little as a result of the whiskey that he had consumed in copious amounts.

"We also stopped participating in the political arena," uncle Toby carried on, "we were too busy enjoying the fruits of our independence that we saw politics as the realm of our domestic servants and the uneducated. That allowed opportunists who saw the advantages of being in politics for their own personal gains to get in and entrench themselves."

"It sounds like the story of Africa," Margaret joined in for the first time. "You could be talking about Uganda!"

The silence that followed seemed to remind everyone that they were living in a foreign land; that they were enjoying Christmas in Johannesburg, while many in Zimbabwe did not have enough food for their day to day living. Were we being selfish? I asked myself. Did it matter that our country's economy was in free fall, or that there was no solution that immediately presented itself?

"Would we make any difference?" I asked out loud.

No one seemed to have the answer so the silence continued. Rumbie called Tendayi into the house, presumably to go and ask him how serious he was with Margaret – maybe even to express her approval, or not. Mr Moyo stood up to pour himself another whiskey, after which he sat down and promptly fell asleep; Zenzo and Sifiso were slow dancing to a softly playing song by Ringo Madlingozi – 'Sondela'. They were soon joined by Promise and Bridget.

"That is why I am going to Canada my brother," Kupa said to Bongani, "this continent is cursed. Basically, it is fucked! Sorry daddy."

"Young lady, do not use such language in my presence," I said sternly to my daughter.

I noticed that Margaret was smiling to herself and wondered why.

"You are a gentleman, Mr Dube," she said. "My father would have thrown whatever it was he was holding, wet or dry, into my face!"

"So, Toby," Aneka said after some time, "as a hero of the war of liberation yourself, did you enjoy the women that were throwing themselves at you guys?"

Caught completely off guard by the question, uncle Toby shifted in his chair and cleared his throat.

"Please do tell, uncle Toby," Kupa seemed determined to add to her uncle's discomfort.

"Well," he said finally, clearing his throat again, "I was young.."

"Of course you were young! It's forty years ago." Aneka seemed to be enjoying her husband's apparent non enjoyment of this particular discussion, "so you did enjoy taking advantage of the innocent young women..."

"They were not so innocent..."

"So you did sleep with them?"

"Yes!" Uncle Toby was getting agitated, "what of it? It was many years ago!"

"Oh my darling," said Aneka, "is that why you are so good in bed?"

The relief on uncle Toby's face on realising that he was not being accused was only made funnier by the embarrassment he was showing at having the most intimate details of his private life revealed in public I realised then that the wine that Aneka had been drinking all afternoon had taken away her normal inhibitions. Bongani and Kupakwashe moved away some distance, obviously embarrassed to hear such intimate details of the sex lives of adults. It struck me then that there had been a time that I had been shocked that my mother... come to think of it, does she and Mr Moyo still...?

"Surely not," I said out loud.

"Surely not what?" Rumbie asked as she and Tendayi came out of the house, arm in arm.

"Err" I stammered, "I'll tell you about it later." She looked at me suspiciously but did not insist.

"Your mother has crashed out on the sofa, poor thing. She must be tired from the bus journey."

"The beers she was drinking did not help either!" I said lowering my voice, "Look at the husband, we might have to carry him up to his room."

"It is Christmas after all," Rumbie said, "and it is our silver wedding anniversary. How perfect that our whole family is here to celebrate with us. My only regret is that my parents did not live long enough to be here today" She sounded angry. Her parents had died at different times, of perfectly curable diseases, but because the health system in Zimbabwe had collapsed, and they did not tell us in time because they did not want to bother us, they both died. Her mother had died first and I had always had the feeling that her father did not contact us deliberately because he had nothing to live for.

"What do you think of that Margaret?" She changed the subject suddenly, "I think she is so pretty."

I looked across at where Tendayi and Margaret were sitting, their faces almost touching as they were deep in conversation. She was really beautiful.

“Too dark for me,” I said to my wife.

“Oh come on,” Rumbie said, “I saw how your face lit up when she walked in. I think you are jealous of the boy, if you ask me.”

“Well, I’m not asking you. What about your other son, you think there’s anything happening on that front there?”

“He is a bit of a closed book that one, but he’ll surprise us one of these days. My worry is Kupa. She’s thirty one this year and she’s never even introduced us to anyone. You think she’s straight?”

“Of course she’s straight. She’s just not met the right person. Anyway, I don’t like to think of some strange man groping her all over!”

“Like you do to me Mr Dube?”

“I don’t ‘grope’. I make love to you.”

“Of course my darling. You are the only man in the world who knows how to do that!”

“Are you guys sleeping or what?” Zenzo was limping towards us, “come on up and dance. It’s Christmas!”

Apart from Mr Moyo who was still slumped in the chair, everyone else was on the dance floor, and it was still ‘Sondela’ playing.

“There are literally thousands of songs on that MP3 player. How come you are only playing one?”

“It’s Sifiso and I’s favourite song and I put it on repeat. But now I don’t know how to take it off!” Zenzo looked sheepishly at me.

The party got going in earnest after this and we danced long into the night.

"I'm shoooo happy that you took me away from that Zimbabwe." Zenzo cornered me at some point in the early hours of the morning. "Imagine where Sifiso and I would be!" He hugged me and squeezed me tightly, lifting me off my feet, "Thank you THANK YOU!" He stood back and looked at me. "It's a pity Samson could not be helped hey?" He said, looking sad, "But he is resting now, thankfully. No more running for Samson." Samson, we had heard from Mr Moyo and my mother had died in a storm the week before in circumstances that were not clear.

I looked at the dancers as they swung on the dance floor and realised that whatever else happened, these were the lucky ones. These were among those who had been fortunate enough to escape from their freedom. What would it take, I wondered, for them to ever want to go back to Zimbabwe again?

www.ingramcontent.com/pod-product-compliance
Lightning Source LLC
Chambersburg PA
CBHW020911060726
47591CB00004B/1192

* 9 7 8 1 7 7 9 2 9 9 6 8 0 *